Postcolonial Practice of Ministry

Postcolonial Practice of Ministry

Leadership, Liturgy, and Interfaith Engagement

Edited by Kwok Pui-lan and Stephen Burns

LEXINGTON BOOKS
Lanham • Boulder • New York • London

Published by Lexington Books
An imprint of The Rowman & Littlefield Publishing Group, Inc.
4501 Forbes Boulevard, Suite 200, Lanham, Maryland 20706
www.rowman.com

Unit A, Whitacre Mews, 26-34 Stannary Street, London SE11 4AB

British Library Cataloguing in Publication Information Available

Library of Congress Cataloging-in-Publication Data

Kwok, Pui-lan, editor.
Title: Postcolonial practice of ministry : leadership, liturgy, and interfaith engagement / Kwok Pui-
    lan and Stephen Burns.
Description: Lanham : Lexington Books, 2016. | Includes bibliographical references and index.
LCCN 2016019537 (print) | LCCN 2016020020 (ebook) | ISBN 9781498534482 (cloth) | ISBN
    9781498534499 (Electronic)
Subjects: LCSH: Pastoral theology. | Postcolonial theology.
Classification: LCC BV4011.3 .P69 2016 (print) | LCC BV4011.3 (ebook) | DDC 253--dc23 LC
    record available at https://lccn.loc.gov/2016019537

Printed in the United States of America

Table of Contents

Acknowledgments

This book is based on a conference on "Challenging the Church: Postcolonial Practice of Ministry" held at the Episcopal Divinity School in Cambridge, Massachusetts, on November 15, 2014. We would like to thank the presenters and participants of the conference for their support and enthusiasm. Many contributors of the book attended the conference and had opportunities to share their work and exchange ideas as they were working on their chapters. The conference was made possible by a generous grant from the Lily Foundation to the school and we are very grateful for the support. We are indebted to our faculty colleagues collectively for shaping the place as one where the kinds of questions we are engaging in the book can be asked and are welcomed. We are grateful to Patrick S. Cheng and the staff at the school for their assistance in organizing the conference.

We thank the contributors, many of whom are pioneers in postcolonial studies of ministry, for sharing our vision and for working closely with us in the editing and production processes. We are fortunate to have Lisa Devine and Andrew Heintz, our student assistants, who provided invaluable editorial assistance; the book is more accessible and consistent because of their careful reading and insightful comments. We are grateful to Sarah Craig at Lexington Press for her trust in the value of this anthology from the beginning. It has been our pleasure working with the professional staff at Lexington Press, who provided guidance and encouragement during the production process. We also want to thank Spencer Bogle for preparing the index in a timely fashion and the Episcopal Divinity School for providing support from the Theological Writing Fund to cover the expense.

Kwok Pui-lan
Stephen Burns

Introduction

Postcolonial Practice of Ministry

Stephen Burns

You have in your hands a new landmark in postcolonial theology. It represents a further development of the impact of postcolonial studies upon the theological academy, showing how postcolonial theology can be brought into dialogue with a range of practical theologies.

One way to get a background sense of why this is new might begin by consulting the various editions of *The Modern Theologians* edited by David Ford, a much-used textbook.[1] First published in 1989, Ford's "introduction to Christian theology in the twentieth century" included nothing on postcolonial perspectives. This omission at that point in time was inevitable, for as R. S. Sugirtharajah writes elsewhere, "Postcolonialism reached biblical studies late in the 1990s."[2] Yet, when a second edition of Ford's book, published in 1997, was restyled as "an introduction to theology since 1918," it was similarly quiet about postcolonial optics. Only in the third edition, of 2005, was there inclusion of a chapter addressing postcolonial matters, written by Sugirtharajah himself.[3] It was not about practical theologies, though.

Sugirtharajah's chapter in Ford's textbook was one among a skein of so-called "perspectival theologies" (situated alongside African theology, Black theology, Latin American liberation theology, and so forth). These constituted Part Five of Ford's collection, which was itself ancillary to what are deemed "classics" constituting Part One: Karl Barth, Dietrich Bonhoeffer, Paul Tillich, Henri de Lubac, Karl Rahner, and Hans Urs von Balthasar. Note that apart from all being men, the supposed classics of theology in the last one hundred years were all European. Moreover, Sugirtharajah's chapter also gave a clue as to where theological appropriation of postcolonial perspectives first took root: a discipline called "Postcolonial Biblical Criticism." Sugirtharajah's chapter identifies Fernando Sergovia, Muse Dube, Roland Boer, and Laura Donaldson as some of the pioneers of the discipline.

Even though Sugirtharajah's own publications have focused on biblical studies, they are nevertheless a very important gauge of ways in which postcolonial theory came to impact broader theological terrain,[4] so

1

I have selected him among a number of important postcolonial scholars as a focus for some further reflections. In the first place, Sugirtharajah is identified by other postcolonial scholars as the "inaugurator of postcolonial biblical criticism" as well as "its most prolific practitioner,"[5] a person whose work one would expect to encounter in exploring postcolonial theology. Second, he tends to be central to discussion of postcolonial theology, at least in Britain, my own culture of origin. Sugirtharajah is Sri Lankan and worked in India before moving to Britain where he has had a long-term base in Birmingham. I appreciate his expressed charge to European theologians to engage the entanglement of "European expansionism and the rise of their own discipline."[6] By 2005, the time of his chapter in *The Modern Theologians*, Sugirtharajah had put out his *The Bible and the Third World* of 2001 (significantly subtitled "precolonial, colonial, and postcolonial encounters"), *Postcolonial Criticism and Biblical Interpretation* of 2002, and *Postcolonial Reconfigurations: A New Way of Reading the Bible and Doing Theology* of 2003.[7] These three books were the beginnings of a flurry of several more volumes by Sugirtharajah that would begin to stretch from biblical studies to wider disciplines developing postcolonial perspectives. These included not only ones written in his own hand, but also some in which he gathered the writing of others in anthologies and readers. By 2005, when the third edition of Ford's textbook was published, at least postcolonial biblical studies was emerging in theological consciousness.

Sugirtharajah began to introduce the term postcolonial in the second edition of his collection of what he then called "contextual Bible study," *Voices from the Margins*.[8] His epilogue to that second edition started to discuss the categories of the colonial and the postcolonial, and included the important assertion that "colonialism is not simply a system of economic and military control, but a systematic cultural penetration and domination."[9] Exposing and resisting "historical, political, and economic domination" is, he suggested, part of what is involved in the postcolonial agenda, as well as tackling the "more damaging" legacy of "psychological, intellectual and cultural colonization."[10] Over time, Sugirtharajah has continued to insist that the postcolonial agenda involves the attempt to "decolonize the mind," citing the Kenyan novelist and literary critic Ngugi wa Thiong'o and the Indian theologian Stanley Samartha for the epitaph.[11]

MAPPING MEANINGS OF "POSTCOLONIAL" IN THEOLOGY

Discussion of postcolonialism continually involves questions of what it entails, where it focuses, and what agendas it espouses.[12] Since the emergence of postcolonial criticism in theological terrain, somewhat different approaches have been taken by various writers, some more weighted to an emphasis on the geopolitics of old and new empires, and others emphasizing dynamics marking a distinctive discursive discourse. That notwithstanding, Sugirtharajah's outline of meanings of the term in his *Postcolonial Reconfigurations* continues to broadly depict the range of attention, both deepening and expanding what he said in the mid-1990s.[13]

First, postcolonialism has a historical sense, concerned with the social, political, and cultural conditions of the current world order, giving special attention to the effects of colonization. When understood in this way, scrutinizing notions of a "third" and "first" world, of "development" and "progress," are crucial. Very importantly, Sugirtharajah points to the tasks of highlighting the ambiguities of decolonization and to identifying ongoing colonization, albeit in transmuted forms.[14]

Second, postcolonialism is a critical discursive practice, a way of analysis marked by certain dynamics and kinds of conflicts: notably, openness to oppositional readings of texts, events and histories by drawing out understandings that have been suppressed, and foregrounding victims and their plight. Analyzing strategies of "othering" and contesting them are key in this. And in this second sense, postcolonial perspectives can be "stretched," as it were, beyond concentrations on particular geopolitical locations once formally embroiled in other nations' empires, so that they can be used to tackle any instance of intolerance for debate, difference, and dissent.

Third, the term "postcolonial" can refer to what Sugirtharajah calls "the political and ideological stance of an interpreter engaged in anticolonial and anti-globalizing" theory and practice. Identifying "vicious aspects of modernity" is crucial to this. Exposing dominance and challenging notions of authority—political, epistemological, and of other kinds—is vital too.

There are, of course, various ways in which these three senses can overlap and intersect, and that is to be welcomed, given the major mark of postcolonialism to which Sugirtharajah's later work especially draws attention: preoccupation with questions of identity, hybridity, and diaspora.

BEYOND BIBLICAL CRITICISM TO OTHER THEOLOGICAL DISCIPLINES

These three clusters of postcolonial concern are not only themselves crisscrossing; they also, in various hybrid ways, overlap with other traditions and schools of thought. For example, insofar as postcolonial theology can be identified within or in relation to the family of liberation theologies,[15] some of the most influential contributions to postcolonial theological endeavor beyond biblical studies have been in dialogue or consort with feminist theology. This dialogue is found notably in the work of Kwok

Pui-lan,[16] whose approach has been to enable an intentional intercultural style of feminist thinking, as well as keeping the significance of gender central to the postcolonial project. This instance of hybridity has certainly been a formidable advance on ways in which gender was not scrutinized in too much early Latin American liberation theology,[17] and Kwok herself has not been shy of pointing to overdue and underdeveloped attention to feminist issues in Sugirtharajah's own work.[18] At the same time as accenting hybridity, however, Sugirtharajah has warned of the dangers of postcolonial theology being "hijacked" and "co-opted by the Christian mainstream."[19]

SCHOLARSHIP, THEORY, AND INCREASING REACH

One of Sugirtharajah's books is called *Caught Reading Again*, about "scholars and their books,"[20] and it includes contributions from among others, Marcella Althaus-Reid, Roland Boer, and Kwok Pui-lan. While the place of postcolonial scholarship is increasingly recognized and included in the theological academy—as Sugirtharajah's chapter in Ford's collection itself suggests—*Caught Reading Again* underscores the revisionist agenda postcolonial scholars will bring to their readings and disciplines, seeking not only inclusion but decisive change. This relates to another important development in Sugirtharajah's own work over time, which has been an increasing certain resistance to "heavy theorizing;" for as he suggests, "Theorizing looks like a specialized business, accessible only to those with arcane epistemological tools,"[21] and hence, is vulnerable to the kind of cooption about which he and others have become concerned. Perhaps the discourse of postcolonialism is at risk of being drafted by and contained in the academy—turned into an intellectual "theme park," as Marcella Althaus-Reid might say. Hence, Sugirtharajah's (at the time of writing) latest major book *The Bible and Asia* warns against the imposition of "artificial structures" by "already worked-out and complex theory" and ways in which that can "obfuscate." Muriel Orevillo-Montenegro is one among a number of other scholars who have also called attention to the challenge that postcolonial theology must resist an overly academic emphasis if it is to avoid "the trap it is seeking to demolish."[22] It cannot, she avers, fall into "mystification and moralism." The latter could, all-too-easily, become totalizing; the former exclusionary in a different way. She pointedly insists that postcolonial theology must not "play safe" behind a veil of "vogue discourse" which would "blur our vision of making God's reign on earth a reality."[23]

TOWARD POSTCOLONIAL PRACTICAL THEOLOGY

This concern is also very much at play in the first book to attempt to address postcolonial questions to patterns of Christian worship: Michael Jagessar and I suggested that "there is within the discourse on postcolonial criticism the tendency for this to remain within the academic realm," and we noted that ideas emerging in the academy "are yet to reach congregational contexts." Attending to worship is, we claimed, a means "to facilitate the postcolonial optic reaching the gathered community," a way for "postcolonial insights to reach a broader 'public.'"[24] There is a need for postcolonial criticism to be engaged in more intentional ways with Christian practices, events, and communities beyond the academy. There is an important task to enact postcolonial theology in shared practice: hence, this volume, *Postcolonial Practice of Ministry*.

What theological curricula tend to cluster in the "fourth area"—fourth, after biblical, historical, and systematic styles—is often gathered under the rubric of "practical theology" and is variously defined, although broadly concerned with Christian communities, their practices, and the particular roles of various representatives in the community.[25] And so it embraces at least worship and liturgy,[26] pastoral and practical theology,[27] and reflection on the practice of ministry, lay and ordained.

Despite the evolving, and sometimes contested, nature of this disparate discipline, one thing is clear: that it has not, until very recently, been subject to very much attention with respect to what are described above as postcolonial concerns.[28] And, arguably, the disciplines clustered under the rubric of practical theology are, like postcolonial theology, increasingly vulnerable to obfuscating theorizing, not least given the need or felt need to provide academic "foundations" for a discipline that has seen a dramatic rise in professional degrees across the university sector in many contexts. That being as it is, another way of looking at the increasing emphasis on method and theory in practical theology can be framed in terms of a transformation "from hints and tips to hermeneutics"[29] shaping the discourse, which might suggest a growing maturation. A shadow side of this might, however, be that to the detriment of a focus on practice; it entangles participants in discourse about uncertainty or lack of agreement about how to relate, reconcile, or choose between leaning on so-called "secular" understandings of human persons, via social sciences of one kind or another, and determining what the supposedly "theological content" of practical theology might be.[30] Strikingly, Emmanuel Y. Lartey, among others, has argued that pastoral theology, quite in contrast to systematic theology, should be defiantly *un*systematic in its hermeneutical processes, and so he writes about resolute refusal to "engage in theoretical discourse that fails to engage unpleasant or inconvenient aspects of human life" and intentional embrace of "tentative," "provisional," "poetic," "apophatic," "elusive," and "enigmatic" modes and moods.[31] Hermeneutics may be an advance on hints and tips, but can become its own cul-de-sac.

To date, work in the fourth area which has made explicit use of post-colonial thinking has included a first attempt to make connections with liturgical theology in Michael Jagessar and Stephen Burns, *Christian Worship: Postcolonial Perspectives* (2011), much of which was consolidated by Cláudio Carvalhaes' collection *Liturgy in Postcolonial Perspectives* (2015).[32] HyeRan Kim-Cragg made interdisciplinary connections between worship and Christian education in her *Story and Song* (2012).[33] In pastoral theology, Melinda McGarrah Sharp's *Misunderstanding Stories* and Emmanuel Y. Lartey's *Postcolonializing God* both appeared in 2013,[34] with Lartey's book also attending to "rituals of remembrance, cleansing, healing and re-collection," as part of what he calls "postcolonializing liturgical practice." We are delighted that all of these scholars are included in the present collection, all of whose books, in different ways, turn their practical theologies toward Christians and their communities, and sometimes also to their interfaith partners.

CURRICULA ISSUES

Michael Jagessar and I had a major concern of relating postcolonial perspectives, strategies, and agendas with lectionary and distinctive ways of engaging "word" in liturgy, and to do the same for the wider liturgical context of word: that of gesture and ceremonial scene in (either long-inherited or makeshift) space for events for and by an assembly. In her own explorations of lectionary provisions offered to Christian communities as part of their Christian education, Kim-Cragg makes what I think is a particularly significant turn for facing the challenge of moving postcolonial insight out of danger from what Sugirtharajah called hijack, cooption, and obfuscation. She invokes Maria Harris' work on curriculum for the church, *Fashion Me a People*.[35] Kim-Cragg picks up Harris' discussion that distinguishes between "a curriculum of education" and "a curriculum of schooling." The former, Harris suggests, refers to the interplay of several modes of learning, including "education in, to, and by service, community, proclamation, worship and teaching." By contrast, schooling is a term she reserves to "only one of the many valuable forms through which education occurs, that form which generally happens in a place called a school, a form focused on processes of instruction, reading of texts, conceptual knowledge, and study."[36] These are helpful categories through which to reflect on the shift from scholars and their books to Christians and their communities. The work of scholarship relates especially to schooling, whilst Christian communities have a broader curriculum of education. That latter curriculum is itself comprised of at least three powerful modes: its explicit, implicit, and null aspects. The explicit curriculum, according to Harris, "refers to what is actually presented, consciously and with intention. It is what we say we are offering, what is found in our table of contents." It is also closest of the three to scholars and their books. The implicit curriculum, by contrast, "refers to the patterns or organization or procedures that frame the explicit curriculum: things like attitudes or time spent or even the design of a room." In the implicit curriculum, scholars and their books are seen in a wider context, in terms of the institutions, communities, and bodies (even buildings) in which they work, which might otherwise be "left implicit, not spoken of or paid attention as part of the educational process."[37] The implicit curriculum invites attention to the current practices of the institutions in which scholars teach, research, and write about other times and places. The implicit curriculum highlights a contemporary analog to dynamics on which scholars may themselves focus, dynamics scrutinized by Sugirtharajah such as "white men bearing gifts," diffusing the Bible in their colonial expansion, pedaling texts, colporteuring scripture, in "the east," in the past.[38]

Elizabeth Conde-Frazier develops Harris' categories in ways that thicken and texture understanding, asserting that "social location, gender, race, and ethnicity all very much form the curriculum," as do "gestures, intonations, inflections, vocal volume, manner of pacing and the many different looks I give my students."[39] "How I dress" is also, according to Conde-Frazier, part of the curriculum, along with "the relationship between teacher and student."[40] Not only architecture but classroom arrangement is formative, as well as processes to which students are subject, "the distance that professors take from the subject they teach," the "policies operating that socialize us," "the make-up of the [governing] board . . . and the values inherent in their decisions."[41] All of these factors as they intersect need to be considered with great care, not least because as Conde-Frazier avers, "The nature of the relationships that we have with one another as staff, professors, and administrators is felt by our students and it teaches them an entire content about power and powerlessness, class, gender, and race relations."[42] The implicit curriculum invites questions about the congruence of what communities with an explicit curriculum practice in light of what they teach, what they say about themselves, how they organize, advertise, and promote themselves, and much else.

Harris defines the null curriculum thus: "A paradox. This is the curriculum that exists because it does not exist; it is what is left out. But the point of including it is that ignorance or the absence of something is not neutral. It skews the balance of options we might consider, alternatives from which we might choose, or perspectives that help us to see."[43] So while the implicit curriculum is what does not have attention drawn to it until it is named as also relevant, the null curriculum is "areas left out," "procedures left unused." Harris calls attention to examples including "two-way dialogue, extensive consultation . . . and participation in deci-sions by all concerned."[44] Conde-Frazier is clear that the "null curricula creates biases."[45]

Harris' categories of the explicit, implicit, and null curriculum lead to very interesting questions. On the one hand, it might be proposed that implicit and null curricula are minor matters in a curriculum of school-ing. But surely Sugirtharajah's own expressed concerns would cause problems for any such assumption: for when asked about "a tendency among members of the biblical guild to dismiss some of the newer meth-ods by racial/ethnic scholars as exotic, not rigorous, and not of much scholarly value," Sugirtharajah had a robust response: "In the context of the biblical guild, 'scholarly' usually means sustaining or preserving certain concerns and interests, replicating particular sets of values, and reinforcing certain power relations." Mention of "scholarly" can be "a camouflage for power exercised by a few."[46] What he identifies is the pernicious maintenance of an implicit curriculum in the culture of profes-sional biblical studies, whilst his choice of the word "camouflage" also suggests intent to hide the power at work in the scenario he describes. For that reason, the way in which some scholars such as David Esterline have written about a "hidden curriculum" rather than implicit curricu-lum may be aptly put to use here.[47] Sugirtharajah also raises concern that "racial or ethnic" scholars writing "out of their life experience," and per-haps with "a great deal of emotion, passion, and expressions of anger," are perhaps being seen by western "colleagues" as confrontational, a characterization by which they are vilified and demeaned, and thought not to be doing theology in the "proper" or "rational" way. As Sugirtha-rajah himself maintains, "It all depends on what you mean by scholar-ly."[48] As many postcolonial scholars have pointed out, without necessari-ly using Harris' or related language, the explicit curriculum, conscious-ness, and norms of professional, university-based, study of the Bible can all-too-readily shunt to sidelines, hide and smother, both persons and methods and means of learning, eliding as much as is focused and clar-ified.

No one has said this with more fierce clarity than Musa Dube, whose essay in honor of Sugirtharajah is called "Curriculum Transformation," in which she "dreams" of decolonization in theological study.[49] She makes an unflinching assessment of her own theological education, at the University of Botswana, Durham (Britain), and Vanderbilt (USA) univer-sities, The Claremont Colleges (USA), and the World Council of Churches in Geneva, Switzerland. She pinpoints numerous common pit-falls in academic courses which form the explicit curriculum—for exam-ple, using colonizing discourses about "developed" and "developing" countries, which only serve to "normalize" these ascriptions. Or, disin-genuous reference to "two-thirds-world" and "third-world," which in terms of global space and its populations, refer to much more territory than the numerals involved suggest. Quite pointedly, she notes that on all three continents in which she has been a student, more curricula space was given to so-called first-world perspectives than is justified by the idea that they represent one-third of persons across the planet—which they do not. Further, these discourses are common, she notes, even in places where rhetoric of inclusion and equal opportunity might be firmly in place. By inference, the people in these places should have been studying materials to avoid these pitfalls. But they preserve their own privilege and hierarchies by continued deployment of such rhetoric married to little enacted concern. Dube asks an excellent question, "Do commitments to equal opportunities and inclusive language translate into disavowal of colonizing ideologies?" Her answer: too often, no. Dube challenges institutions to more pervasive concern for the values that they claim to teach and avow they espouse. As she identifies, if genuine concern is to manifest in practice, "individual commitment, accountable solidarity, academic leadership, and institutional commitment to curriculum transformation"[50] will all need to be harnessed together.

SEMINARY CULTURE

Moreover, whatever might be made of the relationship between explicit and other curricula in university contexts, worship in seminaries, the educational settings which prepare the leadership of Christian communities to do their ministry, takes places alongside study of worship. Persons live in (or by one means or another intentionally form) community in ways which are not necessarily incumbent on university students. Even within the curriculum of schooling in seminaries, practical theology (certainly, pastoral theology) is likely to have a larger role than in many university-based theology programs. Chapel (actual or perhaps virtual, or with some analog in a shared rule of life for a dispersed seminary community), fieldwork in which "practical skills" for ministry are integrated into theological education (or at least the attempt is valued), and questions of vocation toward an ecclesial and wider public all shape the environment. In Harris' terms, the whole amounts to a curriculum of "education in, to, and by service, community, proclamation, worship, and teaching." Seminaries, which are by no means all alike, are marked by the characteristic that they intentionally embrace (some more effectively than others) more than a curriculum of schooling. In seminaries, the need for congruence between different curricula is a test of their integrity; and problems to which Dube points need to be sorted out so that curricula can be aligned.[51]

Dube's essay in honor of Sugirtharajah models the kind of scrutiny that needs to be exercised across seminary institutions, their different kinds of curricula, their culture and climate, their classrooms, chapels, common spaces, patterns of governance, decision-making processes, mission statements, and lived commitments. Seminaries, of course, are only a start to a needed transformation in the wider church, but they are a crucial place in which change must happen if the church's leaders are to learn to support postcolonial causes. What is learned in them needs also to be addressed in many other settings.

In seminaries as in other places, there are many dangers of what Robert Heaney calls "cheap postcolonialism": "using postcolonial rhetoric in a way that does not equate to critically postcolonial practice."[52] Particular problems can cluster around disjunctions which transpire when postcolonial perspectives might be promoted in classrooms and in academic syllabi, but find little trace (let alone traction) elsewhere in the institution. Its community life or liturgical celebration or "hands-on" practice or governance, and so on. The dangers are perhaps especially acute in situations where, by design or neglect, a system of governance confines a faculty (which may be made up of postcolonial scholars) to influence largely or only in the curriculum narrowly understood in terms of schooling. Something more integrated and much more demanding is needed in which the classroom and the public claims of an institution (its explicit curriculum) are credibly connected to the wider context in which students learn, community is formed, decisions are made, policies are enacted, worship takes place, and ministry is encouraged. For seminaries in North American settings, for example, work against cheap postcolonialism would require intentional welcome to postcolonial optics across the whole of what the Association of Theological Schools speaks of, albeit somewhat opaquely, as the "entire" or "total curriculum," a "theological curriculum, comprehensively understood."[53] Everything counts, for as Conde-Frazier insists, "Curriculum takes shape within an institutional structure and serves to cultivate an institutional culture,"[54] and the structures and the culture are themselves part of the curriculum. Care for the continuity and congruence between different kinds of curricula needs to be established in a postcolonial shift from scholars and their books to Christians and their communities.

The spectrum of postcolonial concerns promises or threatens a revolution to seminary communities, just as it does to wider Christian and religious circles. Seminaries occupy an interesting hybrid space between academy and church in which it is important that postcolonial practices are worked out, moving from academy to church, from books to community, from theorizing to practices.

THE CHAPTERS

We very much hope that *Postcolonial Practice of Ministry* will be part of the turn to which this introduction is pointing. Of course, what follows is a series of essays. But they are all about particular dimensions of life in the church, they are all concerned with ministry, they are all about practice. There are three clusters: the first on pastoral ministry (Emmanuel Y. Lartey, Melinda McGarrah Sharp, Mona West, and Stephanie Mitchem), the second on worship (HyeRan Kim-Cragg, Michael Jagessar, Lim Swee Hong, Jenny Te Paa Daniel, and Cláudio Carvalhaes), and the third on interfaith partnership (Sheryl Kujawa-Holbrook, Jonathan Tan, Jenny Daggers, and Melanie Harris). Although the chapters are clustered in this way, they might have been arranged otherwise—for example, in terms of how the authors employ the notion of "postcolonial" in their thinking, which is not always the same. As indicated earlier with reference to Sugirtharajah's *Postcolonial Reconfigurations*, thinkers use the same term somewhat differently, or in a hybrid kind of way with different weightings placed on different meanings. One of the main differences in what follows is, then, between those who focus primarily on geopolitics, on places in the period after formal colonization, and those who might have geopolitics in mind but accent more postcolonial theory, making more use of postcolonial criticism. The former tend to speak of the "post-colonial," while the latter do not use a hyphen. Others want to use "postcolonializing" to indicate it is a process. This and other differences apart, this collection serves as a gathering place for various related perspectives, ranging across our chosen three focal clusters of leadership, liturgy, and interfaith collaboration. It is, we believe, a "first," a forum in which postcolonial and practical theologies collide across a wider range of concerns than any of the aforementioned ventures to relate the two disciplines. Not least as a first, it points to all sorts of areas in which further investigations could and should occur, even as it sets out an exciting agenda for theological and ministerial engagement as it seeks to propel the turn from hermeneutics to winsome enactment of postcolonial conviction.

BIBLIOGRAPHY

Althaus-Reid, Marcella. *From Feminist Theology to Indecent Theology: Readings on Poverty, Sexual Identity and God*. London: SCM Press, 2004.
Burns, Stephen. "Formation for Ordained Ministry: Out of Touch?" In *Aboriginal Australia and the Unfinished Business of Theology: Crosscultural Engagement*, edited by Jione Havea, 151–166. New York, NY: Palgrave Macmillan, 2014.
———. "School or Seminary? Theological Education and Personal Devotion." *St. Mark's Review* 210 (2009): 79–95.
———. "When Seminaries Get Stuck." In *Liturgy in Postcolonial Perspectives: Only One Is Holy*, edited by Cláudio Carvalhaes, 255–66. New York, NY: Palgrave Macmillan, 2015.
———, Nicola Slee, and Michael N. Jagessar, eds. *The Edge of God: New Liturgical Texts and Contexts in Conversation*. Peterborough: Epworth, 2009.
Carvalhaes, Cláudio, ed. *Liturgy in Postcolonial Perspectives: Only One Is Holy*. New York: Palgrave Macmillan, 2015.

Conde-Frazier, Elizabeth. "Thoughts on Curriculum as Formational Praxis for Faculty, Students and their Communities." In *Teaching for a Culturally Diverse and Racially Just World*, edited by Eleazar S. Fernandez, 126–46. Eugene, OR: Cascade, 2014.

Douglas, Ian T., and Kwok Pui-lan, eds. *Beyond Colonial Anglicanism: The Anglican Communion in the Twenty-first Century*. New York: Church Publishing, 2000.

Dube, Musa W. "Curriculum Transformation: Dreaming of Decolonization in Theological Studies." In *Border Crossings: Cross-cultural Hermeneutics*, edited by D. N. Premnath, 121–38. Maryknoll, NY: Orbis Books, 2007.

Esterline, David V. "Multicultural Theological Education and Leadership for a Church without Walls." In *Shaping Beloved Community: Multicultural Theological Education*, edited by David V. Esterline and Ugbu Kalu, 15–27. Louisville, KY: Westminster John Knox Press, 2006.

Fabella, Virginia, and R. S. Sugirtharajah, eds. *The SCM Dictionary of Third World Theologies*. London: SCM Press, 2000.

Ford, David F., ed. *The Modern Theologians: An Introduction to Christian Theology in the Twentieth Century*. Oxford: Blackwell, 1989, 2 volumes.

———, ed. *The Modern Theologians: An Introduction to Christian Theology since 1918*. Oxford: Blackwell, 1997.

———, with Rachel Muers, eds. *The Modern Theologians: An Introduction to Christian Theology since 1918*. Oxford: Wiley-Blackwell, 2005.

——— and Mike Higton, with Simeon Zahl, eds. *The Modern Theologians Reader*. Oxford: Wiley-Blackwell, 2011.

Harris, Maria. *Fashion Me a People: Curriculum in Life of the Church*. Louisville, KY: Westminster John Knox Press, 1989.

Heaney, Robert S. "Prospects and Problems for Evangelical Postcolonialisms." In *Evangelical Postcolonial Conversations: Global Awakenings in Theology and Practice*, edited by Kay Higuera Smith, Jayachitra Lalitha, and L. Daniel Hawk, 29–43. Downers Grove, IL: IVP Academic, 2014.

Hunter, Rodney, et al, eds. *Dictionary of Pastoral Care and Counseling*. Nashville, TN: Abingdon, 1991.

Jagessar, Michael N., and Stephen Burns. *Christian Worship: Postcolonial Perspectives*. Sheffield: Equinox, 2011.

Kim-Cragg, HyeRan. *Story and Song: A Postcolonial Interplay between Christian Education and Worship*. New York: Peter Lang, 2012.

Kujawa-Holbrook, Sheryl A., and Karen B. Montagno, eds. *Injustice and the Care of Souls: Taking Oppression Seriously in Pastoral Care*. Minneapolis: Fortress Press, 2010.

Kwok Pui-lan. *Discovering the Bible in the Non-biblical World*. Maryknoll, NY: Orbis Books, 1995.

———. *Postcolonial Imagination and Feminist Theology*. Louisville, KY: Westminster John Knox Press, 2005.

———. Review of *Postcolonial Biblical Criticism: History, Method, Practice* by R. S. Sugirtharajah. *Postcolonial Networks Blog*. Accessed March 16, 2016. postcolonialnetworks.com/wp-content/uploads/2011/11/pui-lan-on-Sugirtharajah1.pdf.

———, Judith A. Berling and Jenny Te Paa Daniel, eds. *Anglican Women on Church and Mission*. New York: Morehouse, 2012.

Lartey, Emmanuel Y. *Pastoral Theology in an Intercultural World*. Peterborough: Epworth, 2006.

———. *Postcolonializing God: An African Practical Theology*. London: SCM Press, 2013.

Miller-McLemore, Bonnie. *Christian Theology in Practice: Discovering a Discipline*. Grand Rapids, MI: Eerdmans, 2012.

Orevillo-Montenegro, Muriel. *The Jesus of Asian Women*. Maryknoll, NY: Orbis Books, 2007.

Pattison, Stephen. *Pastoral Care and Liberation Theology*. Cambridge: Cambridge University Press, 1994.

———, and Gordon Lynch. "Pastoral and Practical Theology." In *The Modern Theologians: An Introduction to Christian Theology since 1918*, edited by David F. Ford with Rachel Muers, 408–25. Oxford: Blackwell, 2005.

Premnath, D. N. "Margins and Mainstream: An Interview with R.S. Sugirtharajah." In *Border Crossings: Cross-cultural Hermeneutics*, edited by D. N. Premnath, 153–66. Maryknoll, NY: Orbis Books, 2007.

Ramsay, Nancy, ed. *Pastoral Care and Counseling: Redefining the Paradigms*. Nashville, TN: Abingdon, 2004.

Radford Ruether, Rosemary. *America, Amerikkka: Elect Nation and Imperial Violence*. London: Equinox, 2007.

Sharp, Melinda A. McGarrah. *Misunderstanding Stories: Toward a Postcolonial Pastoral Theology*. Eugene, OR: Pickwick, 2013.

Stevenson-Moessner, Jeanne, and Teresa Snorton, eds. *Women Out of Order: Risking Change and Creating Care in a Multicultural World*. Minneapolis: Fortress Press, 2009.

Sugirtharajah, R. S. "Afterword: Cultures, Texts and Margins: A Hermeneutical Odyssey." In *Voices from the Margins: Interpreting the Bible in the Third World*, ed. R. S. Sugirtharajah, New ed., 457–75. London: SPCK, 1995.

———. *The Bible and Asia: From the Pre-Christian Era to the Postcolonial Age*. Cambridge, MA: Harvard University Press, 2013.

———. *The Bible and the Third World: Postcolonial Encounters*. Cambridge: Cambridge University Press, 2001.

———. *Exploring Postcolonial Biblical Criticism: History, Method, Practice*. Oxford: Wiley-Blackwell, 2012.

———. "Muddling Along at the Margins." In *Still at the Margins: Biblical Scholarship Fifteen Years after Voices from the Margins*, edited by R. S. Sugirtharajah, 8–21. London: T. & T. Clark, 2008.

———. "Postcolonial Biblical Interpretation." In *The Modern Theologians: An Introduction to Christian Theology since 1918*, edited by David F. Ford with Rachel Muers, 535–52. Oxford: Wiley-Blackwell, 2005.

———. *Postcolonial Criticism and Biblical Interpretation*. Oxford: Oxford University Press, 2002.

———. *Postcolonial Reconfigurations: An Alternative Way of Reading the Bible and Doing Theology*. London: SCM Press, 2003.

———, ed. *Asian Faces of Jesus*. Maryknoll, NY: Orbis Books, 1993.

———, ed. *Caught Reading Again: Scholars and Their Books*. London: SCM Press, 2009.

———, ed. *Frontiers in Asian Christian Theology: Emerging Trends*. Maryknoll, NY: Orbis Books, 1994.

———, and Cecil Hargreaves, eds. *Readings in Indian Christian Theology*. London: SPCK, 1993.

NOTES

1. David F. Ford, ed., *The Modern Theologians: An Introduction to Christian Theology in the Twentieth Century* (Oxford: Blackwell, 1989), published in two volumes. A second edition of 1997 was published in one volume as *The Modern Theologians: An Introduction to Christian Theology Since 1918* (Oxford: Blackwell, 1997). The third edition was published as David F. Ford with Rachel Muers, eds., *The Modern Theologians: An Introduction to Christian Theology Since 1918* (Oxford: Wiley-Blackwell, 2005) with a subsequent companion anthology, David F. Ford and Mike Higton with Simeon Zahl, eds., *The Modern Theologians Reader* (Oxford: Wiley-Blackwell, 2011).

2. R. S. Sugirtharajah, *The Bible and Asia: From the Pre-Christian Era to the Postcolonial Age* (Cambridge, MA: Harvard University Press, 2013), 212. See also R. S. Sugirtharajah, *Exploring Postcolonial Biblical Criticism: History, Method, Practice* (Oxford: Wiley-Blackwell, 2012), 58.

3. R. S. Sugirtharajah, "Postcolonial Biblical Interpretation," in *The Modern Theologians: An Introduction to Christian Theology since 1918*, ed. David F. Ford with Rachel Muers (Oxford: Wiley-Blackwell, 2005), 535–52.

4. The back cover of *Exploring Postcolonial Biblical Criticism* claims that the author is "the field's leading proponent."

5. Stephen D. Moore's commendation for *Exploring Postcolonial Biblical Criticism* (back cover).

6. For further discussion, see Michael N. Jagessar and Stephen Burns, *Christian Worship: Postcolonial Perspectives* (Sheffield: Equinox, 2011), 2. I note in turn that some of the texts mentioned below—for example, Melinda A. McGarrah Sharp, *Misunderstanding Stories: Toward a Postcolonial Pastoral Theology* (Eugene, OR: Pickwick, 2013)—emerging from a North American context, make no reference to Sugirtharajah.

7. R. S. Sugirtharajah, *The Bible and the Third World: Postcolonial Encounters* (Cambridge: Cambridge University Press, 2001); idem., *Postcolonial Criticism and Biblical Interpretation* (Oxford: Oxford University Press, 2002); and idem., *Postcolonial Reconfigurations: An Alternative Way of Reading the Bible and Doing Theology* (London: SCM Press, 2003).

8. His earlier and ongoing broader work includes: R. S. Sugirtharajah, ed., *Asian Faces of Jesus* (Maryknoll, NY: Orbis Books, 1993); R. S. Sugirtharajah and Cecil Hargreaves, eds., *Readings in Indian Christian Theology* (London: SPCK, 1993); R. S. Sugirtharjah, ed., *Frontiers in Asian Christian Theology: Emerging Trends* (Maryknoll, NY: Orbis Books, 1994); Virginia Fabella and R. S. Sugirtharajah, eds, *The SCM Dictionary of Third World Theologies* (London: SCM Press, 2000).

9. R. S. Sugirtharajah, "Afterword: Cultures, Texts and Margins: A Hermeneutical Odyssey," in *Voices from the Margins: Interpreting the Bible in the Third World*, ed. R. S. Sugirtharajah, New ed. (London: SPCK, 1995), 460.

10. Ibid.

11. D. N. Premnath, "Margins and Mainstream: An Interview with R.S. Sugirtharajah," *Border Crossings: Cross-cultural Hermeneutics*, ed. D. N. Premnath (Maryknoll, NY: Orbis Books, 2007), 156.

12. Sugirtharjah addresses developments in the genre in his *Exploring Postcolonial Biblical Criticism*, which employs the motif of "journey" as an *inclusio* at beginning and end to envelop various essays on different movements: arrivals, trajectories, decenterings, repackagings, and talk-back.

13. Here drawing on Sugirtharajah, *Postcolonial Reconfigurations*, 4.

14. Sugirtharajah published *Postcolonial Reconfigurations* before Rosemary Radford Ruether put out her *America, Amerikkka: Elect Nation and Imperial Violence* (London: Equinox, 2007). Regardless of whatever Sugirtharajah might make of the contents, the scope of her book suggests one way in which neo-colonialism might be explored with special reference to a particular current context. In *Postcolonial Criticism and Biblical Interpretation*, he had himself asked the question, "Is the United States postcolonial?" (33–36).

15. Sugirtharajah writes of them as "companions in struggle": *Postcolonial Criticism*, 117–23.

16. For example, Kwok Pui-lan, *Postcolonial Imagination and Feminist Theology* (Louisville, KY: Westminster John Knox Press, 2005). Note inclusion of her work in editions of *Voices from the Margin* and her important "attempt to dialogue with the Bible from multiple perspectives as an Asian woman theologian" in *Discovering the Bible in the Non-biblical World* (Maryknoll, NY: Orbis Books, 1995) which is concerned both with "constructing a postcolonial discourse" and foregrounding "issues of racism and ethnocentricism in feminist biblical interpretation." It should also be noted that Kwok was instrumental in the very wide-ranging collection *Beyond Colonial Anglicanism: The Anglican Communion in the Twenty-first Century*, edited by herself and Ian T. Douglas (New York: Church Publishing, 2000) as well as *Anglican Women on Church and Mission*, edited by herself, Judith Berling and Jenny Plane Te Paa (New York: Morehouse, 2012).

17. See, for example, Marcella Althaus-Reid's caustic essay, "Gustavo Gutiérrez Goes to Disneyland: Theme Park Theologies and the Diaspora of the Discourse of the Popular Theologian in Liberation Theology," in her *From Feminist Theology to Indecent Theology: Readings on Poverty, Sexual Identity and God* (London: SCM Press, 2004), 124–42.

18. For example, in her review of Sugirtharajah's *Exploring Postcolonial Biblical Criticism* she notes his own engagement with feminist issues, and presses for attention to alignments feminist theology has latterly made with queer studies. See postcolonial-networks.com/wp-content/uploads/2011/11/pui-lan-on-Sugirtharajah1.pdf

19. R. S. Sugirtharajah, "Muddling Along at the Margins," in *Still at the Margins: Biblical Scholarship Fifteen Years after* Voices from the Margins, ed. R. S. Sugirtharajah, (London: T. & T. Clark, 2008), 11, 12.

20. I allude to R. S. Sugirtharajah, ed., *Caught Reading Again: Scholars and Their Books* (London: SCM Press, 2009).

21. Sugirtharajah, *Bible and Asia*, 12.

22. Muriel Orevillo-Montenegro, *The Jesus of Asian Women* (Maryknoll, NY: Orbis Books, 2007), 177.

23. Ibid., 170.

24. Jagessar and Burns, *Postcolonial Perspectives*, 3.

25. Kathleen A. Calahan and James R. Nieman, "Mapping the Field of Practical Theology," in *For Life Abundant: Practical Theology, Theological Education and Christian Ministry*, ed. Dorothy C. Bass and Miroslav Volf (Grand Rapids, MI: Eerdmans, 2008), 62–91, discuss some significant differences, which can be tradition-specific and in other ways more or less conscious of being shaped by context.

26. These terms are sometimes, and sometimes not, seen as interchangeable by scholars within the discipline. These differences can reflect strong ideological convictions about what kinds of worship are or are not included within the scope of the field—to circle in or out of discussion, Pentecostal worship, for example—and this (though it may be unarticulated) is not unrelated to what Sugirtharajah would call "European expansionism."

27. These terms, too, are sometimes, and sometimes not, seen as inter-changeable by scholars within the discipline. The differences often center around concern about pastoral theology being captive to a "clerical paradigm." For a good discussion of this concern, see Bonnie Miller-McLemore, "The Clerical Paradigm and the Academic Paradigm," in her *Christian Theology in Practice: Discovering a Discipline* (Grand Rapids, MI: Eerdmans, 2012), 160–84.

28. Nancy Ramsay, ed., *Pastoral Care and Counseling: Redefining the Paradigms* (Nashville, TN: Abingdon, 2004) is an important collection, not least because it quite consciously seeks to correct omissions in Rodney Hunter, et al, eds, *Dictionary of Pastoral Care and Counseling* (Nashville, TN: Abingdon, 1991). The correctives are incorporated into the second, expanded, edition of the dictionary, published in 2005. The contributions of Emmanuel Y. Lartey—himself once a Birmingham colleague of both Sugirtharajah and Ford—are significant to both the Ramsay book and the later edition of the dictionary. See also Lartey's *Pastoral Theology in an Intercultural World* (Peterborough: Epworth, 2006), which includes material that first appeared in Ramsay's book. Another Birmingham-based theologian, Stephen Pattison produced *Pastoral Care and Liberation Theology* (Cambridge: Cambridge University Press, 1994) which remains a particularly important contribution from the British context, not least for its insistence on what Pattison calls "socio-politically aware and committed" pastoral care, and that it is itself a corrective to overly theoretical perspectives. Sadly, to my mind, Pattison's work is marginal to Ramsay's book (in a rare reference to him, neither author nor editor catches the wrong spelling of his given name on p. 56, for example). Jeanne Stevenson-Moessner and Teresa Snorton, eds., *Women Out of Order: Risking Change and Creating Care in a Multicultural World* (Minneapolis, MN: Fortress Press, 2009) and Sheryl A. Kujawa-Holbrook and Karen B. Montagno, eds., *Injustice and the Care of*

Souls: Taking Oppression Seriously in Pastoral Care (Minneapolis, MN: Fortress Press, 2010) are important more recent contributions from North America.

29. Stephen Pattison and Gordon Lynch, "Pastoral and Practical Theology," in *The Modern Theologians: An Introduction to Christian Theology since 1918*, ed. David F. Ford with Rachel Muers (Oxford: Blackwell, 2005), 408. Notably, the third edition of Ford's textbook is the first edition to include a contribution on practical theology, itself a recognition of the growing influence of the field in the academy.

30. Here I reflect a deep and enduring tension in practical theology, in which some, determined by psychological disciplines, are accused by others of "therapeutic captivity." I also allude to Lartey's concern in *Pastoral Theology in an Intercultural World* with the "matter of theological content."

31. Lartey, *Pastoral Theology*, 101, 103, 106, 107, 111, 114, 116.

32. Cláudio Carvalhaes, ed., *Liturgy in Postcolonial Perspectives: Only One Is Holy* (New York: Palgrave Macmillan, 2015). Carvalhaes' book belongs in the series "Postcolonialism and Religions" published by Palgrave Macmillan, the first volume of which appeared in 2012: www.palgrave.com/series/postcolonialism-and-religions/PCR/

33. HyeRan Kim-Cragg, *Story and Song: A Postcolonial Interplay Between Christian Education and Worship* (New York: Peter Lang, 2012).

34. McGarrah Sharp, mentioned above; Emmanuel Y. Lartey, *Postcolonializing God: An African Practical Theology* (London: SCM Press, 2013).

35. Maria Harris, *Fashion Me a People: Curriculum in Life of the Church* (Louisville, KY: Westminster John Knox Press, 1989). See Kim-Cragg, *Story and Song*, 41–52.

36. Harris, *Fashion Me a People*, 64–65.

37. Ibid., 68.

38. Here drawing on images used by Sugirtharajah in *The Bible and the Third World*: "White men bearing gifts: diffusion of the Bible and scriptural imperialism" and "Textual pedlars: distributing salvation—colporteurs and their portable Bibles" (pp. 45–73, 140–72).

39. Elizabeth Conde-Frazier, "Thoughts on Curriculum as Formational Praxis for Faculty, Students and their Communities," *Teaching for a Culturally Diverse and Racially Just World*, ed. Eleazar S. Fernandez (Eugene, OR: Cascade, 2014), 128.

40. Ibid.

41. All the quotes are from ibid., 129.

42. Ibid., Conde-Frazier's thoughts are particularly valuable for being set in the context of multiple ways of thickening understanding of curriculum, all of which could be related to what I suggest below. For example, she discusses Kathleen Calahan's notions of "vertical" curriculum (how students move from introductory to more advanced studies), "horizontal" curriculum (the impact different parts of students' experience have on one another), and "diagonal" curriculum (concerned with integration of learning with life experience, identity, privilege and discrimination) and Charles Foster's notions of "pedagogies of performance" (teaching and learning of practices through observation, imitation and rehearsal) and "pedagogies of formation" (how spiritual and professional identity is formed within and outside the classroom, in worship, service, spiritual disciplines, and so on) ("Thoughts," esp. 133–35).

43. Harris, *Fashion Me a People*, 69.

44. Harris, *Fashion Me a People*, 69.

45. Conde-Frazier, "Thoughts," 129.

46. Premnath, "Margins and Mainstream," 157.

47. David V. Esterline, "Multicultural Theological Education and Leadership for a Church Without Walls," in *Shaping Beloved Community: Multicultural Theological Education*, ed. David V. Esterline and Ugbu Kalu (Louisville, KY: Westminster John Knox Press, 2006), 20. "Hidden" curriculum is also Conde-Frazier's preferred term.

48. Premnath, "Margins and Mainstream," 157–58.

49. Musa Dube, "Curriculum Transformation: Dreaming of Decolonization in Theological Studies," in *Border Crossings: Cross-cultural Hermeneutics*, 121–38.

50. Ibid., 124.

51. For more on congruence in seminary curricula, see Stephen Burns, "School or Seminary? Theological Education and Personal Devotion," *St. Mark's Review* 210 (2009): 79–95, and for more on Harris' work as a lens on seminaries, Stephen Burns, Nicola Slee, and Michael N. Jagessar, eds., *The Edge of God: New Liturgical Texts and Contexts in Conversation* (Peterborough: Epworth, 2009), about the Birmingham seminary and The Queen's Foundation for Ecumenical Theological Education.

52. Robert S. Heaney, "Prospects and Problems for Evangelical Postcolonialisms," in *Evangelical Postcolonial Conversations: Global Awakenings in Theology and Practice*, ed. Kay Higuera Smith, Jayachitra Lalitha, and L. Daniel Hawk (Downers Grove, IL: IVP Academic, 2014), 38.

53. See www.ats.edu/uploads/accrediting/documents/general-institutional-standards.pdf 3.2, 3.2, 3.2.1, 3.2.2.3. For further reflection on the work of seminaries in postcolonial perspective, see Stephen Burns, "Formation for Ordained Ministry: Out of Touch?" in *Aboriginal Australia and the Unfinished Business of Theology: Crosscultural Engagement*, Jione Havea (New York: Palgrave Macmillan, 2014), 151–66, and Stephen Burns, "When Seminaries Get Stuck," in *Liturgy in Postcolonial Perspectives: Only One Is Holy*, ed. Cláudio Carvalhaes (New York: Palgrave Macmillan, 2015), 255–66.

54. Conde-Frazier, "Thoughts," 139.

I

Pastoral Leadership

ONE

"Borrowed Clothes Will Never Keep You Warm"

Postcolonializing Pastoral Leadership

Emmanuel Y. Lartey

The worldwide church is living in a particularly contentious time today. On issues of polity, practice, and teaching, differences between North and South, East and West have reached epidemic levels, especially most recently on the matter of human sexuality. A challenge of our times for pastoral leaders can be stated fairly directly and simply. How can leaders facilitate peaceful and harmonious living within the communities they lead? How can local leaders help their communities participate in and make contributions to a global church in which their cultural, theological, and practical differences are respected and do not lead to strife or the breakdown of relations? How may the rich cultural, theological, and practical diversity evident in human community be celebrated through the daily life of communities of faith? The global church desperately needs leaders who are able to facilitate unity in the midst of great diversity.

The western Christian missionary project of the eighteenth and nineteenth centuries coincided with the colonial expansionism of European powers. By and large, missionizing was seen as a civilizing effort, which aimed at converting the natives of every conquered land, homogenizing these subjects and turning them into Christians shaped in the image of their western tutors and masters. The plain historical fact is that much of European Christian interaction with the rest of the world involved efforts to turn "uncivilized" non-westerners into carbon copies of their western

Christian missioners. Catechisms were the educational curricula that were framed to provide the tools for this largely westernizing effort.

The Christian theology, especially that undergirded and fueled missionary zeal and practice, has most often understood itself as stating the ONE Christian belief as it has been understood, believed, and practiced by all Christians of all ages, in all places. The oft quoted "Vincentian Canon" is the Latin phrase: "Quod ubique, quod semper, quod ab omnibus creditum est" (i.e., "that Faith which has been believed everywhere, always, by all"). This expression comes from *The Commonitory* by Vincent de Lérins.

"Moreover, in the Catholic Church itself, all possible care must be taken, that we hold that faith which has been believed everywhere, always, by all."[1] The "canon" refers to a standard or measuring stick. It provided three criteria by which one could determine whether a doctrine was orthodox or heretical. Vincent did not invent the "canon" named after him. He summed up in elegant Latin a longstanding theological method traceable to early Christians in quest of a unified faith.[2] Western Christian missionaries consequently saw their mission in the world as getting all people everywhere to believe and practice the faith of their tutors as a whole. Deviations from this "one true faith" were punished as heretical.

Western-missionized Christians in the colonies, like their tutors, were not trained or given tools to handle diversity or difference in any other way than through "conversion," persuasion, conquest, or suppression. Present-day churches across the globe, steeped in the dualistic, adversarial, and conquest mentality of western missionary Christianity likewise seem particularly unprepared to deal with diversity in a way in keeping with the love ethic of their Christian faith.

However, the reality of the global situation has long been that of diversity and difference; the very nature of global Christianity, reflecting the diversity evident in the Scriptures, has been pluralistic since its inception. The context I am focusing on in this chapter is that of post-colonial communities, especially those Sub-Saharan African nations that began to emerge out of colonial servitude into independence in the late 1950s. At ground level, African Christians have by and large always been "multiple religious practitioners." As a local pastor in Ghana, I soon realized that at almost every turn, lived Christianity had an "official" (by day) version and another "informal" (Nicodemus-like, by night) version. Africans were "Christians by day, pagans by night" as one scholar put it or in fact "Europeans by day and Africans by night." Much of my pastoral ministry consisted of trying to convince African Christians to abandon their African beliefs and religio-cultural practices for western sanctioned "Christian" practices. Being Christian meant being European. Pastoral care began to look very different when I began to listen to and learn from African religious and cultural practitioners at ground level and not pulverize or pummel them into subjugation with western theological constructions. My vision of the Christian faith began to expand. African cultural concepts and practices seemed able to encompass and incorporate the essence of the faith of Jesus and to do so in such a way as to deepen the authenticity and integrity of the African practitioners of Christianity. Reflection on the manifest plurality in the Scriptures, including various visions of the Divine, forms of church, and individual patterns of belief and practice, made it clear to me that the desire to make all disciples throughout the world after the chosen image of Europe was at best wrongheaded and at worst heretically damaging.

In this chapter, therefore, Sub-Saharan African societies are the focus of my concern for the emergence of postcolonializing leaders, who will seek to overcome the damaging hegemony of any one model and incarnate the many-sided wisdom of God. The first question that fuels my analysis is the following: What are the sociopolitical, cultural, and religious characteristics of these communities? In response to this question it is necessary to outline some of the characteristics of the global situation observable in post-colonial economies, especially in the Global South.

SOME CHARACTERISTICS OF POST-COLONIAL COMMUNITIES

The Eruption of Subjugated, Indigenous Knowledge

In many post-colonial nations, the existence of pre-colonial indigenous art, science, and valuable knowledge was denied, suppressed or ignored during and immediately following the colonial era. Although the dominant forms of education in these economies continues to be that bequeathed by western missionaries, there has been what can be described as an eruption of indigenous forms of knowledge and culture. The struggle for independence was not only political and economic, it was perhaps above all cultural and anthropological. Human subjects wanted the freedom to be themselves and express in their own languages the knowledge and philosophies of life of their ancestral heritage. There is thus a noticeable appropriation, articulation, and re-valuing of indigenous culture, creative arts, and concepts in post-colonial communities across the world.

Collapsing of Binary Oppositions

As a direct consequence of this eruption, local and contextual knowledge has begun to be more highly valued in many quarters. A noticeable feature of many of these forms of knowledge is the absence of dichotomous, dualistic, and analytic thinking (which breaks up concepts and experience into discrete disconnected segments). It is commonplace that

African cultures hardly draw sharp boundaries between the sacred and the secular, reason and intuition, science and art. Indigenous subjugated knowledge is, by and large, synthetic, bringing together various aspects and drawing connections and linkages across vastly different features of human life, thus collapsing the binary oppositional thinking by which colonists and neo-colonial rulers had established their superiority.

Pluralities of Discourse, Diverse Truths, Divergent Histories: An Affirmation of Multiple Positions and Perspectives

A result of the scramble for Africa was that African nation-states were carved out on drawing boards in Europe with little or no regard for ethnic, linguistic, demographic, or cultural realities on the ground. Internally, African nation states constitute collections of diverse ethnic groups forced together into countries for the sole purpose of the formation of units of production of specific (and singular) raw materials desired by the controlling colonial European powers. As a consequence of these colonial commercial unit-forming activities, these nations within themselves are full of diversity and difference—linguistic, cultural, and political differences within which multiple positions and perspectives are continually expressed. Attempts at nation building have been hampered by this diversity which has often spurred violent ethnic conflicts between groups within the nations. The rise of military dictatorships in the post-colonial period can partly be accounted for by the need to forcefully keep these diverse peoples together for economic and political reasons.

Plurality is thus a common feature of post-colonial Africa. Churches, political parties, and other social institutions have had to address this constitutionally and in terms of policies and practices in order to survive and in an attempt to thrive. Pastoral leadership that wishes to adopt a postcolonializing ethos must pay attention to multiple positions and divergent perspectives, resisting any hegemonic impulses, whether doctrinal or pastoral. Pre-colonial culture and thought in its non-dichotomizing vein may have much to offer in this regard.

Recognition of Social Constructionism Especially of Identity

Another noticeable feature of post-colonial African life is the realization and articulation of the identity of individuals and communities. Various ethnic groups and several individuals have set about reconstructing their selfhood historically, narratively, and culturally through writing, the arts, crafts, and story-telling. Political leaders who were in the forefront of the struggles for independence such as Kwame Nkrumah, Kenneth Kaunda, Julius Nyerere, Sekou Touré, Leopold Senghor, Nelson Mandela, to mention a few, all produced literature in which the issue of their identity as Africans was pivotal. Moreover, Africans have found themselves as diaspora in various continents throughout the world and have forged identities for themselves in each region that are hybrid mixtures of historical heritage and contemporary realities.[3]

A Resurgence of the Conventional: The Empire Strikes Back

Recognizable in this cultural, religious, and social mix is conservatism and a loudly expressed desire for the conventional, even if this means a return to colonialism. Nostalgia for the "good old days" on the part of some has meant a hankering back to the uniformity and rigidity of the conventional.

In doctrinal terms, it is true to say that Christianity in post-colonial Africa is predominantly characterized by conventional conformity to western doctrinal forms. Historic orthodoxy is alive and very well in Africa. African Christian orthodoxy is in fact being cited and politically utilized against liberalizing tendencies in the West. An example of this is the quest for Nigerian bishops for non-gay-affirming American Episcopalians.

These features characterize the diverse communities of the Global South and call for pastoral leadership that is equipped to respond adequately to the needs embedded within them. Therefore, I now move to a discussion of the forms of pastoral care and leadership, which seem to be needed within these post-colonial contexts.

FORMS OF PASTORAL CARE NEEDED IN POST-COLONIAL CONTEXTS

Current post-colonial social, economic, political, and cultural contexts in Sub-Saharan Africa call for forms of pastoral care, counseling and leadership ministry in the widest sense that is responsive to the social forces identified above. These forms of ministry and the leadership that will inspire it need to have the character and capability to respond to the following needs:

1. *The need for empathic and interpathic listening and appropriate responses to people in the complexities of contemporary contexts.*[4]

Sub-Saharan post-colonial contexts are replete with complexity. They are enigmatic mixtures of pre-colonial, colonial, modern, post-colonial and post-modern technology and culture. Western modernistic scientific cultures exist in close proximity with pre-colonial traditional beliefs and practices. Rural and urban communities all reflect this complexity. The quest for appropriate responses to the human needs that these communities embody requires empathic (in which caregivers from within these communities truly enter into the life views of the care seekers) and inter-pathic (in which caregivers from outside the communities also attempt to enter the life experiences of the care seekers) listening. Deep listening to people is the first skill needed for all who seek to minister in these complex situations.

2. The need for communiopathy and fostering of community building within the rhythms of intercultural encounter.

Western forms of ministry and engagement have often been character-ized as individualistic, reflecting as they do the major cultural patterns of their home countries. Individualism can be differentiated from African personalism as expressed especially in the Bantu normative ethical vision of *Ubuntu*, in which "a person is a person by reason of other persons." However, even personalism does not go far enough in responding to the communal philosophy of life that seems to characterize African tradition-al life and thought. There is a shared communion envisioned and entailed in *Ubuntu*; it is the life-blood of these communal cultural groups and far exceeds the sum of the individual or personal parts. In order to attentive-ly respond to this communalism, I have coined the term *communiopathy*—extending and requiring a communal embracing and expansion of both "empathy" and "interpathy." *Communiopathy* points to an entry into the *pathos* (passion, pain, and deep feeling) of an entire community. Many black theologians and social thinkers have sought to call people's atten-tion to the experience of being black in a black-negating white suprema-cist world. Communiopathy in this case would be entry into the pain and pathos of the black community and thus gaining some perspective on the black experience in the world. Communiopathy is about entering into the collective experience of a whole community or social or cultural group. There is a shared communal aspect to the pain of people who have expe-rienced slavery, colonialism, torture, rape, or war; acknowledging this is paramount in the provision of a caring ministry to such people. In com-muniopathy, the caregiver does not overgeneralize, but rather respects individual differences within shared experience. The genius is to recog-nize what is shared and to be able to distinguish how individual or per-sonal experience may be a variant of or be reflective of the group's expe-rience.

3. The need to empower individuals and groups to challenge and change unjust social, economic, and political structures that militate against their mental health and well-being.

Pastoral caregiving in post-colonial contexts goes beyond individual therapy into forms of social activism necessary for the achievement of the goals of personal counseling. There are social forces that militate against individual mental health and well-being. If these are not challenged and changed, therapy remains a futile and fruitless activity. Where sexism, racism, and oppression exist, the flourishing of individual women, individual people of color and individual workers will always be an elusive challenge, no matter how excellent the therapy they receive individually. The dismantling of unjust and socially oppressive structures must thus be the focus of any persons who seek individual well-being. This calls for wise and mature leadership able to influence and transform social, political, and economic conditions within communities.

4. *Affirming heterogeneity and encouraging each person or group to speak for themselves.*

Complex communities need to be respectful of and encourage the heterogeneity which is the essence of their existence. In all decision-making processes in post-colonial communities, each individual and sub-dominant group must be ensured a voice and a space for their perspectives. It is the task of caregivers, leaders, and ministers in these contexts to advocate for the voiceless, the downtrodden, and the oppressed, and to ensure that they are not invisible in the halls of power. Heterogeneity needs to be seen as normal in any community or social grouping. For this to be accomplished, the voices of "those who differ" from the majority need to be clearly heard and respected, and leaders within all communities need to courageously allow minority voices to be expressed and heard. As the parables of Jesus indicate, rather than merely echoing the voice of a community's dominant majority (the ninety-nine), true pastoral leadership seeks out the isolated and marginalized (the "one sheep") and provides the space for that one to be not only safe but also heard and respected.

5. *Encouraging the principle of* dynamism *rather than exclusively focusing on things archeological.*

Too much of what has passed for ministry or pastoral care for so long in post-colonial Sub-Saharan Africa has been a harking back to bygone years (the missionary era) and the paying of homage to European ancestors. Whilst the voice of the past is needed and can be instructive, this must not be allowed to completely eclipse visions of a future created through faith and hope. Dynamism involves the realization that change is an inevitable part of life. As such, it is important to look also at what is emerging through the inbreaking inspiration of the Holy Spirit. The living God is the God of hope and the future. Postcolonializing pastoral leadership is at home with change and leads communities in transformation. To dismantle colonial structures that no longer provide "warmth" and to implement post-colonial ones requires courageous leadership.

Here the example of the life and practice of Jesus the Christ is deeply instructive.

6. *Need to collaborate with and engage in interdisciplinary work with people whose expertise may be ecological, cultural, economic, political, medical or sociological.*

The wholeness that is sought and needed within our global community is of a holistic nature involving *body-mind-soul-community-earth*. Each aspect of this hyphenated reality deserves careful attention and conscious realization of the intersectionality that results in their interrelated and interpenetrating interaction. A crucial aspect of ministry in post-colonial contexts is its need to be interdisciplinary if it is going to be fruitful. Some of the expertise needed to respond to needs and challenges within communities will often come through partnerships with secular (so-called) institutions.

7. *Need to develop, espouse, and utilize indigenous models of ministry and care that address our existence in this era.*

Swiss professor emeritus Walter J. Hollenweger frequently made the assertion that "the religion of the poor is not poor religion."[5] There are rich and untapped resources within the religious cultures of the poor. Embedded in pre-colonial African and other religious cultures of the Global South are understandings of human community, personhood, and the divine which can energize new approaches to ministry. Examples of these include the Bantu communal and interpersonalist concept of "*Ubuntu*" (South Africa)[6]; *Just Therapy* (developed by family therapists in Aotearoa/New Zealand drawing upon Maori culture)[7]; *Palaver-process therapy* (utilized by pastoral care givers and conflict resolution practitioners in the Democratic Republic of Congo and other central African countries)[8] ; *Soul processing* (developed by African mystic Bro. Ishmael Tetteh, Ghana).[9]

The final part of this chapter explores features of postcolonializng pastoral leadership that engage the realities of the complex and dynamic context outlined and seeks to provide the kinds of pastoral care I have highlighted.

CHARACTERISTICS OF POSTCOLONIALZING LEADERSHIP[10]

Counter-hegemonic Activities

Postcolonializing leadership activities are *counter-hegemonic*, insurgent, and even subversive in nature and character. By their very nature they call into question dominance and hegemony in human relations within the church, community, or world. Where patterns of dominance have solidified into hegemonic structures, postcolonializing pastoral leadership takes the form of insurgency and may be deemed subversive by the powers that be. They essentially problematize, disrupt, and attempt to subvert dominant structures leading to more equitable relations between and amongst people. Many who suffered colonialism's brutal suppression resorted to forms of domesticated discourse as a survival strategy. Consequently, it is possible to discern counter-hegemonic patterns and strategies deeply embedded and latent within the domesticated discourse evident in the communities of faith in the Global South. It is also possible to recognize more overt forms of counter-hegemonic activities. Both overt and latent forms of counter-hegemonic practices deserve attention as postcolonializing leadership strategies. Post-colonial pastoral leaders need the wisdom of serpents and the innocence of doves in their counter-hegemonic work.

Strategic

Postcolonializing leadership activities are *strategic*. In other words, they bring into critical focus the dialogical nature of relations between theory and practice, and result in actions with transformative intent in the church and world. In this sense they may be termed praxiological or practical and theoretical with an action-for-change orientation. These activities at times are overtly political, at other times quietist. However, in all cases, postcolonializing leaders are reflective practitioners of their disciplines and arts who are motivated by the desire for transformation. Postcolonializing activities are not engaged in from the safe, disinterested, and uninvolved distance of purported objective research. The postcolonializer is by no means a disinterested observer. Instead, in an incarnational sense, he is *intentional* and *involved*. Postcolonializing leadership activities betray an interested commitment to involvement with the issues and subjects affected by oppressive colonizing actions, and are engaged in with the express intention of seeking transformed existence for all.

Hybrid/Variegated/Plural

Postcolonializing activities are themselves *hybrid* and promote multidimensional discourses and practices. They are deeply *variegated* and *plural*. *Diversity* is a hallmark, characteristic feature and desired end of postcolonializing processes. As such they are *messy*, in that they question and disrupt sharp and clear boundaries between materials, recognizing the often arbitrary lines of demarcation that are drawn, and calling for attention to complexity and *metissage* in the approach to all matters. Sharp demarcations and neat contents are not to be found in postcolonializing discourse and practices. They are therefore also and always ambiguous and at times contradictory, full of contestation and controversy, wary of over-privileging any one form over all others.

Interactional and Intersubjective

An Akan proverb which addresses the complexities of leadership declares: "Power is like an egg. When held too tightly it may break, or it falls and breaks when held loosely."[11] In direct reference to leadership this adage enjoins care and attention to the potential destructive nature of power wielded without caution, subtlety, and sensitivity.

Postcolonializing leadership activities are consequently deeply *interactional* and *intersubjective*. They emphasize the social and global nature of phenomena and encourage approaches to subjects that engage interactively with all people's experience in the discourse on any subject. Ultimately, they engage analytically and relationally with the agents as well as the practices they wish to critique and transform. Relationality is valued especially when it is set within an ethical framework of equality and respect. Post-colonial pastoral leaders need to work to build teams of caring reflective practitioners who have learnt the art of collaboration.

Dynamic

Postcolonializing activities are *dynamic* in nature. They recognize that issues are in a constant state of change and flux. As such, they attempt to engage in analyses that reflect time, change and movement. Analyzing moving structures can be daunting. However, recognizing that social reality is inevitably fluid is a sign of maturity not to be rejected. Postcolonializing leadership practices presuppose and therefore prepare for change. Postcolonializing pastoral leaders are great change agents and thoughtful managers of change within communities.

Polyvocal

Postcolonializing leadership activities are *polyvocal*. As evidenced in both the Babel (Genesis 11) and the Pentecost (Acts 2) narratives in the Bible, they recognize and encourage many voices to speak and be heard on the subjects under consideration. Never satisfied with solely one perspective on any subject, the postcolonializing pastoral leader actively seeks out other voices, especially submerged, ignored, or rejected voices, to be invited to the table, and there to articulate their own authentic voice. Subjugated voices with submerged and often despised knowledge are given room at the post-colonial table. Educated, middle-class, liberal, progressive voices are not the only ones invited to speak. Nor is there an attempt to silence the speech of the uneducated, differently abled, or culturally different.

Creative

Postcolonializing pastoral leadership activities are *creative*. They call for and produce new forms of being, institutions, and practices in the church, community, and world. They entail a weaving together of disparate materials into innovative forms and practices. Creativity moves well beyond improvisation. In improvisation it is the left-overs and whatever is available in and from the colonial project that are used in the formulation of structures that are implicitly temporary. Creativity requires the generation and utilization of new practices, methods, and materials in the development and promotion of substantially different forms of activity that go beyond the status quo inherited or established as standard by colonizers.

CONCLUSION

As expressed by the Akan saying that forms the title of this chapter, many individuals in churches and communities of faith experience a coldness that originates from the structures in place that are borrowed and, as such, are ill-fitting. These "clothes" either belong to a bygone era or else have not been developed in response to the felt needs and lived experience of the people themselves. Consequently, these people experience their communities of faith as strange and alienating places. Postcolonializing pastoral leaders will be in the forefront of the development of structures, policies, and practices that respond to the complex realities of people's real lives. They will be about the designing, weaving, and crafting out of the world sense and experiences of people within their own cultural realities, of clothes that fit to take the place of the second-hand or borrowed clothes of the colonial. Only such clothes can provide the warmth that is needed in today's church.

BIBLIOGRAPHY

Adichie, Chimamanda Ngozi. *Americanah*. New York: Random House, 2013.
Kasonga, wa Kasonga. "African Christian Palaver: A Contemporary Way of Healing Conflicts and Crises." In *The Church and Healing: Echoes from Africa*, edited by Emmanuel Y. Lartey, Daisy N. Nwachuku, and Kasonga wa Kasonga, 49–65. Frankfurt: Peter Lang, 1994.
Lartey, Emmanuel Y. *In Living Color: An Intercultural Approach to Pastoral Care and Counseling*, 2nd ed. London: Jessica Kingsley Publishers, 2003.
———. *Postcolonializing God: An African Practical Theology*. London: SCM Press, 2014.
Murove, Munyaradzi Felix, ed. *African Ethics: An Anthology of Comparative and Applied Ethics*. Scottsville, South Africa: University of KwaZulu-Natal Press, 2013.

Schaff, Philip, and Henry Wace, eds. *The Commonitory,* Nicene and Post-Nicene Fathers Series II, vol. 11. Buffalo, NY: Christian Literature Publishing Co., 1894.

Tamasese, K., C. Peteru, and C. Waldegrave. *Ole Taeao Afua, The New Morning: A Qualitative Investigation into Samoan Perspectives on Mental Health and Culturally Appropriate Services.* Wellington, NZ: The Family Centre, Lower Hutt, 1997.

Waldegrave C., and K. Tamasese. "Some Central Ideas in the 'Just Therapy' Approach." *Family Journal* 2, no. 2 (1994): 94–103.

NOTES

The title is taken from an Akan saying, documented by Ghanaian Sociologist Professor Kofi Asare Opoku. See "Cooking on Two Stones of the Hearth?: African Spirituality and the Socio-cultural Transformation of Africa," (Asante-Opoku-Reindorf Memorial lecture, Akrofi-Christaller Institute of Mission, Theology, and Culture, Akropong-Akuapim, Ghana, November 4, 2009, 22.)

1. Philip Schaff and Henry Wace, eds., *The Commonitory,* chap. 2, §6; Nicene and Post-Nicene Fathers Series II (Buffalo, NY: Christian Literature Publishing Co., 1894), vol. 11, 132.

2. The author of the *Commonitory* used the pseudonym "Peregrinus"; he was later identified as Vincent of the monastery of Lérins, a group of islands near present-day French Riviera. Vincent's living in the western half of the Roman Empire would explain why the Commonitory was written in Latin. He wrote the *Commonitory* in protest against what he considered to be the novelty of Augustine's teaching on predestination. It should be noted that Vincent lived long before there was a Protestant vs. Roman Catholic split. When Vincent wrote about the Catholic Church, what he had in mind was the undivided Church founded by Christ, not the later Roman Catholicism that Luther and the Reformers protested against. In its original sense, "catholic" meant "according to the whole."

3. For an intriguing recent novel that captures this struggle in the twenty-first century see Chimamanda Ngozi Adichie, *Americanah* (New York: Random House, 2013).

4. The terms "empathy" and "interpathy" are explained extensively in my *In Living Color: An Intercultural Approach to Pastoral Care and Counseling,* 2nd ed. (London: Jessica Kingsley Publishers, 2003).

5. Oft-repeated expression of Professor Walter J. Hollenweger, Professor of Mission, University of Birmingham, United Kingdom, from 1972–1989.

6. For a collection of thoughtful and thought-provoking essays on *Ubuntu,* see Munyaradzi Felix Murove, ed., *African Ethics: An Anthology of Comparative and Applied Ethics* (Scottsville, South Africa: University of KwaZulu-Natal Press, 2013).

7. See K. Tamasese, C. Peteru, and C. Waldegrave, *Ole Taeao Afua, The New Morning: A Qualitative Investigation into Samoan Perspectives on Mental Health and Culturally Appropriate Services* (Wellington, NZ: The Family Centre, Lower Hutt, 1997); and C. Waldegrave C. and K. Tamasese, "Some Central Ideas in the 'Just Therapy' Approach," *The Family Journal* 2, no. 2 (1994): 94–103.

8. See Kasonga wa Kasonga, "African Christian Palaver: A Contemporary Way of Healing Conflicts and Crises," in *The Church and Healing: Echoes from Africa,* ed. Emmanuel Y. Lartey, Daisy N. Nwachuku, and Kasonga wa Kasonga (Frankfurt: Peter Lang, 1994), 49–65.

9. See Emmanuel Y. Lartey, *Postcolonializing God: An African Practical Theology* (London: SCM Press, 2014), 93–97.

10. This section is based on my book, *Postcolonializing God,* xiv–xviii.

11. Akan proverb from Ghana. See Albin Kweku Korem and Mawutodzi Kodzo Abissath, *Traditional Wisdom in African Proverbs* (Accra, Ghana: Publishing Trends, 2004), 94.

TWO

Literacies of Listening

Postcolonial Pastoral Leadership in Practice

Melinda A. McGarrah Sharp

What kinds of practices will religious leaders claim and witness if and when postcolonial pastoral theology is realized in our leadership practices? I learned about postcolonialism neither from books nor from church experiences, but rather from my own embodied life experience.[1] I had finished seminary and was living as a Peace Corps volunteer in a small Afro-Surinamese village with descendants of escaped slaves of Dutch colonizers in the Amazon rainforest of Suriname, South America. I had become fluent in language and was invited to learn cultural forms of many life practices: cooking, cleaning, sharing meals, religion, leading, hospitality, music, funeral and birth rituals, honoring ancestors, health and healing, and more. By means of communal discussion and elder decree, I was given a name. In addition to language and cultural fluencies, however, a deeper intercultural fluency was unfolding and being challenged.

I was asked to train a new group of Peace Corps volunteers about respecting culturally appropriate menstruation practices. The most important thing I had learned was to read specific sacred signs, cultural texts that a new volunteer could easily misread or simply miss altogether. I decided to teach the practice of reading these markers by walking through the small village with the group of new volunteers. In the midst of what I intended to be a respectful presentation, an elder ran to me in the manner of spirit possession—I perceived from what she had previously taught me that she was carrying a heightened presence of ancestors with her in this moment—and she yelled that here I was, someone she had trusted, being the colonizing man once again.[2] I became more fluent in postcolonial intercultural literacy in moments of misunderstanding like this one. While teaching eager volunteers how to read sacred signs and even while careful not to cross any threshold markers, I had outed the village's most sacred spaces to a group of strangers. I both read and misread what was going on. I needed to reread.

POSTCOLONIAL AWAKENING IN PASTORAL THEOLOGY

Postcolonial engagement involves a commitment to disrupt fantastic narratives of distance that structure normative claims about what is going on in the world. Where is here? Where is there? *Pastoral theology* is a discipline of guided self-reflection and courageous communal reflection intended to disrupt fantastic narratives of what is going on in here (in my person, traditionally confined to intrapsychic and interpersonal registers of lived experience) to understand better personal and communal experiences of suffering and yearning for healing that are embodied in contexts that reflect a world of violence. Here I rely on British psychoanalyst D. W. Winnicott's notion of fantasy where "in the fantasying, what happens happens immediately, except that it does not happen at all."[3] Both pastoral theology and postcolonial theory aim to reveal and restore embodied connections between selves and others. Postcolonial conversation partner Frantz Fanon longs, "why not the quite simple attempt to touch the other, to feel the other, to explain the other to myself?"[4] As pastoral theology moves in more intercultural and communal directions from a solely intrapsychic focus to a contextual and intercultural understanding of suffering and healing, a postcolonial commitment to disruption needs to inform the disruptive aims of pastoral theology and vice versa.

I now teach pastoral theology and ethics in the Midwest where my students are dispersed across a wide regional geography. When I mention the p-word (postcolonialism), I can easily lose my audience. *How is postcolonialism relevant to present-day life in middle America?* Is this a live question for you in your context? Does learning postcolonialism require leaving home, traveling over there (wherever there may be), and then returning home?[5] Yes and no. The notion of postcolonialism "over there" relieves anyone who buys into this economy of engagement with complicities. The temptation of irrelevance arises from the very claim of irreverence for the sacred worth of every single human being that is violated through dehumanization whether in postcolonial Suriname or in Ferguson or on the US-Mexico border or right here in my church today. Postcolonial discourse disrupts the notion of "over there" by welcoming disruption as an ingredient to lived experiences. Decolonizing travel might be required both near and far to whatever habits, routines, readings and misreadings structure life practices.

By incorporating human experiences of *both* (1) wounding and (2) complicities in wounding as matters of methodological accountability, pastoral theology is an academic discipline that maintains a posture of changing, revising, rereading, indeed of learning that is also an ingredient in postcolonial practices of ministry. The concept of *reading* carries an inherent multiplicity: as an academic discipline, we share a commitment to research that requires fluency in academic reading. This practice of assigned reading comes quite easily in that students/scholars/ministers can say: "I know how to do this." We can go "over there" to the library, consume, interact, and make an assessment that critically engages bounded texts with all the literal and figurative weight of hermeneutics, or habits of interpretation, behind these practices. Even when considering texts as living sacred conversations, each book records a moment of interpretation with authoritative status. Pastoral theologians hold a concurrent commitment to also read human experiences. In 1936, Anton Boisen had what was at the time the clinically absurd idea that pastoral practice includes "learning to read human documents."[6] This kind of reading demands fluency in the challenging work of listening, hearing, mishearing, overhearing, and recommitting to listening again and again.

Multiple literacies of listening inform pastoral practices of attention that negotiate movement between proximity to and distance from suffering—in Howard Thurman's words, from the places where human beings' backs are against the wall[7] —in an intentional cycle of participation and reflection. Reading living human documents situated in the messy, striated, beautiful living human webs[8] that structure, make, and undo shared contemporary postcolonial realities also has authoritative status. Therefore, I identify literacies of listening as resources to challenge churches and to challenge readers around the process of becoming a postcolonial pastoral minister, theologian, leader, student, and teacher.

IMMERSION PEDAGOGY: PREPARING FOR READINGS AND MISREADINGS

I turn our attention to three literacies of listening within immersion pedagogy as a learning context.[9] I once taught an immersion course for students in a transformational leadership for women in ministry program. We covenanted to learn in borderlands by leaving home to disrupt notions of "there." We traveled to Nicaragua to deepen longstanding seminary connections with a community of Nicaraguan women leaders who invited US-American women to learn how to lead and love in more mutually empowering ways. This structured opportunity for disruption included recognition that some of the best teachers for the class were "over there."

What practices best prepare readiness for disruptive encounter? A *myth of complete preparation* surrounds practices of reading assigned to prepare postcolonial ministry practices. It is so tempting to think, "if I only read enough and the right kinds of texts beforehand, then I will be ready." The illusion of being so prepared as to anticipate everything guards against the very disruption required for the challenging work of postcolonial pastoral ministries. The drive to be fully prepared dulls the very creative capacities that will rejuvenate pastoral ministry open to postcolonial practices.[10] Texts remain an invaluable if incomplete tool to prepare responsible participation in the listening and speaking involved in experiences of leaving "home." I place the word home in quotes, as it is a concept that becomes interrogated in immersion pedagogy.

Pastoral theology makes the audacious claim that life experiences present texts on par with library books of the most competitive presses.[11] I believe literacies of listening involve reading, not as a matter of mastery or as an end in itself, but rather as a preparatory gesture that matures in intercultural and intersectional human encounters where practices of listening within diverse contexts are vital to the disruptive nature of postcolonial pastoral ministries. Three structural elements of preparation, or literacies of listening, deserve postcolonial attention: (1) selecting readings and fashioning reading guides or reading engagement assignments based on learning outcomes that matter and make a postcolonial difference; then (2) attending as completely as possible to learning process in practice(s); and finally (3) allowing disruptions to thicken awareness of the multiple literacies of listening demanded in postcolonial pastoral ministries across contexts today.

READING THAT PREPARES AWAKENING

Reading is a first literacy of listening that involves a traditional hermeneutical method of assigned texts to awaken readers to possibilities of transformation. For the Nicaragua immersion course, I discerned five textual genres that support a postcolonial awareness and listening practice: narrative, historical, economic, self-reflexive, and theological reading. *Narrative readings* included Margaret Randall's decades of interviews in the book *Sandino's Daughters Revisited: Feminism in Nicaragua*—in advance of meeting women leaders whose lives had been shaped by these very narratives of their mothers and grandmothers.[12] Women leaders were, are, and will be central to religious, social, familial, and political (even military) leadership in Nicaragua in light of decades of disappeared and absent men. *Historical reading* from political scientists, historians, and journalists helped frame some of these complexities, including the mixed role of the United States. To help us grasp present-day life in Nicaragua, a third genre of *economic reading* included up-to-date internet-based resources on local models of micro-lending and the current year's Papal declaration that the local priest was highlighting to the faith community we would be visiting.

Reading geared toward transformation through disruption inspired two additional preparatory activities: first, *self-reflexive reading* raised the notion that vulnerability is a disruptive capacity that supports transformative learning. For example, literary scholar Nancy Mairs' *Carnal Acts* demonstrates self-reflexive perspective on vulnerability and embodied transformation through reading encounters with various audiences including herself.[13] Finally, I assigned a fifth genre of *theological reading* to raise a crucial question for postcolonial ministry: how are theological concepts translated across communities and to whose benefit? To identify elements of a theology of accompaniment that informs leadership practices we would encounter, I chose the recorded conversational texts of liberation theologian Gustavo Gutiérrez and public health physician Paul Farmer, *In the Company of the Poor*, where Gutiérrez and Farmer account for reading each other's texts in ways open to disruptive conversion.[14]

Assigned reading helps prepare for leaving home, learning, and traveling in intercultural communities. After reading, students then wanted to see the historical markers and murals we read about. Students wondered how we would be received as representatives of and inheritors of local implications of United States political history in the region. Further, students self-identified as privileged people who should already know much more about US-American interventions in Nicaraguan history and current free-market and fair trade practices. Students longed to meet Nicaragua's daughters; students wanted to understand micro-loans as an empowering economic practice of particular communities of women. We wanted to see what transformative power public art held across contexts. Assigned reading helped prepare us for sustaining the vulnerability, courage, and misreading that would also be required.

MISREADING AWAKENS A LEARNING PROCESS

While traveling on and walking beside Nicaraguan streets and highways, we beheld many public murals and memorial markers for the revolutionary men and women that we had read about. One student, pointing to a stone marker proclaiming the site of an assassination, said, "Oh, this one is just like our crosses on the side of the road." And our orientation shifted immediately into disorientation. No, martyrdom in Leon and Nicaragua, and highway accidents in the United States do not share all the same analogous features, even as instances of death are always worth remembering. The theme of memorials and memory filtered throughout the week-long intensive immersion course. It was clear that cross-cultural analogies suggesting understanding more often supported a process of misreading.[15] We tested our prepared literacy with experience, moving us physically, emotionally, spiritually, and communally past unilateral texts and into an embodied multiplicity.[16]

Misreading is a second literacy of listening that activates a process of learning. Misreading recognizes and invites disruptive moments that shift orientation into disorientation, rupturing seemingly settled questions or certain claims about "what is going on?" and "why?" and the deeper questions of "what is my role in all of this?" and "why should I care?" I have been sensitive to misreading since my own jarring experiences within committed partnerships over time.[17] What does misreading look like on the front end of intercultural relationship building?

Misreading is a *postcolonial practice* cultivated in courageous communal interaction with texts across contexts. Postcolonialism is not so much a definition to be mastered, but rather a posture of listening in the midst of tension and challenge, in places where a kind of *blindness* that may start as a byproduct of possible good intentions or worthy missions, has in actuality been carefully and strategically maintained.[18] According to biblical scholar Musa Dube, a postcolonial reading of a text is a process of wrestling with "characters, geography, travelers, gender and unspoken intentions to highlight how these work in justifying the domination of one by another."[19] How do narrative, historical, economic, self-reflexive, and theological texts "take possession of the minds and lands of [people] who are different"?[20] Likewise, in his classic essay "Canaanites, Cowboys, and Indians," Robert Warrior imagines "a society of people delivered from oppression . . . where the original inhabitants can become something other than subjects to be converted to a better way of life."[21] US-North American church people often practice going "over there" to see and serve "the least of these." To paraphrase the Nicaraguan leaders who partnered with this class, "Tell your students and ask them to tell their churches that we are tired of being your least of these."[22]

Accompanying assigned reading for US–North American women, a copy of *Sandino's Daughters* in Spanish was sent to our Nicaraguan counterparts. We would later learn that what was a book, an assigned reading, a matter of pre-immersion check-lists and packing for many students, would serve as a significant opening into probing identities and histories to accompany our emerging Nicaraguan–US American women partnership. After gaining a basic literacy of listening through preparatory reading particular texts, we needed to practice an additional literacy of listening by reading in intercultural communal practice to learn our mutual misunderstandings.

Once awakened to potential learning through reading texts, misreading as a literacy of listening awakens possibilities of transformational accountability. Drawing on practical theologian Elaine Graham and womanist ethicist Emilie Townes, I define *transformational accountability* as an orientation toward pastoral practice that is both embodied in "concrete examples of engagement"[23] and oriented toward an overarching goal of transformation of selves, communities, habits, and institutions structured to constrain possibilities of mutual human recognition.[24] Transformational accountability meets Winnicott's concern that humans too often live "in a world that [is] all the time distorted . . . by [an] inability to feel concerned with what the other person was feeling . . . [while having] acute empathy for all downtrodden persons in the world."[25] Weaving ethics and care practices, pastoral theologians draw on psychological theories, social sciences, critical theory, and more to better attend suffering in human experiences. When considering misreading as an important literacy of listening for postcolonial practices of ministry, at least three resources contribute to transformational accountability: (1) processes of insight; (2) transitional moments; and, more recently, (3) complicity.

Traditionally, psychoanalysts saw insight, or "aha" moments as significant means of change where consequences of insight demand careful examination. Freud's drive to facilitate moments of insight served the goal of uncovering truth. More recently, the meaning of "insight" has moved from a static individualistic accomplishment to a process embedded in thickly textured relational dynamics.[26] Psychoanalyst Nancy McWilliams writes, "Despite the dethronement of insight from its position as the *sine qua non* of psychological change, for analytic therapists and for most clients, understanding remains a central goal."[27] While understanding is indeed a lofty goal, it remains elusive if not actively resisted by the classic colonial trap of "I already understand you" that foists various "you's" into traumatic cycles of non-recognition. Instead of mutual understanding, fantastic narratives are mediated and maintained by intercultural distance with a clear here/there impasse. I turn to theologian conversation partners like M. Shawn Copeland to imagine "enfleshing" such narratives in proximate relationships with an "aha" that evokes shared risk.[28]

Winnicott is helpful in understanding how misreading—what he calls being reminded of being simultaneously awake and wrong—can deepen mutuality within human relationships. A (mis)interpretation such as "oh that must be just like the crosses on the side of the road I've seen before," is itself an invitation into deeper listening because it reveals a fantastic orientation to understanding such markers between familiar and new contexts.[29] However, there is nothing inherently postcolonial about Winnicott's analysis until it is brought into conversation with postcolonial theorists conversant in psychoanalytic thought such as Frantz Fanon and Ashis Nandy, the literary voices of Toni Morrison, Zora Neale Hurston or Jenny Sharpe, and practical theological reflection from leaders in and beyond this volume.[30]

As a second theoretical connection, Heinz Kohut's self-psychology considers how groups of people and individuated human beings come to a sense of self-understanding. What he calls experience-near (or "here") and experience-distant (or "there") relationships form spaces in which human beings work out who we are as people and as communities. Is the space within and between relationships oriented toward intercultural connection and/or estrangement? Whose voices count "in here" and whose voices are relegated "over there"? I find Kohut helpful in that he recognizes that experience-near relationships become the best chance of understanding, but that experience-distant relationships are normative. An engagement with postcolonial theorists then probes why experience-distant spatial organization is normative and who benefits and suffers from just such a webbed geography.

Pastoral practices need to awaken to a postcolonial urgency out of perhaps unintended pre-existing complicities that inform contemporary contexts of life practices arranged by theologies of empire.[31] As pastoral theologians move from solely individualistic models of suffering and healing toward communal, contextual, intercultural, and indeed postcolonial models of suffering and healing, we have begun to address complicity more directly. Injustices that structure churches, schools, borders, and daily life practices also work to structure visibilities and invisibilities of suffering and accompanying access and barriers to access around healing. Recognizing complicities is not only part of wounding, but also part of healing.

Pastoral theology contributes the field's in-depth resources around processes of insight, transitional moments, and, more recently, complicity to misreading as a literacy of listening. However, participation in postcolonial practices also evokes a collaborative rereading of these distinct contributions before and as part of recommending life-giving postcolonial strategies and practices of ministry.

When preparing for the immersion experience to learn to partner with Nicaraguan women, my students purchased *Sandino's Daughters* in English and read it before "going anywhere." In Nicaragua, gathering her sisters around her, we witnessed our Nicaraguan guide pointing to various pictures in the Spanish version of the text, asking who knew these stories which were their stories. She told one story after another after another. We misread this book as merely assigned reading and learned under the shade of star fruit trees that what was so accessible, published, and printed for us was inaccessible to the audience for whom the book was life. Who were we to be the bearers of our sister's stories?

REREADING AWAKENS A BEAUTIFUL EMBODIED TENSION

A third literacy of listening is rereading—once aware of being in the midst of a learning process where recognition of misreading breaks into assigned reading and prepared questions, *rereading* offers an opportunity to awaken to a beautiful embodied tension of postcolonial pastoral ministry within practices. It is so easy not to listen, declares pastoral theologian Emma Justes.[32] Rereading offers an opportunity for deeper listening. This idea still needs constant birthing.

A striking embodied invitation to reread happened for the immersion course in Nicaragua. It was hard to tell if we were welcome or not outside of a church we visited. We wanted to see particular revolutionary murals we had read about. Would the church door be unlocked for us and on what grounds? After some time and much deliberation on behalf of this group of curious, well-intentioned strangers, the invitation that we as guests were trying to activate, was negotiated. It was almost too easy; the negotiation's speed hinted of a power play rather than a step toward mutual trust. When we walked through the pointed, fenced door, white walls met us. No murals.

Like many places, including the United States' border wall that divides present-day United States' southern border from present-day Mexico, Nicaragua has a history of installing and dismantling public art. Thankfully, as our eyes were adjusting, we noticed that the white walls were cloths pinned so closely to the walls covering each panel as to appear as paint. An unnamed worker at the church, who claimed to have no important role, began to describe what was under the murals. Would he lift the cloths? What should we make of our group's shared sense of entitlement to see behind the cloths? What kind of risk would our unidentified guide navigate in ceding to the request of strangers?

Eventually and through translation, our guide lifted one panel just enough to give us some room to look beneath. As we crouched in a group prayer of expectant seeing, he lifted the cloth higher until, with a fully extended arm, he invited everyone to take a picture. Guided by a strange nonverbal momentum, we then moved to another mural and then, after time, another. Our delight and wonder was as palpable as the uncertainty and fear around being invited to consume guarded panels with our eyes and iPhones.

One mural panel depicted a masked child held between two distinct generations. The child's worn blue jeans and a t-shirt, according to our guide, represented being caught in empire's discounted uniform. As we walked, we were moving through layered narratives toward the altar area. Our guide offered to move the altar curtain to show us what was behind a white-skinned Jesus we could already see prominently hanging in front of a large white cloth that was held firm by a pulley system anchored to floor hooks. This panel could not be unhinged by only one person, so the guide invited a student to share in the uncovering process, issuing a reverse invitation also quickly negotiated. Intercultural negotiation across language and other barriers worked to unmask the altar mural as the curtain lowered down to rest as folds of altar carpet.

Behold: Mothers of the disappeared, children dancing, grief, joy, hope, women rising, and a communal representation of Jesus. Our guide shared the personal impact of the revolution and contra wars in his family, the hopes displayed. *Why were the murals covered?* Well, he said, some people think that they are too political. When asked, I agreed to help re-anchor the cloths—another troubling negotiated invitation, both uncomfortable and powerful. While re-covering the altar mural by re-pullying up the cloth wall, our guide suggested that resurrection is by nature political. Mothers of the disappeared is a haunting image present, but not depicted, in many worship spaces. What does it mean to paint the mothers into the altar space and then to cover them up? To cover over this mural, to repave or remove signs of trauma, to mask martyrs as accidents, and then to uncover, to recover, to behold and live in community with this suffering?

Physical unmasking and masking offers an embodied rereading. The immersion class enacted the postcolonial dilemmas we had read in terms of Fanon's recognition, Mairs' public courage, and various invisible political subversions or strategic threats to oral and printed communication. Listening in the company of a guide who calls himself unimportant and nameless turns out to be a literal key, guiding attention, opening imaginative horizons, building trust, navigating body language, unlocking the church, raising bolted curtains, so tightly covering living murals as to be mistaken as wall paint.

Postcolonial pastoral practice involves navigating reading, misreading, and rereading in intercultural spaces, across language barriers, in conditions that are less than ideal. These three literacies of listening involve various forms and depths of risk—often unequally shared, mapped by power plays, and many times invisible by will, oversight, or simply a failing of curiosity. *Reading* reveals a "there," *misreading* disrupts the "there," and *rereading* can dismantle over "there" in order to open new possibilities of intercultural communion. In this particular course, the mural unmasking, viewing, remasking story is embedded in a larger rereading process. The final course project included an annotated, public art installation, months after the course ended, where symbols, words, and experiences were re-interpreted for a public audience. Not surprisingly, images from the murals we had seen appeared throughout the many parts of the collective art installation. In addition, a postcolonial worship service planned in partnership with our Nicaraguan sisters included an unscripted conversation between a Nicaraguan partner and myself about reading, misreading, and rereading *Sandino's Daughters.* Rather than reporting or resolving the postcolonial dilemma around access to this text, we talked together, each in our own language, and laid the book on the altar as open question, an invitation into rereading.

LEARNING LITERACIES OF LISTENING: POSTCOLONIAL PASTORAL PRACTICES

I began by linking (1) a postcolonial commitment to disrupt fantastic narratives of distance that structure normative claims about global dynamics into conversation with (2) pastoral theology's disruptive practices of guided self-reflection that serve cross-contextual understanding and empathy. I was awakened through a process of reading, misreading, and rereading while serving as a Peace Corps volunteer. Now as a pastoral theologian imagining postcolonial pastoral practices, I contend that postcolonial pastoral theology intends to disrupt fantastic narratives of what is going on personally and cross-contextually to understand better personal and communal experiences of suffering and yearning for healing in a world of violence. It is quite tempting to conclude that a process of going "over there" is the primary work of postcolonial practice. At the same time, we ought not dismiss the importance of exiting and entering awareness of contexts always at play within practicing transformational accountability as a postcolonial commitment. Yet, disrupting the tightly bolted "over there" is an ultimate task of postcolonial pastoral practice.

Reading, misreading, and rereading signify formative moments in a process of collaborative postcolonial pastoral leadership. Immersion pedagogy is not about distancing a mythical "over there" from a mythical "right here and now." Immersion is a postcolonial practice that can sharpen listening because seminary learning, church leadership, and human relationships are all immersion experiences. What are the contours of habitual reading practices? Where am I making room to acknowledge and learn literacies of misreading and rereading? How do leaders prepare for the invisible and contested border crossings that are navigated across the thresholds of our lives together?

What can the fruit of an immersive encounter manifest for worshipping communities? By cultivating practices of listening in community with many known and unknown neighbors dying to live, we can begin to recognize the abundance of "strange fruit" institutionalized and invisible.[33] With creative resolute activists and scholars, including contributors to this volume, it is important to recognize "strange fruit" is indeed structured into the architecture of our life together where privilege is not only about "me over here" being better than "you over there," but privilege is also about being satisfied with simplistic reading that categorizes human beings. Instead, invest in communal practices of reading, misreading and rereading. Postcolonialism is an indictment of complicity as sin, while recognition of complicities is also an ingredient to postcolonial healing ecclesiologies.

Constructive postcolonial practical theology requires a vibrant moral imagination that can contemplate possibilities of complicity and resistance concurrent with possibilities of participatory empowerment. What might postcolonial pastoral leaders need in a list of best postcolonial practices? Certainly we must name and examine church practices that reflect deep moral commitments: careful navigation of boundaries accountable to the ever-present risk of abuse of power; recognition of misunderstanding stories; cultivation of listening practices that privilege reinterpretation; advocacy for reading as a human right; and continuous participation in opportunities for courage and risk.

What might this look like in worship? To enter memorial and living stories in such interculturally mixed company involves a process of transformational accountability. *First, navigate invitations into deeper immersions.* This involves permission seeking that turns on investment in trust-building, recognition of borrowed trust, and learning lineages of good reasons for mistrust. How? Insist that permission to participate is not a given on behalf of any party. Construct liturgies of trust with room for unscripted moments and reinterpretation. Review hymns for language that constricts possibilities of misreading. Divest from fantastic narratives of church. Cultivate opportunities to listen differently through global social networks across generations. Make room for critical distance. Identify colonial models of travel that include a narrative of choice regarding where to go and not go. Invest in public art, recovering and uncovering methods, histories, and works of communal art. *Second, invest in a process of mutual becoming.* Only then can any actual unmasking occur. Unmasking is a metaphorical description of the movement from estrangement of non-recognition to deeper community where, even if sustained for only a moment, mutual recognition provides the condition for the intimacy of mutual understanding. Literacies of listening are a resource that I, as a pastoral theologian and ethicist with postcolonial commitments, offer to challenge the church around the process of becoming a postcolonial pastoral minister, theologian, leader, student, and teacher.

In conclusion, consider the following rereading of a quote from the book *Hiking the Horizontal* by Liz Lerman, acclaimed choreographer of diversely embodied public performances. Lerman writes, "if it is important to get the arm right, the move right, or the notion that only one movement will do, then teach *that* and your students will get it. Just don't sit in a circle."[34] Here Lerman outlines the politics of learning a practice where the practice is dance in her case. The work of postcolonial pastoral ministry in practice can't be to define "the arm" or "the move," but rather to commit to a creative cycle, which is ever invitational, open to correction, and in the process of becoming itself a circle in the midst of every possible force—force from the outside trying to squish it into a hierarchy of "right arms" and "right moves," and force from the inside threatening to break the circle when I retreat into fixing it, ignoring it, or not caring about how my humanity is ever mysteriously wrapped up in wonder with yours.[35] Imagine and cultivate postcolonial pastoral practices of transformative accountability, that as Mercy Amba Oduyoye says, "grows as the other is moved to grow . . . a circle, a vision of cooperation, mutuality and care."[36] A postcolonial pastoral theology and the practices of ministry that can be named postcolonial live in the creative tension between these forces, and in so doing work toward coming together.

BIBLIOGRAPHY

Achebe, Chinua. *Things Fall Apart*. London: William Heinemann Ltd. 1959.

Blair, Elizabeth. "The Strange Story of the Man Behind 'Strange Fruit.'" *National Public Radio*, September 5, 2012, www.npr.org/2012/09/05/158933012/the-strange-story-of-the-man-behind-strange-fruit.

Boisen, Anton T. *The Exploration of the Inner World: A Study of Mental Disorder and Religious Experience*. Chicago: Willett, Clark, 1936.

Brock, Rita Nakashima, and Rebecca Ann Parker. *Saving Paradise: How Christianity Traded Love of This World for Crucifixion and Empire*. Boston: Beacon Press, 2008.

Cooper-White, Pamela. *Many Voices: Pastoral Psychotherapy in Relational and Theological Perspective*. Minneapolis: Fortress Press, 2007.

Copeland, M. Shawn. *Enfleshing Freedom: Body, Race, and Being*. Minneapolis: Fortress Press, 2010.

Doehring, Carrie. "Teaching an Intercultural Approach to Spiritual Care." *Journal of Pastoral Theology* 22, no. 2 (2012): 1–24.

Dube, Musa W. "Toward a Postcolonial Feminist Interpretation of the Bible." In *Hope Abundant: Third World and Indigenous Women's Theology*, ed. Kwok Pui-lan, 89–102. Maryknoll, NY: Orbis Books, 2010.

Fanon, Frantz. *Black Skin White Masks*, trans. Charles Lam Markmann. New York: Grove Press, 1967.

Gill-Austern, Brita L. "Engaging Diversity and Difference: From Practices of Exclusion to Practices of Practical Solidarity." In *Injustice and the Care of Souls: Taking Oppression Seriously in Pastoral Care*, edited by Sheryl A. Kujawa-Holbrook and Karen B. Montagno, 29–44. Minneapolis: Fortress Press, 2009.

Graham, Elaine L. *Transforming Practice: Pastoral Theology in an Age of Uncertainty*. London: Mowbray, 1996.

Griffin, Michael and Jennie Weiss Block, eds. *In the Company of the Poor: Conversations with Dr. Paul Farmer and Fr. Gustavo Gutiérrez*. Maryknoll, NY: Orbis Books, 2013.

Justes, Emma J. *Hearing beyond the Words: How to Become a Listening Pastor*. Nashville, TN: Abingdon Press, 2006.

Lartey, Emmanuel Y. "Practical Theology as a Theological Form." In *The Blackwell Reader in Pastoral and Practical Theology*, ed. James Woodward et al., 128–34. Malden, MA: Blackwell, 2000.

Lerman, Liz. *Hiking the Horizontal: Field Notes from a Choreographer*. Middletown, CT: Wesleyan University Press, 2011.

Mairs, Nancy. *Carnal Acts*. Boston: Beacon Press, 1996.

McWilliams, Nancy. *Psychoanalytic Case Formulation*. New York: Guilford Press, 1999.

Miller-McLemore, Bonnie. "Revisiting the Living Human Web: Theological Education and the Role of Clinical Pastoral Education." *Journal of Pastoral Care and Counseling* 62, no. 1–2 (Spring-Summer 2008): 3–18.

Oliver, Mary. *Red Bird: Poems by Mary Oliver*. Boston: Beacon Press, 2008.

Randall, Margaret. *Sandino's Daughters Revisited: Feminism in Nicaragua.* New Brunswick, NJ: Rutgers University Press, 1994.

Rieger, Joerg. *Christ and Empire: From Paul to Postcolonial Times.* Minneapolis: Fortress Press, 2007.

Sharp, Melinda A. McGarrah Sharp. *Misunderstanding Stories: Toward a Postcolonial Pastoral Theology.* Eugene, OR: Pickwick, 2013.

———. "Proximity to Suffering: Not Whether but How and Why Race Matters in the Classroom." *Race Matter in the Classroom Blog, Wabash Center,* October 9, 2014. Accessed March 11, 2016. wabashcenter.typepad.com/antiracism_pedagogy/2014/10/proximity-to-suffering-not-whether-but-how-and-why-race-matters-in-the-classroom.html.

Thurman, Howard. *Jesus and the Disinherited.* New York: Abingdon-Cokesbury, 1949.

Townes, Emilie. "Ethics as an Art of Doing the Work our Souls Must Have." In *The Arts of Ministry: Feminist-Womanist Approaches,* edited by Christie Cozad Neuger, 143–46. Louisville, KY: Westminster John Knox Press, 1996.

Warrior, Robert. "Canaanites, Cowboys, and Indians." *Christianity and Crisis,* September 11, 1989, 261–65.

Winnicott, D. W. *Playing and Reality.* New York: Routledge, 2005.

NOTES

1. I did read Chinua Achebe's *Things Fall Apart* (London: William Heinemann Ltd., 1959) in high school, but as an excursion where the risk to me was only in reading without demand for what I will name below as transforming accountability in practice.

2. See Melinda A. McGarrah Sharp, *Misunderstanding Stories: Toward a Postcolonial Pastoral Theology* (Eugene, OR: Pickwick, 2013).

3. D. W. Winnicott, *Playing and Reality* (New York: Routledge, 2005), 37.

4. Frantz Fanon, *Black Skin White Masks,* trans. Charles Lam Markmann (New York: Grove Press, 1967), 231.

5. Brita L. Gill-Austern, "Engaging Diversity and Difference: From Practices of Exclusion to Practices of Practical Solidarity," in *Injustice and the Care of Souls: Taking Oppression Seriously in Pastoral Care,* ed. Sheryl A. Kujawa-Holbrook and Karen B. Montagno (Minneapolis: Fortress Press, 2009), 29–44.

6. Anton T. Boisen, *The Exploration of the Inner World: A Study of Mental Disorder and Religious Experience* (Chicago: Willett, Clark, 1936).

7. Howard Thurman, *Jesus and the Disinherited* (New York: Abingdon-Cokesbury, 1949); and Melinda A. McGarrah Sharp, "Proximity to Suffering: Not Whether but How and Why Race Matters in the Classroom," *Race Matter in the Classroom Blog, Wabash Center,* October 9, 2014, wabashcenter.typepad.com/antiracism_pedagogy/2014/10/proximity-to-suffering-not-whether-but-how-and-why-race-matters-in-the-classroom.html.

8. Bonnie J. Miller-McLemore, "Revisiting the Living Human Web: Theological Education and the Role of Clinical Pastoral Education," *Journal of Pastoral Care and Counseling* 62, no. 1–2 (Spring-Summer 2008): 3–18.

9. Within pastoral theology, the case study is a traditional means of immersing theological reflection in lived experiences. Case study genre is itself a contribution of pastoral theology to the postcolonial conversation because case studies highlight the importance of beginning with experience as a starting point for theoretical construction/conversation. Within theological education more broadly, immersion pedagogy in which students travel near or far from theological institutions to learn immersed in community meets the Association of Theological Schools's curricular standard of "global awareness and engagement" through opportunities for practice, participation, and cultivating responsiveness (Commission on Accrediting, *General Institutional Stan-*

dards, Association of Theological Schools, 2010, www.ats.edu/uploads/accrediting/documents/general-institutional-standards.pdf, 8–9).

10. Emmanuel Y. Lartey, "Practical Theology as a Theological Form," in *The Blackwell Reader in Pastoral and Practical Theology*, ed. James Woodward et al. (Malden, MA: Blackwell, 2000), 128–34.

11. Yet, the intimidation that accompanies a living reading that opens up intercultural vulnerability can be paralyzing—coupled with the exhausting nature of listening and translating and then on top of that the pressing suffocating current events that mock the exhaustion—borders on the absurd.

12. Margaret Randall, *Sandino's Daughters Revisited: Feminism in Nicaragua* (New Brunswick, NJ: Rutgers University Press, 1994). I also assigned Sister Joan Uhlen's unpublished personal diary, "A Mission Journal," that chronicles her life and work in Nicaragua from 1948–1992, in which she carried forth and supported a liberation theology style base community model of pastoral leadership. We would be living in the physical structure that was the realization of one of Sister Joan's dreams of building a physical and spiritual community center where basic needs and justice would be available alongside the Bible and Eucharist.

13. Nancy Mairs, *Carnal Acts* (Boston: Beacon Press, 1996).

14. Michael Griffin and Jennie Weiss Block, eds., *In the Company of the Poor: Conversations with Dr. Paul Farmer and Fr. Gustavo Gutiérrez* (Maryknoll, NY: Orbis Books, 2013).

15. Pastoral theologian Emmanuel Y. Lartey advocates using the word "intercultural" rather than "cross-cultural" or "multi-cultural," an argument he lays out succinctly in "Practical Theology as a Theological Form."

16. Pamela Cooper-White, *Many Voices: Pastoral Psychotherapy in Relational and Theological Perspective* (Minneapolis: Fortress Press, 2007).

17. The notion of "jarring experiences" is introduced and unpacked in Carrie Doehring, "Teaching an Intercultural Approach to Spiritual Care," *Journal of Pastoral Theology* 22, no. 2 (2012): 1–24.

18. Melinda A. McGarrah Sharp, "Strategic Blindness: Famous Examples from Research and Everyday Complicities," (paper presented at University of Tulsa, Tulsa, OK, April 11, 2014).

19. Musa W. Dube, "Toward a Postcolonial Feminist Interpretation of the Bible," in *Hope Abundant: Third World and Indigenous Women's Theology*, ed. Kwok Pui-lan (Maryknoll, NY: Orbis Books, 2010), 93.

20. Ibid.

21. Robert Warrior, "Canaanites, Cowboys, and Indians," *Christianity and Crisis*, September 11, 1989, 261–65.

22. Discussion on "JustHope," in Context Matters Course, Phillips Theological Seminary, Tulsa, OK, October 7, 2014.

23. Elaine L. Graham, *Transforming Practice: Pastoral Theology in an Age of Uncertainty* (London: Mowbray, 1996), 172.

24. Emilie M. Townes, "Ethics as an Art of Doing the Work our Souls Must Have," in *The Arts of Ministry: Feminist-Womanist Approaches*, ed. Christie Cozad Neuger (Louisville, KY: Westminster John Knox Press, 1996), 143–61.

25. Winnicott, *Playing and Reality*, 177–78.

26. Nancy McWilliams, *Psychoanalytic Case Formulation* (New York: Guilford Press, 1999).

27. Ibid., 15.

28. M. Shawn Copeland, *Enfleshing Freedom: Body, Race, and Being* (Minneapolis: Fortress Press, 2010).

29. Winnicott's theory of fantasy is characterized by separation from actual relationships among human beings (*Playing and Reality*, 35–50).

30. My hope is that my book *Misunderstanding Stories* begins this theoretical partnership.

31. Joerg Rieger, *Christ and Empire: From Paul to Postcolonial Times* (Minneapolis: Fortress Press, 2007) and Rita Nakashima Brock and Rebecca Ann Parker, *Saving Paradise: How Christianity Traded Love of This World for Crucifixion and Empire* (Boston: Beacon Press, 2008).

32. Emma J. Justes, *Hearing beyond the Words: How to Become a Listening Pastor* (Nashville, TN: Abingdon Press, 2006), xi.

33. Copeland, *Enfleshing Freedom*, 121–24. Copeland's text enriches pedagogical examinations of Holiday's "Strange Fruit" based on Meeropol's poem, which is indeed a tragically strange way to open an early morning course session. Elizabeth Blair, "The Strange Story of the Man Behind 'Strange Fruit,'" *National Public Radio*, September 5, 2012, www.npr.org/2012/09/05/158933012/the-strange-story-of-the-man-behind-strange-fruit.

34. Liz Lerman, *Hiking the Horizontal: Field Notes from a Choreographer* (Middletown, CT: Wesleyan University Press, 2011), 249.

35. Mary Oliver, "What is the Greatest Gift?" in *Red Bird: Poems by Mary Oliver* (Boston: Beacon Press, 2008), 76.

36. Mercy Amba Oduyoye, "Poem," in Kwok, *Hope Abundant*, 17.

THREE

Metropolitan Community Church as a Messy Space for Revisioning the Other Side of Pastoral Ministry

Mona West

Metropolitan Community Church (MCC) is a denomination founded in 1968 by a Pentecostal preacher named Troy D. Perry, who had a vision for a church that would accept and celebrate lesbian, gay, bisexual, and transgender (LGBT) people. After being defrocked and forced out of his pastorate because he was a gay man, Perry found himself in deep despair—a despair that led to a failed suicide attempt. Out of that struggle he heard God's voice speak in his heart to say, "I love you, Troy. I don't have any step-sons or step-daughters." A year before the Stonewall riots which would officially launch the Gay Rights movement, Troy Perry took out an ad in a gay newspaper in Los Angeles, California, announcing a worship service open to all people, especially gay and lesbian people, which would take place in his living room on October 6, 1968. Twelve people showed up that day. A sermon was preached, an offering taken, and communion celebrated. MCC was born.

Today, MCC exists in Africa, Asia, Australia/New Zealand, Canada, Europe, Latin America/Caribbean, and the United States with 164 affiliated churches and 37 emerging ministries. There are approximately 20,000 members of MCC worldwide, with 300 ordained clergy serving as pastors, chaplains, spiritual directors, seminary professors, and directors and staff of LGBT and related organizations.

For the past 46 years, MCC has been at the forefront of the LGBT liberation movement. In 1969, Troy Perry launched the struggle for marriage equality by being the first clergy person to officiate a marriage between a same sex couple and subsequently sue the state of California for the right for that marriage to be legal. In the 1980s, MCC clergy and congregations were at the epicenter of the AIDS pandemic in the United States offering pastoral care, funerals, and memorial services when no one else would venture to even touch a person with AIDS.

In recent decades, MCC scholars have led the way in articulating a queer biblical hermeneutic and queer theology that is rooted in the experience of queer communities.[1] This queer hermeneutic has extended into the realm of pastoral theology with the publication of the anthology *Queering Christianity: Finding a Place at the Table for LGBTQ Christians,* whose contributors are all MCC clergy except for one.[2]

Using a postcolonial optic, this chapter will use MCC as a case study to explore the intersections between postcolonial theory and queer experience by applying the concepts "otherness," "third space theory," and "hybridity." It will also examine the ways in which colonialism and imperialism have shaped models of pastoral ministry that have created a clergy "middle class" and have cast the pastor as CEO of the church as a business. This is a model that leads to conflict, burnout, and perpetuates a clergy/laity binary. From this exploration, an initial revisioning of the "other side" of pastoral ministry will be offered which is networked, rooted in performance, engaged in playfulness, and risks "indecency."

POSTCOLONIALISM, QUEER THEORY, AND MCC

Kwok Pui-lan claimed that "while postcolonial theory exposes and questions binarism, queer theory goes a step further to challenge deep-seated heterosexual biases in our society and even in postcolonial criticism. Colonialism is not just about political and economic domination, it has much to do with the repatterning of desire."[3] I would like to explore three aspects of postcolonial theory as they relate to queer experience, especially in MCC: otherness, hybridity, and third space theory.

Many postcolonial theorists draw on the work of Edward W. Said, who claimed that the Orient is a concept created by western colonial power to control the East, using the term "other" to perpetuate a binary which sees the West as civilized and superior and the East as untamed and inferior. HyeRan Kim-Cragg, in her book *Story and Song: A Postcolonial Interplay between Christian Education and Worship,* observes that non-westerners (blacks, First Nations, Asians, Hispanics) in the United States are also made "other" by dominant white Anglo-Americans for socioeconomic reasons by characterizing them as "lazy, sensual, inferior, or uncivilized."[4]

A similar dynamic of "orientalism" or "otherness" began in the early nineteenth century with the invention of the binary terms "heterosexuality" and "homosexuality," assigning sexual normalcy to heterosexuality and sexual deviance to homosexuality. This binary was perpetuated in the 1940s by sex researcher Alfred Kinsey, who developed a six-point scale that attempted to measure the degree of one's homosexuality or heterosexuality by the number of orgasms a person had with a member of the same or opposite gender.[5]

The Web site for the American Institute for Bisexuality features the work of its founder, Austrian sex researcher Fritz Klein, who has published research indicating that rather than sexual orientation being a fixed and measurable identity as articulated by Alfred Kinsey's scale of 1–6, one's sexual orientation is a multi-variable process involving not only genital activity but also attraction, fantasies, and emotional and social preferences; ultimately, it should be seen as a continuum.

Historian Jonathan Ned Katz utilizes the work of social-constructivists theorists such as Michel Foucault to critique this binary of heterosexuality/homosexuality, which creates the homosexual as "other" by pointing out that "heterosexuality is an invented tradition."[6]

In spite of the work of sex researchers and theorists who claim that sexuality and sexual orientation are not fixed identities and therefore not subject to a binary relationship, binary thinking has continued into the twenty-first century as Christian denominations have wrestled with the issue of ordaining openly queer people to pastoral ministry. In efforts to deny ordination, some churches have made LGBT people "other" by characterizing them as pedophiles, promiscuous, deviants, carriers of disease, sinners, and persons with mental illness.

While "otherness" is an attempt to hold power over the colonized and produces the illusion of pure identity, hybridization describes new realities that are created in the interplay between colonized and colonizer. Expounding on the work of Homi K. Bhabha, Kim-Cragg notes that "hybridization reflects a postcolonial reality that emerged from the relationship between and within the colonized and the colonizers' cultures. The aspects of the dominant European culture are implanted in or grafted onto the colonized culture, submerging its beliefs and values within its own to create a hybrid culture that is neither one nor the other . . . hybridity is an identity that refuses a homogenous purity."[7]

Just as postcolonial hybrid identities such as Asian Americans, African Americans, and Native Americans create mixed realities which can lead to new realities, the hybrid identities of LGBT people have created mixed realities, especially with regard to family configurations which include open marriages in which a "traditional heterosexually married" couple remain in an open relationship as one member of the couple "comes out" as gay, lesbian, bisexual, or transgender; co-parenting between gay men and lesbians through artificial insemination; families of choice which are configured as "tribes" or "polyandrous relationships"; a lesbian couple in which one member transitions from a female gender identity to a male gender identity allowing for legal marriage in states and countries that define marriage between "one man and one woman" (the same can be said for a gay male couple in which one member transitions to a female gender identity). Queer hybrid identities also include transgender realities that do not affect one's sexual orientation as well as "androgynous" or "gender queer" identities that resist any designation as male or female.

These mixed realities have had implications for pastoral ministry in MCC. In their chapters on pastoral care in *Queering Christianity: Finding a Place at the Table for LGBTQI Christians*, Joseph Shore-Goss and Joan Saniuk challenge caregivers of LBGT people to recognize the unique stresses of being queer in a heteronormative culture. They encourage the creation of safe spaces for queer stories to be heard and valued.[8]

Kim-Cragg has also noted that in the context of hybrid identities there is always "the Other within the Other" and there is certainly that dimension with regard to transgender people in the queer community and MCC. Pastoral ministry in MCC must continue to explore the interlocking nature of oppression and name the ways in which sexism, race, and class contribute to transphobia. Joseph Shore-Goss makes four suggestions for transgender harm reduction when offering care to transgender youth: transgender expression must be accepted; caregivers must be advocates; resources must be made available to assist young people in making healthy and safe transitions; resources must be developed to help the families and communities of transgendered youth.[9]

MCC congregations also experience hybridity. Many of the first clergy who helped shape MCC's polity, theology, and liturgy came from other denominations who would not accept them as openly gay. Pastors of our first churches were typically men who had been kicked out of denominations such as Roman Catholic, Methodist, Presbyterian, Lutheran, and Baptist. In many instances, these clergy brought with them the liturgy and theology from their previous denominations and grafted them onto an emerging MCC identity. Today, congregational worship styles and liturgy will vary based on the hybrid identity of most of these clergy.

Hybridity also exists for many MCC members who experience a double or triple belonging as the vestiges of being raised in a heteronormative culture combine with being a member of a queer church and also being from a particular racial or ethnic background. MCC has had its challenges and successes providing authentic worship and educational experiences, especially for its Black and Hispanic members in the United States.

Third space theory is closely related to hybrid identity. As a space of enunciation, it is a performative space that is messy and ambiguous since meanings and symbols of culture have no "primordial unity or fixity." It is a place where borders of identity are permeable, and old identities are re-examined while new roles are explored.[10] As Marcella Althaus-Reid (who was a member of MCC Edinburgh, Scotland) reminds us in her book *The Queer God*, third spaces such as bars and nightclubs can be places where transgressive acts are played out—where our "real selves" show up—a place where the oppressed can plot liberation.[11]

In its early years the only place MCC could find to meet for worship was in gay bars. In the Friendly Atheist blog at Patheos.com, Terry Firma remembers the largest LGBT massacre in the United States that happened in a gay bar. On June 24, 1973 members of MCC New Orleans met at a bar called The Upstairs Lounge; a few of the men even invited their mother to join them. Just before 8 pm the downstairs doorbell rang and upon opening the locked steel door, a man threw a fire bomb into the downstairs of the bar. Because of steel bars on the windows upstairs, 40 people died in the fire that ensued, among them the pastor of MCC New Orleans, Rev. Bill Larson.[12] Rev. Troy Perry immediately traveled to New Orleans to provide pastoral support and attempted to try and find a church building to hold a memorial service for those who had lost their lives. After being turned down by several churches, Rev. William Richardson allowed a service at St. George's Episcopal Church.

For the past forty-eight years MCC churches have been places where transgressive acts are played out. Transgressive acts which include gay marriages, the ordination of queer people, baptisms of queer families, queer preaching, funerals of people with AIDS, Transgender Day of Remembrances—even the act of a queer person attending church, not having to check their sexuality at the door, is a transgressive act.

MCC's open communion table is a powerful space of enunciation. It has been at the center of MCC since the very beginning. Regardless of theology or liturgical worship styles, an open communion is celebrated every week. While the Eucharistic table has been a place of division and discrimination throughout Christian history—and even today queer people are denied participation—it has been a healing and generative third space for members of MCC. At the table there is no division between clergy and laity. Anyone can consecrate communion in MCC. Anyone in MCC can serve the bread and the cup in the Eucharistic feast. The table is a place where LGBT families and couples and tribes who would not be welcome at other tables elsewhere can come and participate publicly and openly in the meal together. The open table is a porous boundary where the promiscuity of God is experienced.

When I think about third space as a dynamic, fluid, and performative space I am reminded of Marjorie Garber's comments in her book, *Vested Interests*, on cross-dressing as a "third" which challenges binary notions of not only gender but race and class:

> The "third" is that which questions binary thinking and introduces crisis—a crisis which is symptomatized by *both* the overestimation *and* the underestimation of cross-dressing. But what is crucial here—and I can hardly underscore this strongly enough—is that the "third term" is

not a term. . . . The "third" is a mode of articulation, a way of describing a space of possibility. Three puts in question the idea of one: of identity, self-sufficiency, self-knowledge.[13]

In an October 2014 edition of the webzine, *The Guardian*, Brazilian MCC pastor Marcos Lord was featured in an article that highlighted his tendency to preach as a drag queen named Luandha Perón.[14] Before he came out as a gay man, Marcos used to think he was possessed by demons. He claims now that Luandha is like a "genie in a bottle" who can be outspoken for the rights of LGBT people in Brazil. As a lay pastor in MCC and a public school teacher, certainly Marcos has discovered that preaching in drag is a third space—a mode of articulation, a space of possibility.

MCC pastors have engaged the liturgical calendar and clergy vestments as third space places of possibility and disruption by celebrating World AIDS Day (which originated with MCC), Gay Pride, and Transgender Day of Remembrance as holy days. Their cross-dressing in clerical collars, albs, stoles, and chasubles in MCC's early days was a mode of articulation for the full acceptance of the gifts of pastoral leadership of LGBT people. The queerest third space I have ever been in was the processional for Rev. Elder Nancy Wilson's installation as Moderator of MCC held in the National Cathedral of Washington, DC. People were in leather vestments, boas, mitres, copes and rainbow stoles; and while mimicry can have a subversive dimension to it, the caution for MCC is that we do not "cross-dress" to mimic the power structures of a neocolonial culture that continues to see pastoral ministry as a hierarchy.

COLONIAL INFLUENCES IN PASTORAL MINISTRY IN THE UNITED STATES

Scholars of postcolonialism have noted the ways in which Christianity has colluded with empire to colonize groups of people in efforts to occupy territories throughout the globe.[15] While colonialism may be seen as a phenomenon involving empires such as Britian, France, and Spain dominating countries such as in Asia and Africa, it is also a phenomenon that describes the continental expansion of the United States through genocide and the forced removal of Native peoples as well as through slavery.[16]

The collusion of Christianity and empire in the United States has led to the creation of liturgies, hymnody, and educational programs that perpetuate colonialism in Christian churches and seminaries.[17] This collusion has also led to models for Christian ministry that view the church as a business and the pastor as the CEO. These models lead to clergy burnout and perpetuate a binary of clergy/laity. Clergy burnout is so prevalent, that many denominations are launching major initiatives to understand the causes and provide some support for clergy. Duke University just finished a seven-year study of United Methodist clergy in North Carolina and discovered that these clergy have higher rates of diabetes, arthritis and high blood pressure, compared to other people in the state.[18] The Lilly Endowment has established its Clergy Renewal Programs in an effort to provide opportunities for clergy to step away from the demands of pastoral ministry in order to create space to tend to their spiritual, physical, and mental health. MCC has recently received a grant from the Carpenter Foundation to launch a clergy wellbeing project of its own.

In her August 8, 2010, Huffington Post blog, "Soul Care and the Roots of Clergy Burnout," therapist Anne Dilenschneider noted that the causes of clergy burnout stem from a notion of clergy effectiveness, which is rooted in the production efficiency methodology of corporate America. She observes that one motivation lurking behind all these wellbeing initiatives is the goal of more clergy effectiveness. "Burnout needs to be solved so clergy can be more effective."[19]

David R. Wheeler noted in an article in *The Atlantic* on July 22, 2014, that the rise in bi-vocational ministry and the increasing inability for churches to pay a full-time salary to seminary graduates are indicators of the disappearance of the "clergy middle-class career."[20] And in a rebuttal article published in *Sojourners* July 30, 2014, seminary student Tripp Hudgins states that "Christianity has settled on the marketplace as our model for ecclesiology" claiming "I am not your employee. I am your pastor."[21]

Not only does this corporate efficiency model of pastoral leadership lead to burnout, it perpetuates a binary of clergy and laity by distancing the pastor from the people in the congregation. This model focuses on organizational structure, with a hierarchical leadership structure in which the pastor is the "expert." Even though there may be a council or board made up of lay leaders, the pastor is often the "chair," "president," or "moderator" of the governing body of the church. Ministry is often agenda driven using a command and control model. Often we hear the phrase used by clergy, "this is my church."

This kind of distancing from the congregation often leads to conflict, which can contribute to burnout, and can also lead to clergy misconduct. The recent efforts of judicatories from many mainline denominations to provide boundary training and create sexual misconduct policies is an indicator that this colonial model of pastoral effectiveness perpetuates a clergy/laity binary by seeing the laity as "other" in postcolonial terms.

REVISIONING PASTORAL MINISTRY

MCC has been a third space for pastoral ministry for forty-eight years and that has been and continues to be a messy space. We find ourselves living in the tension between "decency and indecency" as we navigate issues such as marriage equality while honoring and blessing polyamorous relationships, being a denomination as well as a movement, creating systems and structures that guide our congregational and leadership formation while being open to emerging models of ministry globally.

MCC currently has stated in its bylaws that in addition to being a teacher, preacher, and spiritual leader, the pastor is also head of staff and moderator of the board of directors. In tension with this "pastor as director" model, MCC is also a place where the other side of pastoral ministry has been and can be revisioned.

How might living more fully into our hybrid identity as pastoral leaders make our boundaries more permeable so that there is no clergy/laity binary and no need for "boundary training"? In this wiki world, what if we embraced the model of a network for pastoral ministry which leads to less hierarchy and more collaboration and provides an "open source model" for doing church?

Diana Butler Bass has imagined in her book *Christianity after Religion*, that twenty-first century congregations which are part of what she is calling a new awakening will understand ministry as performance.[22] She calls leaders to "act up and act out for God's love"—using a familiar phrase from AIDS activism. What if pastoral ministry were more performance based? And I don't mean "performance" in the sense of "job performance." Pastoral ministry as performance leads to mutual ministry. Bass claims, "the dichotomy between actor and audience is a false one. Performers and viewers inform, inspire, and respond to one another. Ideally, there is no such thing as a passive audience. Instead, audiences conspire with actors to create unique performances. To perform awakening means we must all participate . . . with interchangeable roles."[23]

In his book, *Coming Out Spiritually: The Next Step*, Christian De La Huerta names the spiritual functions LGBT people have had for millennia in cultures throughout the world. Historically "homoerotically inclined" or "gender-variant" people in indigenous cultures have been honored as Revolutionaries, Outsiders, Consciousness Scouts, Sacred Clowns, Keepers of Beauty, Caregivers, Mediators between worlds, Shamans, Divine Androgynes, and Gatekeepers.[24]

Queer people's spiritual legacy as tricksters, keepers of beauty, go-betweens, shamans, and healers points to the importance of playfulness in pastoral ministry. Jaco Hamman has noted the importance of play for practical theology in his article on play in the *Wiley-Blackwell Companion to Practical Theology*. He claims play is a means to spiritual arousal, tied to persons and state of mind more than place or situation; it calls forth imaginative spontaneity, invites the unexpected and promises possibility.[25] A model of pastoral ministry based on playfulness would be hard-pressed to see congregation members as "other."

Finally, MCC can be a place to think about risking indecency in pastoral ministry. In her essay, "Coming to the Table in Leather," MCC pastor Lea Brown fears that, at least in North America, MCC seems to have forgotten or stopped believing in our message that our spiritual power is grounded in the truth of our sexual experience.[26] In her essay, she shares her own story of full inclusion in MCC as a clergy person, who celebrates communion openly as a leather person and as someone who practices sadomasochism and domination-submission. The mutual consent and pleasure she experiences in the communities with which she plays have profoundly impacted the way she understands and connects to the divine source in all of life. How might Lea's story encourage all pastoral leaders not to separate their sexuality from the spirituality, to see themselves as sexual people, and to ground their spiritual power in their sexual experiences?

POSTSCRIPT

While MCC can serve as a case study for revisioning pastoral ministry from a postcolonial perspective, there are still questions we and the queer community in the United States must ask ourselves moving into an open future. In email exchanges with my colleague, Rev. Margarita Sanchez de Leon, on May 30, 2014, and November 7, 2014, we pondered the relationship between equality and diversity. The queer community struggled for equal rights in the military to have "don't ask, don't tell" repealed in the United States, but we have failed to ask "what does it mean to belong to a military structure that has been responsible in the past and in the present for imposing colonizing policies on others?" MCC has queered the Bible, queered theology, and queered Christianity. Where have been our efforts to "queer"—subvert, resist—political and social models that have influenced our hierarchical structure as a denomination and kept us from becoming more diverse as a religious movement?

MCC claims to be a global movement. Economically, the concept of globalism has served to justify the power of main financial monopolies on small structures. In what kind of globalism do we believe? What does it mean to be a global church in a postcolonial world?

MCC will continue to claim and occupy third space as messy space and a space of enunciation and possibility as we struggle with these questions and welcome more, and as we seek to let go of the ways we have been shaped by a colonial legacy while also risking the unknown of the future.

BIBLIOGRAPHY

Althaus-Reid, Marcella. *The Queer God*. London: Routledge, 2003.
Bass, Diana Butler. *Christianity after Religion: The End of Church and the Birth of a New Spiritual Awakening*. New York: Harper Collins, 2012.
De La Huerta, Christian. *Coming Out Spiritually: The Next Step*. New York: Tarcher/ Putnam, 1999.

Dilenschneider, Anne. "Soul Care and the Roots of Clergy Burnout." *The Huffington Post*, August 12, 2010. Accessed September 10, 2015. www.huffingtonpost.com/anne-dilenschneider/soul-care-and-the-roots-o_b_680925.html.

"Duke Clergy Health Initiative: Summary Report." Duke Clergy Health Initiative. divinity.duke.edu/sites/divinity.duke.edu/files/documents/chi/2014%20Summary%20Report%20-%20CHI%20Statewide%20Survey%20of%20United%20Methodist%20Clergy%20in%20North%20Carolina%20-%20web.pdf.

Firmer, Terry. "Remembering the UpStairs Lounge: The U.S.A.'s Largest LGBT Massacre Happened 40 Years Ago Today." Friendly Atheist Blog, July 24, 2013. Acessed September 10, 2015. www.patheos.com/blogs/friendlyatheist/2013/06/24/remembering-the-upstairs-lounge-the-u-s-a-s-largest-lgbt-massacre-happened-40-years-ago-today/.

Garber, Marjorie. *Vested Interests: Cross-dressing and Cultural Anxiety*. New York: Routledge, 1992.

Goss, Robert. *Jesus Acted Up: A Gay and Lesbian Manifesto*. New York: Harper Collins, 1993.

———. *Queering Christ: Beyond Jesus Acted Up*. Cleveland, OH: Pilgrim Press, 2002.

———, and Mona West, eds. *Take Back the Word: A Queer Reading of the Bible*. Cleveland, OH: Pilgrim Press, 2000.

———, Thomas Bohache, Patrick S. Cheng, and Mona West, eds. *Queering Christianity: Finding a Place at the Table for LGBTQI Christians*. Santa Barbara, CA: Praeger, 2013.

Guest, Deryn, Robert Goss, Mona West, and Thomas Bohache, eds. *The Queer Bible Commentary*. London: SCM Press, 2005.

Hamman, Jaco. "Playing." In *The Wiley-Blackwell Companion to Practical Theology*, edited by Bonnie J. Miller-McLemore, 42–50. Malden, MA: Wiley-Blackwell, 2012.

Hudgins, Tripp. "Holy Poverty at Seminary." *Sojourners*, July 30, 2014, accessed September 11, 2015, https://sojo.net/articles/holy-poverty-and-seminary.

Jagessar Michael N, and Stephen Burns. *Christian Worship: Postcolonial Perspectives*. Sheffield: Equinox, 2011.

Katz, Jonathan Ned. *The Invention of Heterosexuality*. New York: Dutton, 1995.

Kim-Cragg, HyeRan. *Story and Song: A Postcolonial Interplay between Christian Education and Worship*. New York: Peter Lang, 2012.

Kwok, Pui-lan. "Changing Identities and Narrativities: Postcolonial Theologies." In *Complex Identities in a Shifting World: Practical Theological Perspectives*, edited by Pamela Couture et al., 115–26. Zürich: LIT, 2015.

———. "Postcolonialism, American History, and World Christianity." *The Ecumenist* 48, no. 2 (2011): 1–7.

McLoughlin, Beth. "The Brazilian Church That Welcomes Gay Believers into the Fold." *The Guardian*, October 19, 2014. Accessed September 10, 2015. www.theguardian.com/world/2014/oct/01/brazilian-church-welcomes-gay-believers.

Wheeler, David R. "Higher Calling, Lower Wages: The Vanishing of Middle-Class Clergy." *The Atlantic*, July 22, 2014. Accessed September 10, 2015. www.theatlantic.com/business/archive/2014/07/higher-calling-lower-wages-the-collapse-of-the-middle-class-clergy/374786/.

NOTES

1. Robert Goss, *Jesus Acted Up: A Gay and Lesbian Manifesto* (New York: Harper Collins, 1993); Robert Goss, *Queering Christ: Beyond Jesus Acted Up* (Cleveland, OH: Pilgrim Press, 2002); Robert Goss and Mona West, eds., *Take Back the Word: A Queer Reading of the Bible* (Cleveland, OH: Pilgrim Press, 2000); and Deryn Guest, Robert Goss, Mona West, and Thomas Bohache, eds. *The Queer Bible Commentary* (London: SCM Press, 2005).

2. Robert E. Shore-Goss, Thomas Bohache, Patrick S. Cheng, and Mona West, eds., *Queering Christianity: Finding a Place at the Table for LGBTQI Christians* (Santa Barbara, CA: Praeger, 2013).

3. Kwok Pui-lan, "Changing Identities and Narrativities: Postcolonial Theologies," in *Complex Identities in a Shifting World: Practical Theological Perspectives*, ed. Pamela Couture et al. (Zürich: LIT, 2015), 120.

4. HyeRan Kim-Cragg, *Story and Song: A Postcolonial Interplay between Christian Education and Worship* (New York: Peter Lang, 2012), 28.

5. Jonathan Ned Katz, *The Invention of Heterosexuality* (New York: Dutton, 1995), 97.

6. Ibid., 182.

7. Kim-Cragg, *Story and Song*, 37.

8. Joseph Shore-Goss, "Pastoral Care for Transgendered Youth," in Shore-Goss et al., *Queering Christianity*, 297–321; Joan Saniuk, "Putting on Wedding Drag: Pastoral Care for Healing and Wholeness in the Queer Congregation," in ibid., 323–38.

9. Shore-Goss, "Pastoral Care for Transgendered Youth," 313.

10. Kwok, "Changing Identities and Narrativities," 117.

11. Marcella Althaus-Reid, *The Queer God* (London: Routledge, 2003).

12. Terry Firmer, "Remembering the UpStairs Lounge: The U.S.A.'s Largest LGBT Massacre Happened 40 Years Ago Today," Friendly Atheist Blog, July 24, 2013, acessed September 10, 2015, www.patheos.com/blogs/friendlyatheist/2013/06/24/remembering-the-upstairs-lounge-the-u-s-a-s-largest-lgbt-massacre-happened-40-years-ago-today/.

13. Marjorie Garber, *Vested Interests: Cross-dressing and Cultural Anxiety* (New York: Routledge, 1992), 11.

14. Beth McLoughlin, "The Brazilian Church That Welcomes Gay Believers into the Fold," *The Guardian*, October 19, 2014, accessed September 10, 2015, www.theguardian.com/world/2014/oct/01/brazilian-church-welcomes-gay-believers.

15. Kwok Pui-lan, "Postcolonialism, American History, and World Christianity," *The Ecumenist* 48, no. 2 (2011): 1–7; Michael N. Jagessar and Stephen Burns, *Christian Worship: Postcolonial Perspectives* (Sheffield: Equinox, 2011).

16. Kwok, "Postcolonialism," 2.

17. Kim-Cragg, *Story and Song*, and Jagessar and Burns, *Christian Worship*.

18. Duke Clergy Health Initiative, "Duke Clergy Health Initiative: Summary Report," divinity.duke.edu/sites/divinity.duke.edu/files/documents/chi/2014%20Summary%20Report%20-%20CHI%20Statewide%20Survey%20of%20United%20Methodist%20Clergy%20in%20North%20Carolina%20-%20web.pdf.

19. Anne Dilenschneider, "Soul Care and the Roots of Clergy Burnout," *The Huffington Post*, August 12, 2010, accessed September 10, 2015, www.huffingtonpost.com/anne-dilenschneider/soul-care-and-the-roots-o_b_680925.html.

20. David R. Wheeler, "Higher Calling, Lower Wages: The Vanishing of Middle-Class Clergy," *The Atlantic*, July 22, 2014, accessed September 10, 2015, www.theatlantic.com/business/archive/2014/07/higher-calling-lower-wages-the-collapse-of-the-middle-class-clergy/374786/.

21. Tripp Hudgins, "Holy Poverty at Seminary," *Sojourners*, July 30, 2014, accessed September 11, 2015, https://sojo.net/articles/holy-poverty-and-seminary.

22. Diana Butler Bass, *Christianity after Religion: The End of Church and the Birth of a New Spiritual Awakening* (New York: Harper Collins, 2012), 258.

23. Ibid., 261.

24. Christian De La Huerta, *Coming Out Spiritually: The Next Step* (New York: Tarcher/Putnam, 1999), 7–43.

25. Jaco Hamman, "Playing," in *The Wiley Blackwell Companion to Practical Theology*, ed. Bonnie J. Miller-McLemore (Malden, MA: Wiley-Blackwell, 2012), 43.

26. Lea Brown, "Coming to the Table in Leather," in Shore-Goss et al., *Queering Christianity*, 355–70.

FOUR

In Conversation

Womanist/Postcolonial/Pastoral

Stephanie Y. Mitchem

To envision postcolonial pastoral ministry from a womanist theology is to enter into a framework that is changed multiple times. This is a dialogue with relevant aspects of postcolonial thought, entering a global framework that may exclude black American women and men. Further, the inclusion of black women in the United States in postcolonial conversations alters the framework of their oppression discussions, opening to re-encounter the global reach of colonization. Womanist theology and ethics have long challenged the primary American epistemological constructions built around white-male-capitalist ideologies that construct hierarchies and determine scales of human value. In the United States, we take these different epistemological frameworks for granted, until something happens and the differences become blindingly obvious. White colleagues tell me that viewing the movie *The Help* in theaters at the same time as black audiences, became socially uncomfortable as the black side of the room broadcast their disgust with what was happening on the screen at different plot points and did not find other points humorous. It is comforting to think there is a single "American" story when postcolonial studies clearly emphasize that there is not.

Throughout this chapter, I will enunciate some aspects of a womanist pastoral practice and ministry in terms of ministering, leading, and healing that have postcolonial dynamics. The terms ministering, leading, and healing, under modernist constructions, were developed as disparate concepts; a bit of one might show up in the other, but disciplines were set up in distinctive categories with identifiable genus and species. Ministry often demanded a separation from the mundane, material world. Leadership was often thrown into a frame of politics, especially in the United States where it is determined by elections, and healing was remanded to mainstream medicine.[1] None of these disciplines welcomed, much less celebrated, the inclusion of black women as professionals in the fields. With few exceptions, black women continue to be pushed to sidelines of ministry, politics, and medicine since each of these fields developed hierarchal structures that reflected white, male, capitalist, mainstream American societies. Framing a womanist category of ministering/leading/ healing encompasses specific historical developments and a unique epistemology that converses with postcolonial concepts.

At times, a painful reception to black women's efforts to heal/minister/lead reflects the racism embedded in American society. I opened this chapter with two moments seared in memory from my own ministering life. I taught a Bible study in a church that was in one part of the country. A white woman in the class raised her hand to ask where black people came from since Adam and Eve were first, implying that they were certainly white. I do not remember how I answered that question. I do know that most black women are subjected to much insanity, perhaps based on a mistaken belief that we are the soft landing, the mammy figure, who will accept anything. Because these white racist ideologies are embedded in society, the breath-taking question—where did black people come from?—was possibly not deemed an insult by the questioner. In another part of the country, I worked as an administrator at a university and became known as a person committed to combating the dean's unjust policies. During a closed-door meeting, she jumped up, ran across the room and screamed in my face. I responded by staring at her, well aware that my genuine response would have had unpleasant consequences for me as a black woman. The dean represents the diverse/not diverse game played by some educational administrators in the United States, those who invite a token few black people in but remind us every day that we are not at home. Institutionalized racism functions efficiently in the United States and is, as Emilie Townes states, "the systematic construction of truncated narratives designed to support and perpetuate structural inequities and forms of social oppression."[2] While this chapter considers a womanist approach to pastoral ministry relevant to postcoloniality, we do not live in the rosy post-racial world some postmodern scholars want to paint. Engaging the postcolonial must entail strategizing against the different faces of racism and so this becomes part of the fabric of a womanist pastoral theology and practice.

Mainstream religions, like other American institutions, built constructions around white-male-capitalist ideologies. Kelly Brown Douglas challenges how black churches may have adopted such ideologies through the promotion of civility: "That which is considered civil in this narrative is what is considered acceptable to white society. The intent of the narrative is to craft an acceptably white image of black people . . . it is an outward looking narrative."[3] Setting up hierarchies of importance in church structures; defining where women can walk and who might be ordained; explaining our relationships with God or each other based on the meanings of holiness: each of these may have some white/male views that most religions find ways to enforce. Whether in the seminary, university, private, or public school, the academy generally can too often serve as the protected breeding grounds for white male views. The presumed universality of these views denies that they were initially based on and developed from a particular culture and time period. Meanwhile, the lives of women are marginalized and placed in the category of anecdotal accident. There are challenges across higher education when raced and gendered analyses are dismissed.

Katie G. Cannon has eloquently named the thoroughness and pain of these multiple dismissals:

> When Womanists refuse to play the game of illusive objectivity, a game that is incapable of tolerating ambiguity, ignores emotions, weeds out passion, resists spontaneity, maintains rigid predictability, and celebrates the isolated solo-self, then the prescriptive authorities impose theoretical frameworks categorizing our truth as a lie. Each and every time that we are not willing to dissect people, places and things; that we stand over against the intellectual propensity to tear apart foundational experiences, meanings, and elements by way of suprarational technical, abstract, referential facts, then we get demoted to the status of second-class thinkers.[4]

There are yet other challenges specific to church practice. For instance, putting some Kente cloth on the altar or a black person in the sanctuary without making any substantive changes in beliefs or practices too often represents denominational ideals of diversity. Religious constructions to support particular views are certainly the right of a given denomination, and these may range from specific theologies (God said women can't do that) to related practices (therefore, she cannot do that). Yet these constructions must be understood to embrace certain epistemological frameworks while excluding others in myriad ways to reinforce the status quo. These exclusionary processes become a self-sustaining, repetitious loop, like the music in a dentist's office. The very concept of ministry had been dropped into that loop and defined or revised so narrowly that only a select few could be understood as ministers. One enduring problem with the repetitive ideological loop is that the validity of any constructions that the loop cannot appropriate and control must be denied entrance. These components construct a framework in America that has been the ground on which black women's works of healing and leading and ministering in their communities takes place.

Historically, two sets of occurrences happened simultaneously in America. The first set built a society in which black people in the United States were enslaved, denied citizenship, excluded from voting, and generally defined as subhuman for centuries. The second set is related to the first: black women were given their own special stereotypes in these categories. From mammies to sluts, these stereotypical constructions reinforced ideas of black women's functions in American society with roles that were deemed for the benefit of white people.

These two sets of occurrences are not redundant or able to be folded one into another. Linda Tuhiwai Smith provides analysis that exposes layers of colonization:

> Colonized peoples have been compelled to define what it means to be human because there is a deep understanding of what it has meant to be considered not fully human, to be savage. The difficulties of such a process, however, have been bound inextricably to constructions of colonial relations around the binary of colonizer and colonized. These two categories are not just a simple opposition but consist of several relations. . . . Unlocking one set of relations most often requires unlocking and unsettling the different constituent part of other relations.[5]

Smith, a Maori scholar, indicates the significant but complicated layers of analysis that are necessary for colonized/indigenous people to signal their own humanity. Research had been a component of colonization; it should now become a way for the formerly colonized to seek social justice. In that aim, research to benefit the formerly colonized will not necessarily look the same as it did for the colonizer.

There are some scholars who would avoid placing African Americans in the same category as other colonized people: there have been instances where black Americans have fully participated in colonial projects at home or around the globe, assisting in the oppression of other people of color. In that same vein, African Americans do not have their own country. While there is some merit to these distinctions, the reality is that black Americans have consistently been disenfranchised, not allowed to fully participate in society and, most importantly, have not typically had economic or social power to originate and sustain oppression of others. This argument would require a much longer discussion but an example may assist. I was a resident of Detroit, Michigan. The population was and remains majority African American, and the city's government was composed mostly of African Americans; the argument was often made that black people had power of policy and economics. This "evidence" of black empowerment has proven to be a chimera in recent years as policy, economic, and even voting rights have been taken from these citizens by fiat of the state. Detroit could be said to be a colony of the state of Michigan in 2014.

The topic at hand is a womanist pastoral theology, in dialogue with the postcolonial, that is born of histories that are often invisible to the eyes of the colonizers. Black women's histories and lives draw on concrete references that craft new approaches to leading and ministering. What are these approaches? How do they look? Why are they to be understood within such an approach to pastoral theology? Perhaps the best place to start is with home training.

HOME TRAINING

Aunt Maggie: "The biggest devils are in the church."
Aunt Maggie: "Get up off your knees and do something."
Aunt Maggie: "Lilies grow even on dung heaps."

African Americans have been aware that we were (are) mistreated for the "flaw" of being black. African Americans crafted new statements of our humanity, as Linda Tuhiwai Smith indicated. These alternate forms are also ignored or misunderstood but they remain affirmations and fully human expressions of hope for better days.

Ministry by black American women has necessarily been a movement against various forms of colonialism, including the patriarchy of black men. As a matter of a postcolonial perspective, I am broadening the concept of "pastoral" and "ministry" to include leadership. I am not suggesting that everything black women do is pastoral or that everything is ministry. But I emphasize here that ministry means more than "service to God" or a humble service to others. A story often told about the Underground Railroad conductor, Harriet Tubman, is also the subject of a painting by Jacob Lawrence—"Forward." As Tubman was leading a group of enslaved Africans from the southern states into the relative freedom of the north, one of the travelers became afraid and wanted to return to enslavement, risking the lives of all the escapees. According to legend, Tubman pulled a gun on the fearful one and instructed him to go forward or die. This kind of action is not the gentle, self-effacing image of a wounded-healer kind of minister that has too often been presented in pastoral ministry courses. Too often, pastoral ministry and theology are reduced to ritual performances, missionary work, and church building. Seminary courses reflect these foci: Christian education, music ministry, evangelism, missions, church polity, preaching, finance, and other epistemological boxes that continue to operate as white male upper-class training processes. Harriet Tubman would not have had time for these courses; most likely, she would not be viewed as pastor "material." Postcolonial studies challenge us out of these epistemological boxes.

In traditional African American churches, black women have often been excluded from significant roles in public, preaching ministry. Jarena Lee was born in the late 1700s and felt called to public ministry as a preacher within the African Methodist Episcopal (A.M.E.) Church. Richard Allen, considered the founder of the A.M.E. Church, after years of her determined requests, eventually authorized her to preach, but some, too many, communities did not accept her. Lee became an itinerant preacher, covering thousands of miles in her lifetime of ministry. Her role was pivotal in the ways she spread the concept of the A.M.E. Church. Today, several A.M.E. women still report their communities' resistance to their calls to be in ordained ministry. But, like eighteenth-century preacher Jarena Lee, in the words of contemporary womanist scholar Cheryl Townsend Gilkes, "If it wasn't for the women, they wouldn't have a church."[6]

Yet, across generations, from Jarena Lee to contemporary struggles to be involved in churched ministries, black women have not stood silently in the wings waiting for their churches' calls. The processes of asserting our humanity were continued over time and place, despite the persistent, damning constructions that sought to define our existences into control. Moreover, our home training from childhood helped many of us think about "ministry" and leadership outside the box of the church.

The opening quotes were from my Aunt Maggie, and I often heard these words growing up. That the "biggest devils are in the church" provided an analysis of holiness itself: church people did not have exclusive rights to sanctity. Church was to be respected as an institution, yet we were to remember that people were not divine. The slavish commitment of some women and men to anything that comes out of church leaders' mouths was antithetical to the ways of my family. The analysis went beyond that. Religion had its place, but it did not take the place of personal responsibility and action. "Get up off your knees and do something" brought prayer to the practical and material. As a scholar, I will now discuss the connections between theory and praxis; as Aunt Maggie's niece, I know that I learned these connections from her.

No human person was to be excluded, including the one who might be deemed undesirable to the rest of society. Knowing that good and beauty can grow in surprising places—lilies on dung heaps—changes the views of poor or differently-abled or Othered persons and therefore human rights are more easily understood.

Such sayings are often used in black communities, teaching through proverbs. The home training may begin there, but is furthered through other community education. In the mid-twentieth century Bernice Johnson Reagon, the founder of Sweet Honey in the Rock, was firm in her religious beliefs, which she expressed through gospel music. Dr. Reagon refers to the Civil Rights icon, Ella Baker, as her political mother and tells the lessons she learned:

> She always greeted everyone. . . . She taught us that no movement could exist without individuals and that any movement organization

had to take care of its people. . . . Miss Baker put nothing in front of teaching others to organize for themselves. She urged us as organizers to understand how to create structures that allowed others in the group to also be leaders as well as followers. Her power was in her wanting to increase others' sense of their own power and their access to power.[7]

These stories of wisdom, from proverbs to training in the trenches, comprise portions of the formational training for black women. Unlike the seminary of the past, this formation is not a long period of separation from life in order to study it, but day-to-day analyses on the fly. Unlike the old seminary approach to training, situational rather than theoretical ethics take precedence. Scripture is applied and prayer is enacted. Today, seminary life itself is changing, brought about by new social realities, revisions in our economic lives, reconstitution of our gendered identities. Seminaries are now trying to keep doors open and enrollments up through on-line components or inviting older candidates. But one thing remains constant: people must apply to seminaries, come with certain skill sets, and can be rejected. The ministerial training itself sets up a kind of uniformity that belies diversity. There is still an element of exclusivity to the work of most seminaries and, by extension, their churches.

There is an open-ended self-selection in a black women's formation. Not everyone will risk as did Harriet Tubman; not everyone will take Ella Baker's lessons to heart as deeply as did Bernice Johnson Reagon during the Civil Rights movement. Some black women will commit and some will not understand. Reagon stated, "We were high school and college students, wives, mothers, workers, educated and uneducated, churched and unchurched, sober and non, and grandmothers—our elders. It was not reasonable to think that there would be constant harmony, but with effort, we did stay together."[8]

A WOMANIST PASTORAL THEOLOGY IN A POSTCOLONIAL KEY

Framing a womanist pastoral theology that resonates with postcolonial thought will incorporate all these aspects. But there is much more to incorporate. Linda Tuhiwai Smith discusses some components that are part of building theories that fit the lives of indigenous and oppressed peoples: "Part of the exercise is about recovering our own stories of the past. This is inextricably bound to a recovery of our language and epistemological foundations. It is about reconciling and reprioritizing what is really important about the past with what is important in the present."[9] Stories of Harriet Tubman or Bernice Johnson Reagon become ways to recapture language and ideas that are embedded in African American women's lives.

These stories help Toni C. King and S. Alease Ferguson to identify what they define as black womanist leadership, using the field of leadership studies. King and Ferguson define the sharing stories among black women as a "kitchen table" transmission of leadership. The kitchen table is the place where "much of the socialization and cultural rites of passage occur. The kitchen table, seen as insignificant domestic space, is actually a place of power, utilized by women to give and receive support, problem solve, plan, and create."[10]

King and Ferguson draw from the work of Alice Walker to define womanism and see it on an ethical continuum with black feminism not so much drawing in the theological. In their view, black feminism is based on "(1) the legacy of struggle; (2) the search for voice and the refusal to be silenced; (3) the impossibility of separating intellectual inquiry from political activism; and (4) the direct application of empowerment to everyday life."[11] They distinguish a black feminist/womanist posture when "African American women of all strata strive for a measure of self-acceptance and appreciation such as that articulated by Alice Walker when she described womanists as intentional leaders."[12]

The authors clearly define what leadership means from this black feminist/womanist perspective: "The desire, ability, and efforts to influence the world around us, based upon an ethic of care for self and other and fueled by a vision that one sustains over time."[13] A definition indicating the good of society based on "an ethic of care" does not necessarily align with the view of most mainstream administrators or politicians. Influencing the world in mainstream views may be delineated by an ethic of capitalism: that is, only focused on the fiscal bottom line, wherein racism names white power and control as the acceptable status quo.

Understanding the differences in their approach to leadership reflects longstanding difficulties with capitalist/racist conceptualizations of leadership that are embedded in our disciplines. We get caught, as Linda Tuhiwai Smith stated, in the "constructions of colonial relations around the binary of colonizer and colonized."[14] Noelle Witherspoon Arnold analyzes similar shortcomings in educational leadership trends that reflect multiple layers of the current colonizer/colonized binary:

> Current trends are problematic in that [they] fragment spiritual and religious leadership, rendering religion insignificant . . . leadership and management have been treated as synonymous and merely denotes holding the position of leader, possessing certain traits, or implying that leadership is purely about the leader and not the relationship to others. . . . The field tends to pay little heed to conducting research on female leadership and certainly leadership by females of color when the field desperately needs to do so.[15]

Arnold then follows with a question that is particularly pertinent for this essay: *What of an ethical leadership style that is grounded in a religio-spiritual tradition of black women?*[16]

In contrast to King and Ferguson, Arnold draws from established concepts of womanist theology, noting that Alice Walker's definition of womanism (as adapted by womanist ethicist Stacey Floyd Thomas) includes: (1) radical subjectivity; (2) traditional communalism; (3) redemptive self-love; (4) critical engagement; and (5) appropriation and reciprocity. "To these, I add what I call (6) Spirit-love to highlight the religious spirituality that binds these principles together. By expanding these tenets," Arnold contends, "womanism . . . becomes a model framework in this research for exploring religion in everyday life and becomes a vital epistemology for exploring religious spirituality." [17]

Identifying the spiritual traditions of black women connects stories, proverbs, and home training. King and Ferguson define the idea of kitchen table leadership to develop the idea of a Motherline transmission of knowledge among African American women. That is, "women who pass on values of an African-centered worldview, women who help daughters learn to read the social clime, heal from dominant culture oppression, fashion a culturally grounded identity, form and carry out resistance aimed at a particular social context or institution are the Motherline." [18] This idea shakes up the meaning of leadership in any setting even as it helps to expand the idea of ministry. Like Ella Baker and Bernice Johnson Reagon's Motherline, we can learn that prayer is not a liturgical production, but actions based on visions that will enrich a given community.

In an additional essay, Toni C. King identifies old traditions at kitchen tables and in stories that comprise the transmission of values that become and sustain the visions that are part of her life. "Stories became for me the foundation for engaging self and others in the process of reflexivity— focusing the lens and method of inquiry on one's self. This process of working through the issues, sorting through experience, sense making, imaginary-role taking, values clarifying, empathy building, and identity construction were the 'emotional technologies' that I began to develop" [19] Further, she states that "stories and storytelling have played a fundamental role in the preservation of every aspect of black culture." [20]

There is an authority given to the women who transmit wisdom, based on lived lessons, not merely pieces of paper granted by an impersonal institution. To say this differently, enslaved Africans did not follow Harriet Tubman into unknown places because she had a terminal degree. In the twenty-first century, however, as more black women receive advanced degrees, we will need to retain respect for the home-grown wisdom of kitchen tables while we employ our credentials as tools to enrich our communities in new ways.

Healing activities are part of the spiritual traditions of black women. Healing is not a mere concern for an individual body's symptoms but incorporates a holistic view of mind-body-spirit and includes the life of the community. Healing is often descriptive rather than prescriptive; it is a root for speaking truth in the many formats in which black women may find themselves. Aiming for wellness, not an absence of illness, healing depends on the person or community who hears the description to act to make change. Healing is woven into the ministering and leading components of a womanist pastoral practice.

Marsha Foster Boyd wrote of WomanistCare, a small group of African American women in the pastoral care professions including clergy women, social workers, clinical pastoral educators, and professors that began meeting in 1991. Boyd lists five components of WomanistCare pastoral theology: communication, including and especially listening; validation and affirmation of black women's stories; willingness to positively confront each other as well as unjust systems in order to build society; accountability among the members for honesty and integrity; and finally, healing, "so that we are able to help one another overcome." [21]

Drawing from womanist theology as methodology, Noelle Witherspoon Arnold details the lives and thoughts of black women principals to understand the sources of their leadership, especially the religious and the spiritual. Arnold emphasized that womanist theology held value beyond "simply promoting the addition of a religio-spiritual perspective, . . . [and may] provide a bridge from African American perspectives to cross cultural ones to further advance the increasing social justice agenda in schools." [22] The social justice agenda in schools, she contends, had too often been based on theories that were white, male, and middle class, "formulaic and impersonal and applies a universality to the needs of individuals and groups." [23] She seeks these new views, like King and Ferguson, in the stories of black women, past and present.

> Black women's historical spiritual texts have had a transforming presence on society, institutions and individuals. Moreover, I believe that "new" spiritual narratives need to be created to add new voices in insights in spiritual, cultural, and educational thought. Womanists' redemptive self-love is expressed in scholarship that rescues Black women from caricature and produces new paradigms. [24]

The resonance between WomanistCare that began meeting in 1991 and an educator in the early twenty-first century resounds along a Motherline that provides strong soundings for a womanist postcolonial pastoral theology.

If King and Ferguson draw womanist concepts into leadership studies and Arnold uses womanist thought as methodology for her educational leadership studies, Phillis Sheppard utilizes psychoanalysis to state a womanist practical theology. In some ways, this approach is a bold step, but it is a logical next step. Across disciplines, many African American scholars avoided the use of material that spoke only to white perceptions of black realities; in like manner, so much white psychoanalytic research "proved" the mental deficiencies of black people. In 1976, a groundbreaking book by psychologist Robert V. Guthrie emphasized the exclusivity of the white gaze in its title: *Even the Rat was White, A Historical View of Psychology.*[25]

By drawing from black women's stories and from a wide range of scholarship, Sheppard names aspects of experience and religious life that have significance for black women: body shape and size; skin color; sexuality and gender; suffering; love; family; violence; work and career. Sheppard arrives at a statement of a womanist practical theology that centrally focuses on the needs of black women. This requires ministering/healing/teaching that will embrace a womanist theological anthropology and will "(1) be engaged across disciplinary lines; (2) . . . articulate a theology that resists the impact of dehumanizing gaze toward black women and other marginalized groups; (3) develop praxes that address the intrapsychic and social aspect of need; and (4) create spaces for the loving and appreciative gazes that celebrate, challenge and work for the ongoing transformation of black women and the contexts in which they live."[26] Sheppard is calling us to redefine the holy and to see it in black women's bodies and experiences.

With this womanist theological anthropology, there are other aspects related to the statement of a pastoral theology with a postcolonial edge. The meaning of tradition would expand to incorporate the myriad values of black women as well as other excluded peoples, not as footnotes to white/male/capitalist meaning worlds. The recognition of how multiple ethical perspectives are grounded in tradition would require its own long-term study. As an example, the Motherline, King and Ferguson state, "includes the development of a kind of moral compass and capacities to interrogate the ethical implications of real life events or of social and political systems."[27] Implicit in this wider view of tradition is a process of giving a blessing to those who raise serious questions about the normative. Creativity would not then be a force to be controlled and commodified. The concept of empowerment is then embedded into our pastoral practice rather than the source of contention.

WARNINGS

In conclusion, several warnings are sounded. I have aimed to bring womanist pastoral thought into conversation with the postcolonial and have focused on the work of Linda Tuhiwai Smith. Smith provides a warning about the processes of research: "The debates about intellectual and property rights cast the contestation of knowledge in a new frame. . . . Now indigenous peoples have to prove that what was used for centuries to heal an illness was something which was 'discovered' and then had a value added to that discovery through some sort of scientific process."[28] The explorations of womanist pastoral theology have multiple benefits — for scholarship, for religious lives, for leadership, for healing. But, as

Cannon stated, "Whenever the masterminds of intellectual imperialism encode our candid perceptions and scholarly labor as nothing more than culturally laden idiosyncrasies, then we end up with education that is unbalanced, knowledge that is incomplete and a world view that is distorted."[29]

There is benefit to the conversations between womanist pastoral theology and postcoloniality. However, one of the ways that the "masterminds of intellectual imperialism" seek to control us who are often Othered is to try to collapse all our thought into a single room and then starve us to death. Sheppard cites Emilie Townes' warnings against postmodernism, where considerations of "otherness and difference can actually reproduce the oppressive dualism it seeks to dismantle because it lapses into specialized language and abstractions that can eventually 'become tools for hegemony.'"[30] In other words, guarding against the creation of a new controlling master narrative requires its own kind of vigilance. The same is true of the dialogues with postcoloniality, especially as women of color in the United States, the African Diaspora, and on the African continent find ways to further our conversations.

The second warning is related to this one, coming from Noelle Arnold: "The women in this study [of educational leadership] highlight the fact that religion and spirituality can often be insular and unaccommodating. Each principal had an isolated way of thinking that is at odds with reciprocity [a womanist principle Arnold cites]."[31] And in this statement, we reach the ends of interdisciplinarity. Interdisciplinarity does not, at this time in history, undermine or replace the need for the work of individual disciplines. The insularity of some religious thought is a moment where a scholar in one field can throw the conversation back to someone in another; to make a critique of a discipline and find an ending point, is not to end the conversation.

The final warning encourages scholars to continue this conversation. We need more, not less, processes for dialogue. Sheppard, Arnold, King, and Ferguson have already shone a light on the path to more collaborative foci.

BIBLIOGRAPHY

Ali, Carroll A. Watkins. *Survival and Liberation: Pastoral Theology in African American Context*. St. Louis, MO: Chalice Press, 1999.

Arnold, Noelle Witherspoon. *Ordinary Theologies: Religio-spirituality and the Leadership of Black Female Principals*. New York: Peter Lang, 2014.

Boyd, Marsha Foster. "Womanist Care, Some Reflections on the Pastoral Care and the Transformation of African American Women." In *Embracing the Spirit: Womanist Perspectives on Hope, Salvation, and Transformation*, ed. Emilie M. Townes, 197–202. Maryknoll, NY: Orbis Books, 1997.

Cannon, Katie G. "Structured Academic Amnesia, As If This True Womanist Story Never Happened." In *Deeper Shades of Purple: Womanism in Religion and Society,* edited by Stacey M. Floyd-Thomas, 19–28. New York: New York University Press, 2006.

Collins, Patricia Hill. *Fighting Words: Black Women and the Search for Justice*. Minneapolis: University of Minnesota Press, 1998.

Douglas, Kelly Brown. *Black Bodies and the Black Church: A Blues Slant*. New York: Palgrave Macmillan, 2012.

Gilkes, Cheryl Townsend. *If It Wasn't for the Women . . . Black Women's Experience and Womanist Culture in Church and Community*. Maryknoll, NY: Orbis Books, 2001.

Guthrie, Robert V. *Even the Rat Was White: A Historical View of Psychology*. New York: Harper and Row, 1976.

King, Toni C., and S. Alease Ferguson. *Black Womanist Leadership: Tracing the Motherline*. Albany: State University of New York Press 2011.

Mitchem, Stephanie Y. *African American Women: Tapping Power and Spiritual Wellness*. Eugene, OR: Wipf and Stock 2004.

Reagon, Bernice Johnson, and Sweet Honey in the Rock. *We Who Believe in Freedom*. New York: Anchor Books 1993.

Sheppard, Phillis Isabella. *Self, Culture and Others in Womanist Practical Theology*. New York: Palgrave Macmillan, 2011.

Smith, Linda Tuhiwai. *Decolonizing Methodologies: Research and Indigenous Peoples*. New York: Zed Books, 1999.

Townes, Emilie M. *Womanist Ethics and the Cultural Production of Evil*. New York: Palgrave Macmillan 2006.

NOTES

1. In contrast to these views, African American women's scholarship has been citing views of their own. For pastoral theology, Carroll A. Watkins Ali, *Survival and Liberation: Pastoral Theology in African American Context* (St. Louis, MO: Chalice Press, 1999) promotes a culturally relevant grounding for pastoral care. Patricia Hill Collins' *Fighting Words: Black Women and the Search for Justice* (Minneapolis: University of Minnesota Press, 1998) analyzes social contexts for African American women's social justice. Stephanie Y. Mitchem, *African American Women Tapping Power and Spiritual Wellness* (reprint, Eugene, OR: Wipf and Stock 2004) considers routes by which black women enact healing.

2. Emilie M. Townes, *Womanist Ethics and the Cultural Production of Evil* (New York: Palgrave Macmillan 2006), 4.

3. Kelly Brown Douglas, *Black Bodies and the Black Church: A Blues Slant* (New York: Palgrave Macmillan, 2012), 72.

4. Katie G. Cannon, "Structured Academic Amnesia, As If This True Womanist Story Never Happened," in *Deeper Shades of Purple: Womanism in Religion and Society*, ed. Stacey M. Floyd-Thomas (New York: New York University Press, 2006), 26.

5. Linda Tuhiwai Smith, *Decolonizing Methodologies: Research and Indigenous Peoples* (New York: Zed Books, 1999), 26–27.

6. Cheryl Townsend Gilkes, *If It Wasn't for the Women . . . : Black Women's Experience and Womanist Culture in Church and Community* (Maryknoll, NY: Orbis Books, 2001).

7. Bernice Johnson Reagon and Sweet Honey in the Rock, *We Who Believe in Freedom* (New York: Anchor Books 1993), 20, 22.

8. Ibid., 155.

9. Smith, *Decolonizing Methodologies*, 39.

10. Toni C. King and S. Alease Ferguson, *Black Womanist Leadership: Tracing the Motherline* (Albany: State University of New York Press 2011), xv.

11. Ibid., 10.

12. Ibid., 10.

13. Ibid., 11.

14. Smith, *Decolonizing Methodologies*, 26.

15. Noelle Witherspoon Arnold, *Ordinary Theologies: Religio-spirituality and the Leadership of Black Female Principals* (New York: Peter Lang, 2014), 26–27.

16. Ibid., 27, emphasis added.

17. Ibid., 18.

18. King and Ferguson, *Black Womanist Leadership*, 23.

19. Toni C. King, "Don't Waste Your Breath: The Dialectics of Communal Leadership Development" in King and Ferguson, *Black Womanist Leadership,*, 89.

20. Ibid.

21. Marsha Foster Boyd, "Womanist Care, Some Reflections on the Pastoral Care and the Transformation of African American Women," in *Embracing the Spirit: Womanist Perspectives on Hope, Salvation, and Transformation*, ed. Emilie M. Townes (Maryknoll, NY: Orbis Books, 1997), 200–201.

22. Arnold, *Ordinary Theologies*, 217.

23. Ibid.

24. Ibid., 54–55.

25. Robert V. Guthrie, *Even the Rat Was White: A Historical View of Psychology* (New York: Harper and Row, 1976).

26. Phillis Isabella Sheppard, *Self, Culture and Others in Womanist Practical Theology* (New York: Palgrave Macmillan, 2011), 188.

27. King and Ferguson, *Black Womanist Leadership*, 236.

28. Smith, *Decolonizing Methodologies*, 104.

29. Cannon, "Structured Academic Amnesia," 27.

30. Sheppard, *Self, Culture and Others*, 72.

31. Arnold, *Ordinary Theologies*, 229.

II

Liturgical Celebration

FIVE

Postcolonial Practices on Eucharist

HyeRan Kim-Cragg

What comes to your mind when you see and hear the word "Eucharist?" Is it the text that records the ancient ritual as performed by the earliest Christians? Is it the liturgy performed by the celebrant in today's churches? Or is it the participation in the movements of standing and kneeling, the shared silences, the sounds of litany and doxology chanted with others, and the taste of the elements?

This chapter identifies three aspects of Eucharist: the content of the Eucharist as written text, the leadership of the Eucharist performed by clergy, and the elements used in Eucharist. Each of these aspects is in turn viewed from two different sides: Eucharist as a non-literary practice versus a literary one, Eucharist as the work of the people versus the domain of the clergy, Eucharist as a celebration using ordinary versus consecrated food. While these two sides can be at odds with each other, they actually exist together as two sides of the same coin. One without the other is not desirable and may even be impossible. This chapter tries to highlight the complex nature of the Eucharist. It suggests that Eucharist is a hybrid Christian practice that holds contradictory and oppositional notions in tension.

THE PROBLEM OF VIEWING THE EUCHARIST AS WRITTEN TEXT ALONE

When we consider the Eucharist in academia it is usually the written liturgy and its authoritative performance by clergy that gets most attention. This view is also often dominant in the church. This chapter questions why this is the case. Performance studies scholars argue that "the hegemony of textualism"[1] is to blame. These scholars juxtapose textual knowledge with performative knowledge. Our understanding of the Eucharist tends to privilege propositional/textual knowledge over performative knowledge, and grants authority to clergy over the laity. This, however, runs counter to the understanding that the power of clergy and laity must be shared. For the celebration of communion is, when done properly, an act of empowerment rather than one of marginalization. This has implications for our understanding of the Eucharist and for how the practice of the Eucharist impacts the political, economic, and social issues of our time, including those touched on in postcolonial studies.

In order to dislodge this text-based hegemony, we turn to the performance studies work of Diane Taylor. Performance, Taylor writes, as "embodied practice, along with and bound up with other cultural practices, offers a way of knowing . . . as underlies the understanding of performance as simultaneously 'real' and 'constructed,' as practices that bring together what have historically been kept separate as discrete, supposedly free-standing, ontological, and epistemological.[2] Performance, she says, is "a system of learning, storing, and transmitting knowledge"[3] rather than merely an act. It is about how people produce and pass down knowledge.

According to postcolonial theory, the colonial construction and acquisition of knowledge is characterized by the compartmentalization and detachment from daily events, especially in the lives of the ordinary and the subaltern.[4] Colonial knowledge is used as a tool of the privileged, the literate, and the powerful for the sake of normalizing their experiences. It also benefitted their economic, cultural, and political interests. How does this written text-based colonial attitude toward knowledge relate to the practice of the Eucharist? The normative Eucharistic liturgies, the written texts produced in Europe (mostly in the Vatican in the case of the Roman Catholic Church) travel to the various regions across the globe. These texts are inserted or imposed upon the worshipping communities there as authoritative, often failing to reflect or respect the local culture.[5]

There are similarities between how writing and accessing indigenous knowledge were controlled and how the canonized Bible and its access were also limited to the European male priesthood. Taylor notes: "Not only did the colonizers burn their ancient codices, they limited the access to writing to a very small group of conquered males who they felt would promote their evangelical efforts. . . . Those who controlled writing . . . gained an inordinate amount of power."[6] The supposed preservation of indigenous knowledge was accomplished first by destroying it. Then, it was reproduced and appropriated by the local conquered men who were converted to Christianity. They became colonialist puppets, who served the colonialists while benefiting from colonial power. Knowledge, then, as a colonial legacy is compartmentalized as well as gendered and racialized.[7]

The colonial project not only destroyed indigenous knowledge but also distorted it. Indigenous knowledge was said to have been *"lost"* (stolen) but was supposedly *"found"* (discovered) again by those who wrote about indigenous people, their culture, and their tradition. The colonial project of acquiring knowledge is thoroughly unidirectional—it is "us" writing about "them," denying the agency to the peoples that are studied, as much as completely orientalizing in its motive—fetishized the local as primitive, inferior, and uncivilized, incapable of shaping their own identities.[8] When the New World was *discovered,* the indigenous people and their knowledge there *disappeared* since "the conqueror will write the body of the other and trace there his own history," as "the inaugural scene."[9] However, the subversive irony is that not all knowledge was lost and not everyone disappeared.

Though fragmentary, indigenous religious and cultural knowledge around ritual survived and was reproduced, partly because the knowledge was performative. The performative power of the knowledge enabled people to be resilient, empowering people's determination to resist. Taylor helpfully articulates this point by explaining the differences between the written knowledge which she describes as "the archive" and performative knowledge which she calls "the repertoire." The archive conjures up to us the idea of a building where a record is kept. Etymologically derived from the Greek word *"arkhe, "* the archive also points to a beginning. It is "the first place."[10] Thus the archives are where the first and original items of knowledge are kept. The knowledge before "the first place," then, is said to be nonexistent and what we know is "immunized against alterity," as Michel de Certeau contends.[11] The archive is kept in one and the first place at the center, and it is fixed. In contrast, the repertoire as embodied memory is etymologically linked to the idea of an inventory, derived from the Latin word, *"reperiō"* from *re-* ("again") + *pariō* ("invent" or "produce"). It requires people's agency and their presence. Opposite to the archive, the repertoire is not fixed but open to change. It involves contingency and captures the present moment without homogenizing or universalizing. It does not privilege the record of the past as the first and most essential.

The performative knowledge of the conquered as repertoire is beautifully exemplified in the case of the colonial encounter of Spanish friars with the Mexican indigenous people. In her study of the topic, Taylor exposes the European clerics' response to the subversive and hybrid indigenous elements the people embedded in the Eucharistic ritual:

> The friars riled against any mixing and overlapping of belief systems "until the heathen ceremonies and false cults of their counterfeit desires are extinguished, erased.". . . Insisting on strict orthodoxy, they

feared anything in indigenous practice that somehow resembled or overlapped with their own. [And yet] Durán, in the *Book of the Gods and Rites*, draws some uneasy comparisons between the Nahua's practice of human sacrifice and Christian communion, noting "how cleverly this diabolical rite imitates that of our Holy Church.". . . Native peoples came to be seen as perpetual performers, engaged in "idolatrous dissembling, . . . like monkeys, looking at everything, so as to imitate whatever they see people do." On the one hand, European . . . had praised the native peoples' capacity for imitation and used that to argue that they could be taught to be Christians and take the sacraments. On the other hand, the mimicry was inappropriate.[12]

The result of the violent collision of colonial interests with indigenous culture produced in the church liturgy something hybrid that was "almost the same but not quite."[13] The colonial power was disrupted by this effect. That is a paradoxical irony. However fragmentary and limited, indigenous performative mimicry of colonial religious ritual as a hybrid and subversive practice served to put a crack in the wall of Empire.

One of the recent findings of research into the Eucharistic practices of the early church is that the last supper was not cited in liturgical texts for several hundred years after the birth of Christianity. Even institution narratives, deemed the most essential pattern of Eucharistic tradition, were neither used ritually nor included actually as Eucharistic prayer. Institution narratives, Paul Bradshaw claims, "appear to be innovations in eucharistic prayer rather than the continuation of an ancient tradition."[14] These research findings demonstrate that the seemingly intact pattern of the Eucharist as a written text as we know it today is far from resembling early Christian practices. The quest to discover the most accurate and original Eucharistic liturgy (which assumed it must have looked something like the ones currently in use) may therefore be futile. When one understands how diverse, fluid, and multiple the Eucharist practices have always been we see each practice has organically and gradually been converging and diverging from one another. James F. White helpfully puts it this way: "Various types of worship contain differing rates of both fixed formulas for word and action found in books and the spontaneity that ebbs and flows as the Spirit moves and cannot be found in print."[15] The Eucharist carries a hybrid identity whose elements and traditions are mixed and whose practices intermingle with the current traditions and subvert old traditions while at the same time adopting and creating new ones, refusing to settle into one unified text or practice. With this point in mind, we move to the issue of the leadership of Eucharist.

THE PROBLEM OF THE LITURGICAL LEADERSHIP

The two opposite concepts of knowledge as archive and repertoire, discussed in the previous section, do not stand on equal footing. Historically they have different trajectories and power differentials. Hence, a binary position, opting for one and dismissing the other, is neither wise for our discussion nor possible in reality. The relationship between the two has never been clear cut or presented as linear. Instead the two aspects of knowledge have always been intertwined, implicated, and complicated. What is necessary, then, is to acknowledge their uneasy and tangled relationship without failing to critically ask, "Whose memories 'disappear' if only archival knowledge is valorized and granted permanence?"[16] What are the leadership and power dynamics involved in this knowledge production and practice?

These questions acknowledge the Eucharist as a hybrid and ambivalent practice, while also demonstrating how the Eucharist has both text and act, carrying both propositional and performative knowledge. Borrowing Taylor's concepts, it is possible to see that Eucharist involves both archival and repertory knowledge. The so-called "both-and" nature of the Eucharist highlights its hybrid identity. Having this doubleness, we can say that the Eucharist as performance contains a latent resistant power and poses alternative possibilities as an incarnational, untamable, Spirt-filled event.[17] While performative knowledge can be learned and passed down through embodied practice, it cannot be boxed into uniformity and reproduced in the same manner propositional written knowledge can. In the words of Peggy Phelan, "performance cannot be saved, recorded, documented, or otherwise participate in the circulation of representations of representation."[18] Given its ontological nature, that is, that it exists by disappearing, there lies a tremendous power to move beyond the status quo, always orienting toward an unfolding reality that is beyond our present grasp. There is resistance inherent in the nature of performance as it refuses to be contained in an archive or captured in a museum. Those of us who regularly perform the Eucharist, both as clergy and laity, can affirm this experience. Even if we do it often, and repetitively, it is never the same. We can never totally and forever capture what it is in the same way. In Eucharist, there is alterity and irreducibility that liberates and reverses the status quo.

Keeping in mind the subversive and irreducible power embedded in the performative aspect of the Eucharist, let us further explore the role of the Eucharist as performance of resistance against violence. William T. Cavanaugh in *Torture and the Eucharist* argues that Eucharist in terms of what the experience holds is subversive. This is so not only in terms of what constitutes its message. Its subversive nature is also constituted in its medium in who is involved in its celebration. It is political to proclaim that God is the one to whom we owe respect before the state. This is especially so when the state *appears* to be more powerful as when it asserts its power unjustly with military force. The Eucharist resists violence by the way it is enacted. It is never an individual private act. It is done through the social body of the community and by a group of people in public making their presence visible. Reflecting on the context of Chile under the Pinochet regime, Cavanaugh contrasts the Eucharist with the use of torture committed by the state. The state tried to make its crime against humanity invisible and used it to isolate people. He writes, "Modern torture is predicated on invisibility" as exemplified by the disappearance of tortured bodies. The consequence of torture is left undone since it cannot be known, shared, or disclosed. Thus the violence causes double pain. Or one may say the body has been murdered twice, once by the police secretly (privately) and then by public ignorance. However, there is a counter-narrative performed in the Eucharist which claims that "pain can be shared," in and by the public, Cavanaugh continues, "precisely because people can be knitted together into one body."[19] The Eucharist makes invisibility visible. The Eucharist gathers people rather than isolates them. The Eucharist makes a private affair into a public act. As long as the community recognizes and remembers the violence that has occurred, death is not the end of the story. Victory does not totally belong to the state; members might have been lost but never forgotten.

Remembering and not forgetting is a critical imperative for building up the human community. Keeping memory alive makes humans resilient. The Eucharist plays a key role in this preservation of memory—this ultimate remembering. The event of the Passover and the Last supper with Jesus are remembered in the form of a rite. For the point of view of those in power these rites and the memory they represent have often been perceived as dangerous. [20] Why? Because the memory of Jesus' death and resurrection signifies the ultimate powerlessness of temporal authorities in matters of life and death. In our remembering, brutal violence is named. In our remembering, injustice and oppression against the innocent and the powerless are revealed. Even though Jesus' life was taken away, he remains alive among Christian communities who commemorate his death as a way toward the ending of violence and the bringing of justice. That is why it is necessary to remember because it gives us the courage to face suffering and death. *Anamnesis* in Eucharist, Johann B. Metz writes, "forces us to look at the public *thartrum mundi* not merely from the standpoint of the successful and the established, but from that of the conquered and the victims."[21] The Eucharist in this regard is a public performance of telling the story from the point of view of the conquered and the victims. It is a subversive memorial acclamation that Jesus' death was not in vain and that his life lives in us as long as we remember it.

The subversive, countercultural, and resistant nature of the Eucharist, however, is only one bright side of the story. One must look closely at the other shadowy side. As I have argued elsewhere, like the Bible, the Eucharist has an ambivalent nature. It can be both liberating and oppressive for women and other marginalized groups.[22] For the critique of misogyny and sexism manifested in the Eucharist, we turn to the feminist liturgical scholars and theologians. Marjorie Procter-Smith, reflecting on the experiences of women, contends that communion has become *disunion* because women have been denied both access to the Eucharist and authority to officiate it. Their abilities were denied as ordained ministers and priests for reason of being impure.[23] Furthermore, there has been too much emphasis on the atonement, a theology of Eucharist that justifies the unjust sacrifices in the name of patriarchy. The irony of a theology that touts the holiness and purity of the blood of Jesus Christ that was shed for us is painfully obvious when seen against the practice of denying women access to the Eucharist during their time of menstruation. Such demonization of women's blood and the denial of women's participation in Eucharist is in stark contrast with the glorification of Jesus' blood and the total control of the male clergy. One wonders if the blood of women is fundamentally different from that of men, when one looks at the Church's ambivalent and contradictory attitude. Another feminist theologian, Letty Russell, sharpens this point: "the usual pattern of blood sacrifice is that it takes place as an exclusive male ritual in which the pattern is one of taking life and shedding blood, in contrast to the women's role of shedding blood to *give* life."[24] Such obsession with the blood of Jesus Christ and the male clergy's obsession of the control over the Eucharist demonstrate how patriarchy perpetuates and reproduces itself to maintain the male dominance in church and society over centuries. But Christianity is not the only religion to be blamed on this matter. Nancy Jay's research shows that a sacrificial, patrilineal system existed before Christianity and can be found in other cultures and other religions.[25] At the end, it was a gendered role, chiefly associated with childbirth and childrearing that was at play in the construction of the basis of patriarchal social order. In that context and for that purpose, sacrificial purity ritual is established and Eucharist as a Christian blood sacrifice ritual, where Jesus is the purifier,[26] has been promoted. Creating a male dominant patrilineal system in society goes hand and hand with creating a male dominant clerical authority in church. They mutually influence and benefit each other.

In short, atonement theology of the Eucharist creates difficulties. Highlighting the blood sacrifice of Jesus "normalizes sadistic and masochistic dynamics," as Carter Heyward noted.[27] It potentially justifies violence, fueling imposed sacrifice of the vulnerable for patriotism or family or other cause, while endorsing and acquiescing the abuse of the innocent including women, children, and the elderly. Cognizant of these challenges, we turn to the final aspect of Eucharist, the elements.

THE PROBLEM OF COMMERCIALIZED EUCHARIST ELEMENTS

The following of the historical use of bread and wine is important for maintaining a constancy in worship.[28] However, wheat bread and wine represent Europe, though they are connected to the Mediterranean culture from which Jesus came. Both wheat and wine are produced in that region. In many places, especially in the Global South, wheat and wine are far less accessible; they are certainly not the common food of ordinary people. And yet, Christians in these places make efforts to follow and imitate European-Mediterranean Christians by using wheat bread and wine. Russell Yee in *Worship on the Way* makes a convincing and challenging case regarding the difficulty of the food used in Eucharist: "I have worshipped with Christians in Sri Lanka, where there is no tradition of cultivating grapes. I learned that many of these believers have adopted the practice of using a . . . grape-flavored soda for Communion. . . . But is such an attachment to 'grapeness' truly helpful or needed? . . . If Jesus were at a church in Sri Lanka and had available a foreign, artificially-flavored grape soda there beside a rich, fragrant Sri Lanka tea, which do you think he would choose to offer as his blood?"[29]

Also problematic is the issue of the wafer as the body of Christ. You can order wafers now online[30] as selling Jesus' body has become profitable. The Cavanagh Company of Greenville, Rhode Island, established in 1943 now makes 80 percent of the "altar breads" that are consumed in the churches in the United States. Cavanagh has built a brand that dominates the markets in Australia, England, and Canada.[31] So Cavanagh is not only a locally monopolized company, but also runs a transnational globalized business. Once traditionally the work of the monastery, mostly that of nuns, the baking bread has now left the church. It is ironic to note that the bread made for teaching about the Reign of God is manufactured by a profit-driven industry that benefits from capitalism. Andrea Bieler and Luise Schottroff argue that one must see the economic and political significance of the bread and the wine shared at the table because these Eucharistic elements reveal how they become part of an economic system favoring some and oppressing others.[32] The wafer industry has become such a driving force that it has turned the Eucharistic element into a commodity. The title of the article, "Buying the Body of Christ," is not just a catch phrase but embeds a truthful reality.[33] In this atmosphere of commercialization a strange marketing strategy has been developed. Rowan Moore Gerety writes, "In a fortuitous convergence of doctrine between the Food and Drug Administration and the Catholic Church, the Cavanagh Company has taken 'contamination' to mean human touch, and the company maintains a fully-automated production process where employees are forbidden from laying their hands on the wafers." The bread of the Eucharist has been disembodied, abandoning the human touch, its labor, as the company boastfully states: "Our wafers are untouched by human hands."[34] It would be unfair to dismiss that many churches (especially most Reformed Churches) use locally baked bread, some even baking it on their own in the church, considering various shapes and sizes, adding nutritious ingredients and theological meanings of sharing and nurturing at the Table of Jesus Christ.

The Eucharist signifies a symbol of overflowing abundance, embodying the unconditional love of Jesus Christ. God's self-giving love for abundant life is multiple and freeing rather than normative and uniformed. Andrew McGowan's critique is valid here. Looking into food and drink used in early Christian ritual meals, he laments that for far too long we assumed a uniformity of Eucharist practice without sufficient evidence. One cannot pinpoint one kind of food as dominant but it is evident that the food and the drink that the early Christians used were diverse, localized, and pluriform. Indeed, the Eucharist involved the sharing of fruits, vegetables, and fish instead of strictly using bread. Other liquids such as water, milk, and oil were also used instead of using wine.[35] Liturgical theologian Christopher Grundy, building on the work of Bradshaw and McGowan, points out that our Gospel traditions also indicate non-normative and non-unified practices as they show traces of tension and diversity in Eucharistic practice. While the upper room narrative in Mark has subsumed all other narratives of the Eucharist, the meal at Emmaus in Luke and the story of the bread and fish in John have co-existed, been practiced, and served as catechetical tools.[36]

POSTCOLONIAL IMAGINATION FOR CREATING EUCHARISTIC PRACTICES

Thus far, we have examined and posed the three issues that are central to Eucharist and its practice. At the heart of the problems lie both the written text as the Eucharistic liturgy and the patriarchal tradition of the Eucharistic liturgy that are performed and privileged by the few male clergy. The elements used in the rite are themselves deeply colonial, Eurocentric and capitalistic, and thus deserve a postcolonial optic and imagination. It is unnerving to acknowledge the patriarchal, colonial, and market-driven practices and traditions embedded and practiced in the Eucharist.

The early church Eucharistic practices have been hybrid, always holding ambivalent and contradictory positions. Thus, our role as theologians, religious educators, and liturgists is to recognize and tease out the contradictory and empowering cultural and religious traditions that continue to appear in the Eucharist. We need not go back to the precolonial world to retrieve a Eucharist that is untainted by forces of patriarchy, empire, and capitalism. Such never existed. It is important to "honor the violent embodied logic which gradually eclipsed all other ritual meal practices of the early church, while reserving the possibility that this particular logic of practice is no longer the most appropriate or effective."[37] We have a choice to make, Grundy continues, a possibility "in which the grace we discover and strive to embody at our sacramental tables significantly includes the nurture of resilience, the re-programming (through practices) of damage-induced *habitus* for the sake of our continued collaboration with God's persistent work for the kin-dom."[38]

The nurture of resilience as a postcolonial optic empowers whether it be in a theater or in a church or in a march on the street. According to Taylor, even those who are spectators, along with the actors, directors, and writers, are keenly bound up in the events happening on stage at the theater, not only through identification but also through participation. Bystanders and spectators are the ones who are called on to intervene and change the course of the performance.[39] All Christians are spectators in this sense. All Christians have the agency to identify and participate in the event which must be changed. Such intervention can happen in multiple ways. In fact, it is dangerous to have a single story.[40] The single story almost always serves the ones in power and oppresses the ones at the margin. Theologian Willie James Jennings traces the social construction of race as he demonstrates how the remapping of biblical geography as a single story with a single perspective basically identified the victory of Israel as a chosen race with that of British people in the mission of colonialism.[41] It was a single event of conquest. Alternative stories and perspectives coming from multiple places and people as resilience and resistance must be performed and practiced. Even if it seems only one bold and courageous person is doing the work, it is never single-handedly done. Even in a play featuring one person in monologue there are multiple audiences and spectators making an impact on the performance which leads to and creates heterogeneous stories and meanings.

In this regard, one can imagine multiple scenes of Eucharistic resilience. Here are a few examples: A group of ordinary people gather and share a meal, remembering the story of Jesus at the last supper by singing a song, "God Bless to Us Our Bread/Bendice, Señor, nuestro pan"[42] without following any written text. This remembrance performed becomes real, as they share their hunger and impoverished reality due to the ecological degradation of mining. Despite the scarcity of food available to them, they offer their common food of corn in Eucharist. Here is another: there is a subversive performance happening when a woman priest (who has claimed her right to preside despite the opposition and condemnation from church authorities) lifts up the chalice. She is denouncing authority that demonizes women's bodies and dismisses their leadership. When a transgender minister stands at the communion table having overcome the barriers of transphobia in family, church, and society, the wall of heteronormativity and gender binary is broken down. Even if we are not actors in this but only speculators, we become the witnesses who intervene to crack the wall of discrimination open. We are the collective agent that changes the course of the event as Eucharist.

So the journey continues. It would be, thus, appropriate to end this chapter by circling back to the first question raised at the beginning of this chapter, "what comes to your mind when you hear and see Eucharist *now?*"

BIBLIOGRAPHY

Adichie, Chimamada Ngozi. "The Danger of a Single Story." TED website, July, 2009. Accessed January 15, 2015. www.ted.com/talks/chimamanda_adichie_the _danger_of_a_single_story?language=en.

Bell, Catherine. *Ritual Theory, Ritual Practice*. New York: Oxford University Press, 1992.

Bhabha, Homi K. *The Location of Culture*. New York: Routledge, 1994.

Bieler, Andrea, and Luise Schottrof. *The Eucharist: Bodies, Bread, & Resurrection*. Minneapolis: Fortress Press, 2007.

Bradshaw, Paul. *Eucharistic Origins*. New York: Oxford University Press, 2004.

Cavanagh, William T. *Torture and Eucharist: Theology, Politics, and the Body of Christ*. Oxford: Blackwell, 1998.

Conquergood, Dwight. "Performance Studies: Interventions and Radical Research." In *The Performance Studies Reader*, 2nd ed., edited by Henry Bial, 369–80. New York: Routledge, 2007.

Craigo-Snell, Shannon. *The Empty Church: Theater, Theology, and Bodily Hope*. Oxford: Oxford University Press, 2014.

De Certeau, Michel. *The Writing of History*, trans. Tom Conley. New York: Columbia University Press, 1988.

Gerety, Rowan Moore. "Buying the Body of Christ." Killing the Buddha. Accessed December 22, 2014. killingthebuddha.com/mag/dogma/buying-the-body-of-christ.

Grundy, Christopher. "The Grace of Resilience: Eucharistic Origins, Trauma Theory, and Implications for Contemporary Practice." *NAAL Proceedings 2006*, 150–51.

Heyward, Carter. *Saving Jesus from Those Who Are Right*. Minneapolis: Fortress Press, 1999.

Jay, Nancy. "Sacrifice as Remedy for Having Been Born of Woman." In *Immaculate and Powerful: The Female in Sacred Image and Social Reality*, edited by Clarissa W. Atkinson, Constance H. Buchanan, and Margaret R. Miles, 283–309. Boston: Beacon Press, 1985.

Jennings, Willie James. *The Christian Imagination: Theology and the Origins of Race*. New Haven, CT: Yale University Press, 2011.

Kim-Cragg, HyeRan. *Story and Song: A Postcolonial Interplay between Christian Education and Worship*. New York: Peter Lang, 2012.

Kwok, Pui-lan. *Globalization, Gender, and Peacebuilding: The Future of Interfaith Dialogue*. New York: Paulist Press, 2012.

McClintock, Anne. "The Angel of Progress: Pitfalls of the Term 'Post-colonialism.'" In *Colonial Discourse and Post-Colonial Theory: A Reader*, edited by Patrick Williams and Laura Chrisman, 291–304. New York: Columbia University Press, 1994.

McGowan, Andrew. *Ascetic Eucharists: Food and Drink in Early Christian Ritual Meals*. New York: Oxford University Press, 1999.

Metz, Johann Baptist, and Jurgen Moltman. *Faith and the Future: Essays on Theology, Solidarity, and Modernity*. Maryknoll, NY: Orbis Books, 1995.

Morrill, Bruce T. *Anamnesis as Dangerous Memory: Political and Liturgical Theology in Dialogue*. Collegeville, IL: Liturgical Press, 2000.

Phelan, Peggy. *Unmarked: The Politics of Performance*. London: Routledge, 1993.

Procter-Smith, Marjorie. *In Her Own Rite: Constructing Feminist Liturgical Tradition*. Nashville: Abingdon, 1990.

Russell, Letty M. *Church in the Round: Feminist Interpretation of the Church*. Louisville, KY: Westminster John Knox Press, 1993.

Said, Edward W. *Orientalism*. New York: Vintage Books, 1978.

Spivak, Gayatri Chakravorty. "Extempore Response to Susan Abraham, Tat-siong Benny Liew, and Mayra Rivera." In *Planetary Loves: Spivak, Postcoloniality, and Theology*, edited by Stephen D. Moore and Mayra Rivera, 136–46. New York: Fordham University Press, 2011.

Taylor, Diane. *The Archives and the Repertoire: Performing Cultural Memory in the Americas*. Durham, NC: Duke University Press, 2003.

White, James F. *Introduction to Christian Worship*. Nashville, TN: Abingdon Press, 2000.

Yee, Russell. *Worship on the Way: Exploring Asian North American Christian Experience*. Valley Forge: Judson Press, 2012.

NOTES

1. Dwight Conquergood, "Performance Studies: Interventions and Radical Research," in *The Performance Studies Reader*, 2nd ed., ed. Henry Bial (New York: Routledge, 2007), 371.

2. Diane Taylor, *The Archives and the Repertoire: Performing Cultural Memory in the Americas* (Durham, NC: Duke University Press, 2003), 3.

3. Ibid., 16.

4. Here the term "subaltern" is used to indicate both the reality of their powerlessness, unable to be "heard collectively," and their potential path to be "inserted into circuits of hegemony." Gayatri Chakravorty Spivak, "Extempore Response to Susan Abraham, Tat-siong Benny Liew, and Mayra Rivera," in *Planetary Loves: Spivak, Postcoloniality, and Theology*, ed. Stephen D. Moore and Mayra Rivera (New York: Fordham University Press, 2011), 145.

5. Anne McClintock, "The Angel of Progress: Pitfalls of the Term 'Post-colonialism,'" in *Colonial Discourse and Post-Colonial Theory: A Reader*, ed. Patrick Williams and Laura Chrisman (New York: Columbia University Press, 1994), 295.

6. Taylor, *The Archives and the Repertoire*, 18.

7. Kwok Pui-lan, *Globalization, Gender, and Peacebuilding: The Future of Interfaith Dialogue* (New York: Paulist Press, 2012), 61.

8. Edward W. Said, *Orientalism* (New York: Vintage Books, 1978), 4–5.

9. Michel de Certeau, *The Writing of History*, trans. Tom Conley (New York: Columbia University Press, 1988), xxv.

10. Taylor, *The Archives and the Repertoire*, 19.

11. de Certeau, *The Writing of History*, 216.

12. Taylor, *The Archives and the Repertoire*, 45.

13. Homi K. Bhabha, *The Location of Culture* (New York: Routledge, 1994), 112, 86.

14. Paul Bradshaw, *Eucharistic Origins* (New York: Oxford University Press, 2004), 11.

15. James F. White, *Introduction to Christian Worship* (Nashville, TN: Abingdon Press, 2000), 18.

16. Taylor, *The Archives and the Repertoire*, 36.

17. Shannon Craigo-Snell, *The Empty Church: Theater, Theology, and Bodily Hope* (Oxford: Oxford University Press, 2014). She explores church as performance, employing three features of performance as event, interaction, and doubleness. For a detailed discussion, see chapter 1.

18. Peggy Phelan, *Unmarked: The Politics of Performance* (London: Routledge, 1993), 146.

19. William T. Cavanagh, *Torture and Eucharist: Theology, Politics, and the Body of Christ* (Oxford: Blackwell, 1998), 280.

20. Bruce T. Morrill, *Anamnesis as Dangerous Memory: Political and Liturgical Theology in Dialogue* (Collegeville, IL: Liturgical Press, 2000).

21. Johann Baptist Metz and Jurgen Moltman, "The Future in the Memory of Suffering," in *Faith and the Future: Essays on Theology, Solidarity, and Modernity* (Maryknoll, NY: Orbis Books, 1995), 6–7.

22. HyeRan Kim-Cragg, *Story and Song: A Postcolonial Interplay between Christian Education and Worship* (New York: Peter Lang, 2012), 32. I argue that any discussion around the Bible must consider and examine assumptions, which are operative: one is ambivalent, having a contradictory nature and the other is colonial tendency.

23. Marjorie Procter-Smith, *In Her Own Rite: Constructing Feminist Liturgical Tradition* (Nashville: Abingdon, 1990), 149–51.

24. Letty M. Russell, *Church in the Round: Feminist Interpretation of the Church* (Louisville, KY: Westminster John Knox Press, 1993), 143.

25. Nancy Jay, "Sacrifice as Remedy for Having Been Born of Woman," in *Immaculate and Powerful: The Female in Sacred Image and Social Reality*, ed. Clarissa W. Atkinson, Constance H. Buchanan, and Margaret R. Miles (Boston: Beacon Press, 1985), 300.

26. Jesus as purifier is a metaphor that is still very much in use in many churches. My son was recently in a youth gathering at one such church where Jesus was literally compared to a water purifier. Unconverted human beings are identified as tainted water.

27. Carter Heyward, *Saving Jesus from Those Who Are Right* (Minneapolis: Fortress Press, 1999), 175.

28. White, *Introduction to Christian Worship*, 41.

29. Russell Yee, *Worship on the Way: Exploring Asian North American Christian Experience* (Valley Forge: Judson Press, 2012), 134–35.

30. Here are a couple of internet sites: www.amazon.com/Communion-Wafers-1000-Broadman-Press/dp/0805470859, accessed December 22, 2014.

31. Rowan Moore Gerety, "Buying the Body of Christ," Killing the Buddha, accessed December 22, 2014, killingthebuddha.com/mag/dogma/buying-the-body-of-christ/.

32. Andrea Bieler, and Luise Schottrof, *The Eucharist: Bodies, Bread, & Resurrection* (Minneapolis: Fortress Press, 2007), 4.

33. Gerety, "Buying the Body of Christ."

34. Ibid.

35. Andrew McGowan, *Ascetic Eucharists: Food and Drink in Early Christian Ritual Meals* (New York: Oxford University Press, 1999), chapter 3.

36. Christopher Grundy, "The Grace of Resilience: Eucharistic Origins, Trauma Theory, and Implications for Contemporary Practice," *NAAL Proceedings 2006*, 150–51.

37. Grundy in "The Grace of Resilience," 156, elaborates on this term, "embodied logic" as "a certain logical or structural consistency, a coherence of principle, that is exercised in the embodied practices of ritual," drawing from Catherine Bell, *Ritual Theory, Ritual Practice* (New York: Oxford University Press, 1992).

38. Grundy, "The Grace of Resilience," 155–56.

39. Taylor, *The Archives and the Repertoire*, 12.

40. See the TED Talk of Chimamada Ngozi Adichie, "The Danger of a Single Story," TED website, July, 2009, accessed January 15, 2015, www.ted.com/talks/chimamanda_adichie_the_danger_of_a_single_story?language=en.

41. Willie James Jennings, *The Christian Imagination: Theology and the Origins of Race* (New Haven, CT: Yale University Press, 2011).

42. *More Voices* #193 (Toronto: United Church Publishing House, 2007). Words are by Bishop Federico Pagura from Argentina. English translation by John L. Bell.

SIX

Table Habits, Liturgical *Pelau*, and *Dis*placing Conversation

A Postcolonial Excursion

Michael N. Jagessar

In the winter of 2013, while visiting Australia, the English cricket team failed to keep the coveted Ashes trophy. They were convincingly thrashed 5–0 and thus began soul-searching about the state of England's performance in sports. An early exit from World Cup football in 2014 plunged the nation into even more despair. A BBC online article explored how English sport has always been suspicious of "outlandish talent" as sport was "set up for honest yeomen" (sic).[1] This distrust was traced back to the Victorian era and the age of the sporting amateur when what mattered most were loyalty, comradeship, and mutual responsibility. There was no place for anyone or anything *unorthodox*. Such tactical conservatism still characterizes English attitudes to sport today. So much so, that when someone with a different, or transgressing, outlook and way of doing things emerges, managing bodies do not know what to do with them. Pushing the boundaries of orthodoxy and tradition(s) is still viewed with much suspicion.

When *Church Times* provided readers with a list of one hundred best Christian books, it embraced a mix of poetry, prose, spirituality and some theology.[2] The list was presented as inclusive because the writers come from various ecclesial traditions. Yet, all judges were white-British (four men and three women), mainly Church of England, and of the books selected only one is written by a theologian from the South (Gustavo Gutiérrez). While insisting on the influence of books and words, especially their mental impact in shaping ecclesial life,[3] the judges decided to exclude the Bible, liturgy, and hymnals from the exercise. They decided that these are "too seminal, too much woven into the Church's life to be considered books in themselves."[4] Interesting, to say the least!

If worship is where habits are formed and nurtured for living out the liturgy in the world, then what we do in our liturgy is critical for the ministry practices of the whole people of God. What is the role of liturgy in interrupting colonial discourse and advancing the possibility of healing for relationships distorted or even destroyed by hegemonic discourse and agendas? How does colonial memory shape how we share, for example, the eucharistic meal? What complex discourses of power lurk among those who sit in the pews, within ecclesial traditions and with presiders?

Building on the critical conversations in *Christian Worship: Postcolonial Perspectives*,[5] my reflections engage aspects of the theology and practice of eucharist.[6] If postcolonial tactics are more than the effects of historic colonialism, where, I wonder, is the interrogation of the received deposit of faith and of eucharistic theologies happening so as to reveal their role in the shaping of identity, to critique our talkative proclivities and suspicion of mystery, and to decolonize table spaces and table habits? How do we speak of table as expansive, complex, porous, hybrid, fluid, unstable, and as a contested space? How has postcolonial understanding and practice of eucharist challenged notions of fixed meanings and essentialized identities? How have our eucharistic theologies valued diversity and otherness in a manner consistent with trinitarian differentiation? In what ways have our eucharistic practices resisted the notion of totalized and enforced homogeneity by giving agency to particularity, social location and trans-local and multiple identities? How has eucharist been used to address themes of mutual encounter, reciprocity, and self-giving in Christian community? Has eucharist perpetuated divisions in the body of Christ?

"PLAYFUL" QUALIFIERS

The title of my reflections is intended to be playful. The familiar word "excursion," often associated with a trip or jaunt, is deployed here in the sense of a "raid," "deviation," or "digression" with no guarantee that one will return to the same point of departure. Here, excursion is also incursion. *Pelau* (a meal associated with Trinidad) is one of the many meals that exemplifies Caribbean hybridized reality and intercultural encounters, putting home, mouths and stomachs on a renegotiated landscape. Crossing or transgressing various ethnic cooking styles (Indian, Persian, African, Spanish, French, English, and Amerindian among others), *pelau* is often a rice-based meal for Saturdays, producing something delicious from all the week's leftovers. The *pelau* metaphor allows for ambiguity, creolization, and signifying, and it is aptly related to eating and table. "*Displace*" draws on multiple meanings. *Dis*place is about location(s). It is about geographies, spatiality, but not necessarily fixed places. It is also about spaces, displacement, dislocation, and movement (forced or otherwise). Hence, *dis*placed conversation is about the complexity of location and multiplicity of identities that collide and/or are renegotiated. Liberating liturgical God-talk and -walk needs to explore such locations/spaces to better grasp the multilayered heritage of the diverse members that comprise the worshiping community, while sheltering and accepting multiplicity in the context of inherited traditions. Discussions about belonging and identity need to involve a dialogue among the several spaces occupied by different people within the same community. Different people and the different positions they occupy make for diverse notions and feelings about what belonging and authenticity mean, and this has implications for God-talk and practice. So the notion of *dis*place is being employed both as a way of doing eucharistic theological conversation—locating ourselves within our fluid and complex contexts—and is a signifying heuristic "check" of every attempt at majoring in exactitudes and drawing doctrinal, ecclesial, and cultural boundaries on God and God's actions.

LOCATING SELF, THEOLOGY, AND CHURCH

My self-understanding as a minister and theologian is shaped by a number of markers. I am a complex Diasporan Caribbean traveler—an unintentional missionary who landed in Britain by accident. I look Indian but I am not a Hindu or Muslim, though my parents and siblings are. My accent is as deceptive as the places I have lived. While I am a minority in the United Kingdom, I am also privileged (a male heterosexual minister) within that minority context. My faith and spirituality have been informed and shaped by impulses from multiple religious and cultural traditions. I have no choice but to live in the fullness of two or three simultaneously. Hence, my theologizing and ministry practices reflect calypso temper, rainbow and religious textures, and limbo positionality. God-talk is done within the rich world of diversity, identities, hybridity, impurity, many-one-ness, contradictions, ambivalence, fluidity, and tidalectics, Anansi-ism (related to the Caribbean saint and trickster figure), and the exciting possibilities and challenges these offer. Long before Homi Bhabha, Stuart Hall, and other theorists, I have been living hybridity, contradictions, and ambivalence—without naming it.

I found a home in the United Reformed Church (URC) because of its dissenting, nonconforming, and minority heritage. A young church (formed in 1972) with Presbyterian, Congregational, and Churches of Christ antecedents across three nations (England, Scotland, and Wales), the URC is a minority church in the United Kingdom that wrestles with identity issues and punches above her weight in all sorts of ways. We are a church that tries hard to create space and to give agency to all sorts of minorities. So when I was elected as a Moderator of our General Assembly (2012–2014), it was no surprise to anyone. It did not, however, mean that more space was created around the table or that space was being renegotiated to include the difference and culturally shaped gifts I bring. For the most part, I had to fit into a white, male, extroverted, heterosexual, able-bodied framework. The habit of all-around-the-table being *mutually inconvenienced* for the sake of economy of the host (God-in-Christ) remained too uncomfortable and demanding!

I have constantly drawn from, challenged, and critiqued the treasures and multiple blessings that have influenced me. My leaning is toward a multiplicity of views or the in-between spaces of the multiplicities-in-conversation. Hence my embrace of the postcolonial framework as a helpful tool, mindful of the dangers of "neo-colonizing anti-colonialism."[7]

(DIS)PLACING *PLAT PRINCIPAL* CONVERSATIONS

Eating, Hospitality, Exclusion

Besides its theological and ecclesial significance, the central place of eating, drinking, and conversation in our life together cannot be ignored. "Food matters so much so," according to Angel F. Méndez-Montoya, "that God becomes food, our daily bread."[8] The reality, though, is that some have bread, while many starve; some can drink and guzzle wine while many die of thirst or over-indulge so that relationships are damaged. We theologize on bread and wine, while greedy "corp-o-crats" speculate on grains and water and buy up land, dispossessing millions, including those not yet born. Hence, the late Tissa Balasuriya got fed up with the domestication of the eucharist and asked: "why is it that persons and people who proclaim eucharistic love and sharing deprive the poor people of the world of food, capital, employment and even land?"[9] Colonial habits have many avatars and no table is beyond their reach! Worship that does not recognize these contradictions, that legitimizes systemic oppression and domination, and creates victims, either explicitly or implicitly, is not worship in spirit and truth.[10]

While phrases like "radical welcome" and "Christian hospitality" abound in mission statements, many continue to experience exclusion and marginalization, not the least around the tables of churches. The contradictions become even more evident in our lack of asking "who gets to define community?" and how specific definitions of community serve different interests. The theologies undergirding our table habits need to be interrogated.[11] Closer scrutiny of our praxis may reveal that the invitation is to *our* table where the rules of eating, drinking, and conversations operate within proscribed theological perspectives and particular readings of scriptures. What kind of Christ and what kind of Church do we project through our table habits, methods, and theologies? The eucharistic theology we articulate shapes the theologies informing other dimensions of our practice of ministry and life together.[12] Mary Grey refers to the need for a "reconstructive moment" in which crucial doctrines are "re-envisioned," and her words are very timely.[13] A significant part of the challenge before us "lies not in the invention of new ways, but in the discovery of what has always been there, and been hidden or perverted."[14]

Minding Words, Metaphors, Language and Deposit of Faith

From Caribbean writers[15] and Rastafarians I have learnt that our words, grammar, and language are often tied to hegemonic control. They are forced to labor under the weight of our spatial imagination. Hence, I will not be following the colonial rule on capitalizing eucharist, table, or tradition. I agree with Cláudio Carvalhaes that "words are not detached linguistic signs but rather, they carry a load of different meanings according to their cultural usages."[16] As Carvalhaes notes: "the grammatical use of the word Eucharist is directly related to the theological meanings and ritual approvals attached to the word. It is the theological borders that institute the grammatical rules and limits of the vocabulary usage of the word Eucharist."[17] Hence, any critical engagement with liturgy must, as Kwok Pui-lan insists, include more than a translation-project into local language. The cultural and linguistic world of what is often termed "the deposit of faith" must be fully interrogated.[18] So besides grammar and words, some of our inherited liturgical terminologies need to be exposed for their role in gate-keeping and "border controlling" the free and generous exchange of abundant grace![19]

The ways in which the deposit of faith has been and is presented (and dressed up[20]) have to do with how it was represented in the first instance and how it continues to be presented today. Re-presentation and presentation are not value-free.[21] Thus, there is a need to scrutinize the deposit of faith in order to detect, question, challenge, and expose how the dominated are represented by the dominant; the links between power and knowledge; and the ideologies in plots and characterization in texts and their interpretations. What, for instance, in the arriving-at and solidifying of this deposit of faith, happened to marginal and dissenting voices? What is the link between the deposit, empire, and liturgical theology? As R. S. Sugirtharajah observes, "Colonial discourse is staunchly wedded to unvarying and exclusive truth and tolerates no dissent or debate."[22] A postcolonial perspective, writes Kwok Pui-lan, "offers an invaluable vantage point on theology, because it interrogates how religious and cultural productions are enmeshed in the economic and political domination of colonialism and empire building."[23] Moreover, an interrogation of the "given-ness" of the received product will raise questions as to its role in shaping and forming identities.

The goal of a decolonized table is to both interrogate and release space for that which it is intended—rather than ecclesial glimpses of mystery in what turns out to be fenced-in space; eucharistic space is for all people, and borders are named and transgressed. The activities around a decolonized table must, drawing on Emmanuel Lartey's work, be counter-hegemonic and strategic (subversive space), hybrid (interactive-intersubjective space), dynamic and creative, and ambiguous (in-between space).[24] Where such interrogation may lead is anyone's guess! It may be that faithfulness to a free flow of grace and to creating space *for all* may require of us the courage to risk giving up established texts and dump restrictive metaphors.[25]

Eucharistic Prayers, Bible, and Hermeneutics

Given that "there is hardly a sentence in the Eucharistic liturgy that does not echo the Scriptures,"[26] how are postcolonial readings of scriptures and other ecclesial texts impacting eucharistic theology and practice? Paula Gooder and Michael Perham note how contemporary liturgists and Liturgical Commissions work with "texts that have come down the centuries and gone through many revisions and changes," while carrying—"*unconsciously*"—some of the texts "lodged deep inside them" through "years of prayer and worship."[27] This lodging of ideas "deep inside" underscores the urgency and challenge to dislodge colonial habits.

Gooder and Perham note how attempts at "constant harmonization of narrative and ideas runs counter to biblical scholarship" and how "interpretational decision" related to liturgical texts can result in original meaning and intent being altered.[28] Addressing concern about appropriate deploying of biblical texts (in scriptural allusions and references in eucharistic liturgies), the authors see no problem that this may end up "being the opposite of what was clearly intended in the biblical narratives." They reason that we should see allusion as allusion and contend that faithfulness to the text is more about "prayerful attention to its original meaning."[29] While warning about "the forming of a liturgical canon within a canon" they give way to tradition. Because "[t]his technique has such a historic and honored tradition," the authors are hesitant "to say that it *shouldn't* be done." They do, though, insist that there is a need to be "aware of the issues and implications that arise when it *is* done."[30] *How* the interpretation then shapes our table habits and life together is not considered. Certainly, there is a need for liturgists to pay careful attention to the Bible in preparing the liturgy given the ways the Bible has been misused over the years to subjugate.[31] For as Rowan Williams says, "the very act of interpreting affects the narratives as well as the world."[32]

Gooder and Perham do not disclose what kind of interpretative lens they employ nor do they query past or current interpretative biases in the use of others' scriptural allusions. They miss issues involving the colonial contexts of empire in which liturgy has evolved! It is strange that little consideration is given to the implications of multiple ways of rereading scriptures from a variety of perspectives. What would some of these re-readings mean for the use of scriptures in eucharistic prayers and for the rethinking of eucharistic theology? More is involved than "liturgical cen-soring" or merely "overlooking those traditions which have provided theological underpinning for various forms of colonialism and which scandalize most people today."[33] Are crafters of eucharistic prayers aware of the ways their interpretative paraphrasing is compromised and how it may be more a "word about God" rather than "of God"?

Take for instance, the notion of "the body of Christ" as a key idea in eucharistic theology.[34] Richardo Garcia suggests that it can become a "weapon for cultural imperialism," as unwittingly all in Christ are en-couraged to maintain the same mind—as in a "melting pot theory of assimilation" without acceptance of cultural or convictional differences.[35] Do our interpretations allow room for the distinctiveness of identities and for differences within "the body"? Or are identities subsumed in the liturgical rite—as we become "one people," "one loaf," "one loving as-sembly," "one eschatological community"? What space is allowed for multiplicity or many-one-ness? Given that race consciousness plays a central role in the theological constructions of racially marginalized and oppressed communities, how do we make sense of ethnic particularity within the church's theological formulations? How do we reread the interpretive tendencies of Paul's oneness theory that seems to subsume differences?[36] What would happen were we to explore Christian liturgi-cal discourse by looking "beyond the limitations of the Jewish-Hellenistic context and pay attention also to the Jewish-Aramaic influence"?[37] Bibli-cal stories "must not become the dead husks of orthodoxy." Husks must be cracked "open to reveal the seeds they contain." It is from the seeds that new narratives "which resonate with our lived experience" will sprout forth.[38]

REMEMBERING WITH A DIFFERENCE

How can the saving action of the remembered one be done in a way that is transforming for a particular gathering in any age? What is it we are actually remembering? Is our remembering a liberating act? In the con-text of "eucharist as rehearsing God's reign,"[39] what is it we are reenacting?[40] And how does remembering give agency to multiple identities and influence the shaping of identities?

These are important questions especially when colonial and imperial memory may shape the self-understanding and daily experience of many around the table. For instance, there are groups and peoples whose land has been invaded and occupied by foreign powers, or displaced because of forced movement. How does eucharistic remembrance speak to their experience? How can the experience at the table be of mutuality, healing, and transformation where the agenda of empire has caused a lack of bread for many, power imbalances, and penury instead of freedom? Will our liturgical "remembering" reinforce boundaries that advance a cultural, economic, and spiritual superiority of one group or tradition while others are merely supposed to conform? For should we, in the act of remembering, forget power inequalities around the table, we may end up turning a supposed inclusive space into one where subalterns will be unable to find their voice or reluctant to share space with those implicated in the colonial agenda.

We need to be aware that what is "remembered" comes to us "from the liturgical creativity of early communities," rather than from Jesus.[41] We are recalling "the way the Church re-acts the last meal of the Lord."[42] It is crucial to be aware of how an oral tradition evolved into a written one, and how exported and imported texts (eucharistic liturgies) with their literary constructions and representations, are already culturally and ideologically compromised.[43] Jione Havea suggests shifting "our attention from focusing on *book* and *reading* (the realm of hermeneutics) to *story* and *telling*, subjects that vibrate in oral cultures." Can such a shift free up the texts from "the burden of translation"?[44] Would "remembering" be then released from restrictive ecclesial boundaries?

Carmel Pilcher calls for deeper eucharistic remembering[45] that moves beyond recalling to imitating or mimicking Christ in lived response. "It is not enough," she notes, to break bread together at the table "unless we are prepared to work towards equality and justice for all peoples—even in the carrying out of the church's liturgy."[46] Mimicry though, is more than imitation. It may look almost the same, but it is not quite the same.[47] Mimicry, governed by some ambivalence, may be deployed to subtly challenge and subvert the controlling, authoritarian tendencies of the status quo. As a strategy in the negotiation of identities it could be critically used as a resource to interrogate rhetoric around remembering and a subtle way "of shifting power relations" and of performing freedom.[48]

The liturgical habit of remembering at table is vital in shaping the identity of the community. For around the table, "Christian identity is enacted and rehearsed,"[49] shaped, and reshaped, "pulling us beyond individualism and defensiveness" to "identify with others and acknowledge that God has graciously identified with us in Christ."[50] Does "our remembering and re-enacting" allow for variety and multiple identities around the table? Do our eucharistic liturgies lift up and celebrate diversity and hybrid versions of communal identity—neither Jew nor Greek and at the same time both Jew and Greek—and help reconfigure belonging and identity *for all*? This question is especially the case given that the eucharistic meal "gradually became a source of dis-identity from the Jewish community, and a source of self-identity."[51]

The act of remembering is a liturgically enacted counter-politics to those of Caesar. Drawing the church back to the ways of Christ, the eucharist provides resources to resist injustice and violence.[52] So *what* is recalled is important: who or what voices and stories are remembered in the recalling is of crucial importance to what we espouse as eucharistic theology. As Janet Wootton contends, "the eucharist itself ought to be a place for celebrating women's stories. Women are the makers and providers of food. Women's bodies and blood are the nourishers of new life."[53] Hence women's approaches to the eucharist have been "freeing, celebratory and inclusive" rather than focusing on "violent symbolism and sacrifice, and authoritarian restrictions."[54] So what are the implications of remembering Mary's right as a woman and mother of Jesus to say "my body and my blood?" And where in current eucharistic prayers do we give agency to the silent history of minorities and veneration of "saints" from among our deposits of faith and what our "readerly and writerly texts"[55] have buried?

Angel F. Méndez-Montoya makes a case for eucharistic remembering as a playful and uniting movement between God and humanity—neither one having any claim on the eucharist itself, with ownership moving back and forth between them. There is reciprocity and mutuality in giving and receiving in a divine economy. In giving God also receives.[56] Are there possibilities here for a more dynamic understanding of eucharistic theology where no one group can stake any rigid claim—where we are all in need and all are invited to be mutually inconvenienced?

HYBRIDITY AND EUCHARISTIC THEOLOGIES AND PRACTICES

Hybridity is a challenge to our eucharistic theologies and practices. Though the biblical world is replete with hybrid situations, contexts, moments, and intercultural encounters, there is still an aversion to hybridity that must be overcome. For as long as we favor notions of purity, election and being set apart, that which is mixed, hybrid, multiple, ambiguous, and liminal is perceived as mess, danger, threat, or terror. Can it be that "fencing" off our eucharistic tables is reflective of such fear and insecurity?

Edward Foley makes a case for Jesus' table as an experience of hybridity. He suggests that "hybridity as 'third space' provides a fascinating lens for considering the Jesus table as a moment of subversive, ambiguous and liminal encounter."[57] While uncomfortable with identifying Jesus as "colonizer," Foley does note that Jesus was perceived as "one who possessed power and authority."[58] He points specifically to ways in which Jesus deployed his authority "to negotiate that 'third space' while at table" and beyond. In some of the meal encounters, Foley notes the "time-space liminality of the meal" and especially the reversals where (for instance) Jesus the guest becomes the host.[59] The reality of hybridity does not mean that we lack identity; it means that we are not merely ourselves in any simple, immediate, or homogenous way.

Jesus' table ministry was truly an experience of hybridity: disruptive and liminal for both Jesus and those who broke bread with him. What Jesus did to his received religious tradition was to push the boundaries through reversals, redefining table space, conversations and eating habits, and negotiating and articulating a fresh take on God's reign.[60] It was both a "negotiation between Jesus and those with whom he shared a table and common meal"[61] and the religious gatekeepers who took Jesus to task for his eating and drinking habits with dodgy people. In trying to guard the purity of their received faith, tradition and practice, they also contributed to the experience of this "third space." Rereading Jesus' table encounters through the metaphors of third space and hybridity opens up possibilities to rethink our eucharistic theologies and practice. Foley draws on Homi Bhabha's analysis of complex-rich hybrid spaces, and Bhabha's observation that overlap and displacement are where the intersubjective and collective experiences of community and its values are renegotiated.[62] Can it be that in the complex exchange in the in-between space at the table, the Spirit is working overtime to produce mutual inconveniencing, transformation, and new creation with regard to identities and belonging?[63]

LIMINALITY, MYSTERY, AND IN-BETWEEN SPACES

From a Reformed perspective, is it possible that the idea of a "third or in-between space" may offer possibilities for the recovery of a lost dimension of sacramental mystery? If God's grace is as extraordinary as Jesus suggests, why should we impoverish the divine with predictability?[64] I agree with Regina Schwartz that in response to their perception of the idolatry around eucharistic theology and practices of their time, the Reformers lost much in dumping the doctrine of transubstantiation for their various versions of mystery and presence.

Understandably, the Reformers were responding to a situation where the eucharist was turned from being a "means of grace" to "ecclesial control over the sacred." For in attempting to make the "visible invisible," the pre-Reformation Church gave the eucharist a "consolidating" and "strategic function," equating "mystical reality and the visible" and ensuring that it depended upon "hierarchical authority."[65] Mystery—that which is beyond human manipulation—became "instrumentalized."[66] As Schwartz notes: "In one of the more influential co-optations of its sacramental meaning, then, the mystical body came to refer more and more to the absolute monarch and to the body of the monarch, the nation."[67] The Protestant Reformers, preoccupied with idolatry and fearing "instrumentality that sought to control the domain of mystery," ended up re-inscribing instrumentality "not of the Eucharist by the Church, but of the sacred by the state."[68] So while attempting to destroy and restrict the many variations of "idols"—purging churches of icons, art, crosses, liturgical wear, carvings, tapestry, monuments, and ceremonies—the state was simultaneously "embracing images and processionals full of pomp and ceremony."[69]

Eventually the state consolidated and legitimized its power. Hence, "Elizabethan iconography tried to borrow the power of mysticism from medieval Mariology" and link it to "pagan embodiments of power, wealth, and empire." This can be seen in the portraits of Elizabeth "not only holding the globe, but planting her feet on it, spanning the starry heavens and regulating the thunderstorms, thereby projecting the order of the state onto the very cosmos. The divine sphere, once mysterious, is now the Queen's territory."[70] Linking this observation with the corresponding colonial expansion in the "new world" at that time further underscores the hegemonic links with our inherited liturgical traditions and practices.

In their zeal to purge the doctrine of transubstantiation, the Protestant Reformers lost a sense of mystery that "infuses all materiality, spirituality, and signification with the presence of God."[71] This point leads Schwartz to conclude that "[w]hen it is stripped of its mystical sense, even the Eucharist—the *mysterion*—is no longer about faith, hope, and charity, but refers to identity, one that forges insiders, with corporate shared values, and outsiders who do not share them."[72] Perhaps a rediscovery of sacramental "mystery" may open up ways for us to reimagine community in terms of in-between space(s) and a kind of "homelessness" around the table? Not fixed spaces or places that fossilize and polarize identity and belonging, removing "any possibility of a genuine, open-ended engagement with others," or "of seeing community in multiple contexts and through the lens of diversity,"[73] but rather as a third space of a community that displaces all its members because there is more meaning than each of us around the table may be able to comprehend.

SIGNIFYING DESSERTS: BEYOND WORDS AND UNENDING
TABLE CONVERSATIONS

My Muslim and Hindu grandmothers held the view that "we are what
we eat."[74] For them, at the heart of food, cooking, eating, and table is a
sense of abundance, being blessed, divine presence, a delightful nourishing of all, and eating as an act in which we rediscover our transfigured
selves. Of course, they never used all these fancy words to describe the
ecstatic, gastro-ingenious mystery, and the subversive dimensions of
their kitchen space.

I love words. Over the recent years, though, I have come to question
Protestant preoccupation with words, especially their (mis)use in control,
reduction, and seeking after truth in neat, restrictive categories, in ways
that close down conversations and create more polarizations. Regina
Schwartz suggests that our "wordy" eucharistic liturgies with their "sacramental poetry" may be pointing to a larger meaning beyond themselves.[75] Indeed "word" can evoke mystery just as it can contribute to its
demise. It is not insignificant that western Christianity moved miles
away from the Hebrew culture in which words are deployed in endlessly
ambivalent, imprecise, and inconclusive ways that defy closure, inviting
multiple epiphanies, and thriving on surprises. In our trans-techno-glo-
bal world, "we are seduced into thinking that if we know the codes, we
can pin down all meaning, get all mysteries right and have our own way,
without surprise, without deception, without amazement, without gift,
without miracle, without address, without absence, without anything
that signals mystery or risk."[76]

No wonder "words have become cheap and transitory,"[77] tired, dried
up and lifeless. Hence, Barbara Brown Taylor pleads for silence in our
worship, giving the divine "some relief from our descriptive assaults."[78]
It is interesting that in the Jewish tradition the central declaration of faith
is "Hear, O Israel . . ." underscoring listening—the ears, not the lips. The
Christian community departed from this heritage, emphasizing the mandate to go out and share the word. Consequently, "[t]he word was described, defined, delimited by words, so that what Christians said became more decisive than anything they did."[79] Listening to God became
marginal. And faith has sometimes become exceedingly "talkative."

My grandmothers' kitchens and table spaces were imaginative play at
its best, creating an alternative world in impoverished circumstances,
where little turned into plenty, where "but for the grace of God" was real,
where dynamic mix (or creolization) was a given, and where arousal of
the senses was more important than the tendency to rationalize or work
with precise and measured quantities of anything. Their cooking and the
food they "dished out" drew us in and sent us out with a feeling that
there were still more flavors to be discovered, ingest, digest and taste.

"Taste and see," declared the psalmist. My grandmothers would say "amen" to that!

BIBLIOGRAPHY

Abraham, Susan. "What Does Mumbai Have to Do with Rome? Postcolonial Perspectives on Globalization and Theology." *Theological Studies* 69 (2008): 376–93.

Aching, Gerard. *Masking Power: Carnival and Popular Culture in the Caribbean.* Minneapolis: University of Minnesota Press, 2002.

Agard, John. *Mangoes and Bullets.* London: Serpent's Tail, 1985.

Balasuriya, Tissa. *The Eucharist and Human Liberation.* London: SCM Press, 1979.

Barthes, Roland. *S/Z,* trans. Richard Miller. Oxford: Farrar, Strauss, and Giroux, 1974.

Barton, John. *The People of the Book? The Authority of the Bible in Christianity.* London: SPCK, 1988.

Bhabha, Homi K. *The Location of Culture.* London: Routledge, 1994.

Brueggemann, Walter. *Deep Memory, Exuberant Hope: Contested Truth in a Post-Christian World.* Minneapolis: Fortress Press, 2000.

Burns, Stephen, and Michael N. Jagessar, "Thank You for the Night: Images in Worship: Postcolonial Perspectives." In *Worship and Ministry Shaped Towards God,* edited by Stephen Burns, 52–77. Preston, Victoria: Mosaic Press, 2012.

Carvalhaes, Cláudio. *Eucharist and Globalization: Redrawing the Borders of Eucharistic Hospitality.* Eugene, OR: Pickwick, 2013.

Cavanaugh, William T. *Torture and the Eucharist: Theology, Politics and the Body of Christ.* Oxford: Blackwell Publishers, 1998.

Chauvet, Louis-Marie. *Symbol and Sacrament: A Sacramental Reinterpretation of Christian Existence,* trans. Patrick Madigan and Madeleine Beaumont. Collegeville, MN: Liturgical Press, 1995.

Crossan, John Dominic. *The Historical Jesus: The Life of a Mediterranean Jewish Peasant.* Blackburn: Collins Dove, 1991.

De Lima, Glauco. "Preface," in *Beyond Colonial Anglicanism: The Anglican Communion in the Twenty-first Century,* edited by Ian T. Douglas and Kwok Pui-lan, 1–8. New York: Church Publishing, 2001.

Dirs, Ben. "Does English Sport Suffer from its Suspicion of Maverick Talent?" BBC Sport, January 13, 2014. Accessed January 14, 2014. www.bbc.co.uk/sport/0/cricket/25680571.

Dube, Musa W. "Reading for Decolonization (John 4:1–42)." In *John and Postcolonialism: Travel, Space and Power,* edited by Musa W. Dube and Jeffrey Staley, 51–75. London: Sheffield Academic Press, 2002.

Duck, Ruth C. *Worship for the Whole People of God: Vital Worship for the 21st Century.* Louisville, KY: Westminster John Knox Press, 2013.

Elvey, Anne, Carol Hogan, Kim Power, and Claire Renkin. *Reinterpreting the Eucharist: Exploration in Feminist Theology and Ethics.* Sheffield: Equinox, 2013.

Garcia, Ricardo. *Teaching in a Pluralistic Society: Concepts, Models and Strategies.* New York: Harper and Row, 1982.

Foley, Edward. "Eucharist, Postcolonial Theory and Developmental Disabilities: A Practical Theologian Revisits the Jesus Table." *International Journal of Pastoral Theology* 15 (2011): 57–73.

Grey, Mary. "Catholic Feminist Theology." In *Exploring Theology: Making Sense of Catholic Tradition,* edited by Anne Hession and Patricia Kieran, 273–85. Dublin: Veritas Publishers, 2007.

Hanley, Paul. "How We Took Our Pick." *Church Times,* September 26, 2014, 28.

Jagessar, Michael N. "Holy Crumbs, Table Habits and (Dis)placing Conversations: Beyond 'Only One Is Holy'." In *Liturgy in Postcolonial Perspectives: Only One Is Holy,* edited by Cláudio Carvalhaes, 223–40. New York: Palgrave Macmillan, 2015.

————— and Stephen Burns. *Christian Worship: Postcolonial Perspectives*. Sheffield: Equinox, 2011.

Goizueta, Roberto S. *Christ our Compassion: Toward a Theological Aesthetics of Liberation*. Maryknoll, NY: Orbis Books, 2009.

Gooder, Paula, and Michael Perham. *Echoing the Word: The Bible in the Eucharist*. London: SPCK, 2013.

Havea, Jione. "Who is Strange(r)? A Pacific Native Muses Over Mission." *JTCA* 7–8 (2008/2009): 121–37.

Joy, David. "Liturgical Explorations in a Postcolonial Context." In *The Edge of God: New Liturgical Texts and Contexts in Conversation*, edited by Stephen Burns, Nicola Slee, and Michael N. Jagessar, 39–49. London: Epworth, 2008.

Kim, Yung Suk. *Christ's Body in Corinth: The Politics of a Metaphor*. Minneapolis: Fortress Press, 2008.

Kwok Pui-lan. "The Legacy of Cultural Hegemony in the Anglican Church." In *Beyond Colonial Anglicanism: The Anglican Communion in the Twenty-first Century*, edited by Ian T. Douglas and Kwok Pui-lan, 47–70. New York: Church Publishing, 2001.

—————. "Theology and Social Theory." In *Empire and the Christian Tradition: New Readings of Classical Theologians*, edited by Kwok Pui-lan, Don H. Compier, and Joerg Rieger, 15–29. Minneapolis: Fortress Press, 2007.

Lartey, Emmanuel Y. *Postcolonializing God: New Perspectives on Pastoral and Practical Theology*. London: SCM Press, 2013.

Marty, Peter. "Beyond Polarization: Grace and Surprise in Worship." *Christian Century*, March 18–25, 1998, 284–87.

Méndez-Montoya, Angel F. *The Theology of Food: Eating and the Eucharist*. Chichester: Wiley-Blackwell, 2012.

Prior, Michael. *The Bible and Colonialism: A Moral Critique*. Sheffield: Sheffield Academic Press, 1997.

Schwartz, Regina Mara. *Sacramental Poetics at the Dawn of Secularism: When God Left the World*. Stanford: Stanford University Press, 2008.

Spohn, William. *Go and Do Likewise: Jesus and Ethics*. New York: Continuum, 2007.

Sugirtharajah, R. S. "The First, Second and Third Letters of John." In *A Postcolonial Commentary on the New Testament Writings*, edited by Fernando F. Segovia and R. S. Sugirtharajah, 413–23. London: T. & T. Clark, 2007.

—————. "Postcolonial and Biblical Interpretation: The Next Phase." In *A Postcolonial Commentary on the New Testament Writings*, edited by Fernando F. Segovia and R. S. Sugirtharajah, 455–66. London: T. & T. Clark, 2007.

—————. *Postcolonial Criticism and Biblical Interpretation*. Oxford: Oxford University Press, 2002.

Taylor, Barbara Brown. *When God Is Silent: Divine Language beyond Words*. Norwich, UK: Canterbury Press, 2013.

Walton, Heather. "Breaking Open the Bible." In *Life-cycles: Women and Pastoral Care*, edited by Elaine Graham and Margaret Halsey, 192–99. London: SPCK, 1993.

Weller, Philip. *Selected Easter Sermons of Saint Augustine*. London: B. Herder Books Co., 1959.

Winter, David. "There's Nothing Like a Good Book." *Church Times*, September 26, 2014, 23.

Wootton, Janet. *Introducing a Practical Feminist Theology of Worship*. Sheffield: Sheffield Academic Press, 2000.

NOTES

1. Ben Dirs, "Does English Sport Suffer from its Suspicion of Maverick Talent?" *BBC Sport*, January 13, 2014, accessed January 14, 2014, www.bbc.co.uk/sport/0/cricket/25680571.

2. *Church Times*, September 26, 2014; October 3 and 10, 2014.

3. David Winter, "There's Nothing Like a Good Book," *Church Times*, September 26, 2014, 23.

4. Paul Hanley, "How We Took Our Pick," *Church Times*, September 26, 2014, 28.

5. Michael N. Jagessar and Stephen Burns, *Christian Worship: Postcolonial Perspectives* (Sheffield: Equinox, 2011), x.

6. I have drawn from ideas developed in another essay, "Holy Crumbs, Table Habits and (Dis)placing Conversations: Beyond 'Only One Is Holy'," in *Liturgy in Postcolonial Perspectives: Only One Is Holy*, ed. Cláudio Carvalhaes (New York: Palgrave Macmillan, 2015), 223–40.

7. An insight and critique of Gayatri Spivak.

8. Angel F. Méndez-Montoya, *The Theology of Food: Eating and the Eucharist* (Chichester: Wiley-Blackwell, 2012), 3.

9. Tissa Balasuriya, *The Eucharist and Human Liberation* (London: SCM Press, 1979), xi–xii.

10. See Roberto S. Goizueta, *Christ our Compassion: Toward a Theological Aesthetics of Liberation* (Maryknoll, NY: Orbis Books, 2009), 149.

11. Yung Suk Kim, *Christ's Body in Corinth: The Politics of a Metaphor* (Minneapolis: Fortress Press, 2008), 7.

12. Kim Power and Carol Hogan, "Introduction," in *Reinterpreting the Eucharist: Exploration in Feminist Theology and Ethics*, ed. Anne Elvey, Carol Hogan, Kim Power, and Claire Renkin (Sheffield: Equinox, 2013), 2–3.

13. Mary Grey, "Catholic Feminist Theology," in *Exploring Theology: Making Sense of Catholic Tradition*, ed. Anne Hession and Patricia Kieran (Dublin: Veritas Publishers, 2007), 277.

14. Janet Wootton, *Introducing a Practical Feminist Theology of Worship* (Sheffield: Sheffield Academic Press, 2000), 134.

15. For example, John Agard, "Listen Mr. Oxford Don," in *Mangoes and Bullets* (London: Serpent's Tail, 1985), 44.

16. Cláudio Carvalhaes, *Eucharist and Globalization: Redrawing the Borders of Eucharistic Hospitality* (Eugene, OR: Pickwick, 2013), 9.

17. Ibid.

18. Kwok Pui-lan, "The Legacy of Cultural Hegemony in the Anglican Church," in *Beyond Colonial Anglicanism: The Anglican Communion in the Twenty-first Century*, ed. Ian T. Douglas and Kwok Pui-lan (New York: Church Publishing, 2001), 59–60.

19. Wootton, *Introducing a Practical Feminist Theology of Worship*, 29–30.

20. Glauco D. de Lima, "Preface," in Douglas and Kwok, *Beyond Colonial Anglicanism*, 3. See also, Regina Mara Schwartz, *Sacramental Poetics at the Dawn of Secularism: When God Left the World* (Stanford: Stanford University Press, 2008).

21. See R. S. Sugirtharajah, *Postcolonial Criticism and Biblical Interpretation* (Oxford: Oxford University Press, 2002).

22. R. S. Sugirtharajah, "The First, Second and Third Letters of John," in *A Postcolonial Commentary on the New Testament Writings*, ed. Fernando F. Segovia and R. S. Sugirtharajah (London: T. & T. Clark, 2007), 413.

23. Kwok Pui-lan, "Theology and Social Theory," in *Empire and The Christian Tradition: New Readings of Classical Theologians*, ed. Kwok Pui-lan, Don H. Compier, and Joerg Rieger (Minneapolis: Fortress Press, 2007), 19.

24. See Emmanuel Y. Lartey, *Postcolonializing God: New Perspectives on Pastoral and Practical Theology* (London: SCM Press, 2013), xvi–xviii.

25. See Stephen Burns and Michael N. Jagessar, "Thank You for the Night: Images in Worship: Postcolonial Perspectives," in *Worship and Ministry Shaped Towards God*, ed. Stephen Burns (Preston, Victoria: Mosaic Press, 2012), 77.

26. Paula Gooder and Michael Perham, *Echoing the Word: The Bible in the Eucharist* (London: SPCK, 2013), ix.

27. Ibid., x, my emphasis.

28. Ibid., 123.

29. Ibid.,123–24.

30. Ibid., 124.

31. David Joy, "Liturgical Explorations in a Postcolonial Context," in *The Edge of God: New Liturgical Texts and Contexts in Conversation*, ed. Stephen Burns, Nicola Slee, and Michael N. Jagessar (London: Epworth, 2008), 45–46.

32. Rowan Williams, "Postmodern Theology and the Judgement of the World," in *Postmodern Theology: Christian Faith in a Pluralist World*, ed. Frederic B. Burnham (San Francisco: HarperSanFrancisco, 1989), 94, cited in Heather Walton, "Breaking Open the Bible," in *Life-cycles: Women and Pastoral Care*, ed. Elaine Graham and Margaret Halsey (London: SPCK, 1993), 195. See also John Barton "The Bible in Liturgy," in John Barton, *The People of the Book? The Authority of the Bible in Christianity* (London: SPCK, 1988), 77.

33. Michael Prior, *The Bible and Colonialism: A Moral Critique* (Sheffield: Sheffield Academic Press, 1997), 278.

34. Carmel Pilcher, "The Sunday Eucharist: Embodying Christ in a Prophetic Act," in Elvey, *Reinterpreting the Eucharist*, 42.

35. Ricardo Garcia, *Teaching in a Pluralistic Society: Concepts, Models and Strategies* (New York: Harper and Row, 1982), 35.

36. Kim, *Christ's Body in Corinth*, 11.

37. R. S. Sugirtharajah, "Postcolonial and Biblical Interpretation: The Next Phase," in *A Postcolonial Commentary on the New Testament Writings*, ed. Fernando F. Segovia and R. S. Sugirtharajah (London: T. & T. Clark, 2007), 455. He says, a closer look at the story of the early Church through Jewish-Aramaic optics will reveal how much Jewish Christians, for instance, "were the original hybridizers who wished to remain within the Jewish religious parameters and reconfigured their faith in the light of the teachings of Jesus." It was early Christianity and the later Eurocentric one which "flattened significant or cultural differences" into restrictive monotheism or oneness of almost everything, including the mind.

38. Walton, "Breaking Open the Bible," 196.

39. Ruth C. Duck, *Worship for the Whole People of God: Vital Worship for the 21st Century* (Louisville, KY: Westminster John Knox Press, 2013), 187.

40. Burns, ed. *Worship and Ministry Shaped Towards God*, 134.

41. John Dominic Crossan, *The Historical Jesus: The Life of a Mediterranean Jewish Peasant* (North Blackburn: Collins Dove, 1991), 30.

42. Louis-Marie Chauvet, *Symbol and Sacrament: A Sacramental Reinterpretation of Christian Existence*, trans. Patrick Madigan and Madeleine Beaumont (Collegeville, MN: Liturgical Press, 1995), 198.

43. See Musa W. Dube, "Reading for Decolonization (John 4:1–42)," in *John and Postcolonialism: Travel, Space and Power*, ed. Musa W. Dube and Jeffrey Staley (London: Sheffield Academic Press, 2002), 51–75.

44. Jione Havea, "Who is Strange(r)? A Pacific Native Muses Over Mission," *JTCA* 7–8 (2008/2009): 135–36.

45. Pilcher, "The Sunday Eucharist," 33.

46. Ibid., 36.

47. Homi K. Bhabha, *The Location of Culture* (London: Routledge, 1994), 121.

48. Gerard Aching, *Masking Power: Carnival and Popular Culture in the Caribbean* (Minneapolis: University of Minnesota Press, 2002), 32.

49. William Spohn, *Go and Do Likewise: Jesus and Ethics* (New York: Continuum, 2007), 184.

50. Ibid., 169.

51. Frances Gray, "Mystery Appropriated: Disembodied Eucharist and Meta-Theology" in Elvey, *Reinterpreting the Eucharist*, 125.

52. See William T. Cavanaugh, *Torture and the Eucharist: Theology, Politics and the Body of Christ* (Oxford: Blackwell Publishers, 1998).

53. Wootton, *Introducing a Practical Feminist Theology of Worship*, 46.

54. Ibid., 46.

55. Roland Barthes, *S/Z*, trans. Richard Miller (Oxford: Farrar, Strauss, and Giroux, 1974), 5.

56. Angel F. Méndez-Montoya, *The Theology of Food: Eating and the Eucharist* (Sussex: Wiley-Blackwell, 2012).

57. Edward Foley, "Eucharist, Postcolonial Theory and Developmental Disabilities: A Practical Theologian Revisits the Jesus Table," *International Journal of Pastoral Theology* 15 (2011): 63–64.

58. Ibid., 64.

59. Ibid.

60. Ibid., 65.

61. Ibid., 66.

62. Bhabha, *The Location of Culture*.

63. Foley, "Eucharist, Postcolonial Theory," 71. See also Susan Abraham, "What Does Mumbai Have to Do with Rome? Postcolonial Perspectives on Globalization and Theology," *Theological Studies* 69 (2008): 376–93.

64. See Peter Marty, "Beyond Polarization: Grace and Surprise in Worship," *Christian Century*, March 18–25, 1998, 284–87.

65. Schwartz, *Sacramental Poetics at the Dawn of Secularism*, 20.

66. Ibid.

67. Ibid., 22.

68. Ibid., 29.

69. Ibid, 31.

70. Ibid., 32.

71. Ibid., 13.

72. Ibid., 35.

73. Kim, *Christ's Body in Corinth*, 37.

74. Augustine, speaking about the Eucharist: "Receive what you are. Become what you receive." This is adapted from Augustine's sermon "On the Eucharist." See Philip T. Weller, *Selected Easter Sermons of Saint Augustine* (London: B. Herder Books Co., 1959), 104.

75. Schwartz, *Sacramental Poetics*, 6–7.

76. Walter Brueggemann, *Deep Memory, Exuberant Hope: Contested Truth in a Post-Christian World* (Minneapolis: Fortress Press, 2000), 3.

77. Barbara Brown Taylor, *When God Is Silent: Divine Language beyond Words* (Norwich, UK: Canterbury Press, 2013), 38.

78. Ibid., 38.

79. Ibid., 49–50.

SEVEN

Prayer Books, Postcolonialism, Power, and Politics

Some Thoughts from an Antipodean Indigenous Laywoman

Jenny Te Paa Daniel

This chapter offers an indigenous laywoman's perspective on contemporary theological research on worship and liturgy, from the Anglican Church in Aotearoa New Zealand. The surprising reality, given the significant scholarly community among New Zealand Anglicans and the globally coveted status of the New Zealand Prayer Book,[1] is that there is actually very little in the way of substantive analytical theological research, let alone published theological writing on the ecclesial context within which and for which worship and liturgy is offered.[2]

This got me thinking anew about the extant postcolonial ecclesial reality, twenty-four years after a major Constitutional Revision of the Anglican Church.[3] I began to think far more critically about the motivations, the ways, and the outcomes of changes to worship and liturgy, which have long characterized the life of the church in the Antipodes, as it has sought and determined in good faith to respond to various postcolonial ructions affecting civil society over many years.[4]

I began to think in particular about the 1989 New Zealand Prayer Book and how it is popularly assumed, especially internationally, to reflect something of the inherent respect held within the postcolonial New Zealand Church for indigenous people, language, and liturgical form. The New Zealand Prayer Book is indeed a visionary, inclusive, nuanced, and theologically enlightened liturgical resource. Liturgically, it is so utterly deserving of the ongoing global chorus of appreciation it so regularly receives. It was after all one of the first primarily fully bilingual prayer books in the Anglican community.

My extensive experience of working across the Anglican Communion for the past twenty or so years further reveals a widely held perception beyond our shores that the twin *innovations* of the 1989 Prayer Book and the 1992 Revised Constitution position the Anglican Church in Aotearoa New Zealand and Polynesia way ahead of those postcolonial provinces in the Anglican Communion, which have also sought to *redeem* political histories indelibly stained by the narratives of pain and injustice inflicted upon indigenous peoples.

However, as a result of my experience of working as an indigenous lay woman leader both privileged and challenged by significant church leadership responsibility, what then am I to make of the significant behavioral and attitudinal contradictions and abuses, which I have regularly witnessed to also be at play? What about the contradictions between the undoubted and understandable liturgical allure of the New Zealand Prayer Book and the existential ecclesial reality, which I have experienced?

As I began to seriously interrogate the postcolonial ecclesial reality of my homeland against, for example, the bold and admirable claims made in the introductory section of the New Zealand Prayer Book, it soon became apparent that there is indeed a disconnect between the overall liturgical allure of the Prayer Book and the reality of the church as the self-proclaimed missional body of Christ. For example I began to wonder afresh about why in the twenty-first century, the wider and publicly acknowledged sociopolitical influence of the church in seeking the lost and lonely and speaking boldly and prophetically in the public square, especially on behalf of those who are the least in our society, is barely noticeable.[5]

As I began further to seriously interrogate the postcolonial ecclesial reality of my church against the unequivocal claims of the 1992 Constitutional revisions, it further became readily apparent that there is a very serious disconnect between the ideologically based Constitutional provisions for cultural freedom and the constitutionally assumed theological ideal of being truly one in Christ.

This reflection is intended not as a criticism of the Prayer Book nor of the Constitution *per se*; rather, it is a critical reflection upon the way in which I believe the true potential of the New Zealand Prayer Book and of the Constitution, which prescribes right relationality among the Anglican body of Christ has yet to be fully realized by the postcolonial church itself.

I am firmly of the view that were the rhetorical claims of the Prayer Book able to be more credibly matched to the substantive responses of the church to the pressing realities of human need, especially among Maori in Aotearoa New Zealand, then this precious liturgical resource *could well be* key to the unfinished project of truly redeeming and thus reconciling the historically established chasm between indigenous Maori and colonially planted Pakeha Anglicans. Were the church to model such exemplary Gospel-based activism it could deservedly be key to effecting and exemplifying the wider social project of achieving God's justice for all who suffer, all who are marginalized, and all who are in human need.

It follows, however, that the contemporary church, now deeply uncritically configured according to its bold and unprecedented postcolonial Constitutional revisions of 1992, must now faithfully reconsider the essential nature of who and what it has determined to become as God's missional Anglican Church in Aotearoa New Zealand in the early twenty-first century.

Twenty-four years ago, in response to the rightly unrelenting insistence from Maori Anglicans for postcolonial justice within our own household, the Anglican Church revised its Constitution not merely to *accommodate* indigenous interests but instead to share power and resources, to remove the structural impediments for authentic involvement in decision making and to create culturally determined space for autonomous flourishing within one church. The new Constitution created first two, and later three, autonomous and essentially racially based units within the church, which became known as *tikanga*.[6] These were intended to provide culturally safe spaces for each of the *tikanga* partners to enjoy freedom to worship and to flourish according to their respective cultural preferences in terms of language and tradition. It was for Anglicans a globally unprecedented postcolonial response to historically relentless indigenous activism.

Unfortunately, in the inevitably chaotic implementation phase of the new Constitution little or no attention was paid to two critical factors. The first of these was for the church to articulate with clarity and conviction just what was the actual *theological basis* for the radical revision? The second of these was for the church to articulate with clarity and conviction just how it intended to monitor itself in terms of realizing the theological imperatives inherent in its Constitutional revision initiative. Clearly, without the first action, the second was virtually impossible to realize. Twenty-four years later neither articulation has yet been substantively developed.

It is my contention that we must now with profound urgency commit to a project involving a truly representative cross section of the church, who are charged with the task of articulating afresh what it now means to be God's twenty-first-century Gospel people in our unique postcolonial homeland. We must find ways to be vulnerable anew to one another as we seek to discern the deep theological basis for either maintaining or modifying our understanding of the distinctively treaty-based,[7] *tikanga-*

based partnership relationships and obligations we have so uncritically constitutionally constructed with and for one another.

This is our church's yet unrecognized, unfinished business. It is our ongoing, unresolved postcolonial challenge. Without critically reflecting upon the quality of our life *together* as God's twenty-first-century Aotearoa New Zealand and Polynesia Anglican people, I contend the theological quality of our worship, our liturgical life, and our constitutional intentions remain deservedly open to the criticisms of those who consider *tikanga* to be functioning as a divisive ideology rather than as a reconciling theologically grounded ideal.

In order to appropriately contextualize this contemporary challenge there needs first to be a brief consideration of the relevant past. Although unique, New Zealand Anglican Church his/story has deep resonance with the emerging narratives of other colonized indigenous peoples across the Anglican Communion.[8] We each share a historical story of missionary encounter, missionary evangelization, and largely agreeable mutual engagement, which was then inexorably corrupted by the deeply intertwined colonial forces of the Cross, with the Crown. Late nineteenth-century indigenous Anglican history across the Anglican Communion was characterized by the experience of well-intended, but ultimately misguided, missionary benevolence. This resulted in mutually disadvantageous bewilderment and finally acquiescence by increasingly marginalized indigenous Anglicans to the power-laden forces of the colonial church.

Anglicanism in Aotearoa New Zealand began in 1814 as an indigenous church. It began awkwardly at first but then developed steadily such that by the time the first English bishop arrived in 1842, many Maori, perhaps even the majority, were already literate, numerate and very well experienced in the arts of evangelizing each other. Using classic Church Missionary Society (CMS) strategy of translating written material into the vernacular, legendary CMS pioneer leader Henry Williams urged his society to give priority to supplying more books, particularly more Scriptures as "those they at present possess, they generally know by heart."[9] Notwithstanding the fact that missionary concentration was focused upon "saving the souls of the heathen Maori" and to protecting their charges from the ultimately predatory instincts of the colonials, Maori were nonetheless irrevocably transformed and remained willingly formed as faith-filled Christians.

By 1833, missionary George Clarke reported that many schools were now being established by "the natives" themselves. It was estimated that by 1845 there were more than 100,000 copies of both the New Testament and the Prayer Book in circulation among the similarly constituted adult Maori population. By then the majority were voracious readers and most adults could at least recite large portions of both books by heart. Maori were thus well evangelized as a result of this largely mutually agreeable and beneficial ecclesial relationship. Beyond the church, Maori were by now increasingly well experienced in the more worldly affairs of business and trade and were for a time leading the way with economic development. Maori were thus well placed to respond to the colonial overtures for settlement.

In 1839, rudimentary arrangements were in place for the administrative establishment of a colonial outpost replete with classic Rule Britannia overlay. In order to secure the interests of the Crown, a standard treaty was proposed. It was to be one which would establish a good faith binding compact between the people of the land and the newcomers. This was to be a Treaty within which each partner would formally commit to peacefully co-exist within a covenanted relationship of agreed responsibilities and obligations.

The Treaty of Waitangi was signed on February 6, 1840. CMS missionaries, as drafters, translators, and collectors of signatures, very ably assisted the Crown negotiators. Very soon after this period of political settlement the arrival of the first Bishop of New Zealand heralded the formal establishment of the Church of England, replete with its age-old hierarchy of patriarchal order and control. The new settlers from the mother Church of England thus efficiently transplanted their institutional church into the new colony. Many of the settler Anglicans were blissfully unaware that for the previous twenty plus years, Maori had been active, faith-filled, baptized members of the same denominational church.

Ecclesiological struggles soon ensued between the first colonial Bishop George Augustus Selwyn and the leaders of the CMS. Both wanted proprietorial rights over indigenous souls. These unresolved tensions were to completely skew the ecclesial environment and to set the stage for two quite racially distinctive streams within the Anglican Church to emerge. The "natives" were of course destined to remain under the patronage of the missionary church.[10] As with other British colonies of that time, particularly those which later formed the British Commonwealth, many of the leading colonial settlers or establishment Anglicans who came or were sent to New Zealand to assist in its settlement were those also exceedingly prominent as lay people in the judicial, political, and ecclesiastical environment. And so it was that Anglican DNA was very early imprinted also upon the establishment of the new colonial outpost and eventually upon the fully fledged government, which was officially constituted in 1852.

Just five years later in 1857, the first Constitution of the Anglican Church for the fledgling colony was formally signed. Notably, in spite of a forty-three year history of deep and abiding devotion to the Church, Maori were in that first Constitutional moment completely structurally and attitudinally marginalized from any place within the decision making or leadership realms of the establishment Church.[11]

However, the indigenous or missionary Church continued to flourish and to expand its national reach under the benevolent patronage of the CMS missionaries. One of the key sites of empowerment for Maori was the missionary classroom where there was an opportunity for developing and refining the life of the mind and for learning to think and act critically, strategically, and compassionately. Sadly, as the oppressive forces within the colonizing movement gained ascendancy, the brutal reality of treaty betrayal, political treachery, warfare, and introduced diseases would very quickly devastate Maori community and family life. The faith of Maori Anglicans was to be severely tested.

However, given that it was activist evangelical Christians[12] who were originally responsible for the establishment of the CMS, it is perhaps not surprising that within this similarly intellectually and theologically charged ecclesial milieu would emerge those Maori who eventually became the insurgents, the strategists, the activists, and those who refused to capitulate to the often brutally cruel forces inherent in colonial imperialism. There is no question that the lethal colonial combination of the Cross and the Crown, which has indeed wreaked almost irreparable havoc across so many former British colonies, was no less omnipresent in the chaotic context of *settling* Aotearoa New Zealand.[13]

Maori would be relentless in their determination to push back against the oppressive tools of policy and punishment often harshly meted out by both church and state in the protracted processes of colonizing New Zealand. But they were to the largest extent unable to withstand the ravages of war, disease, and subsequently disastrous depopulation. For many, their faith was both the only and the last bastion of hope.

One of the legendary instruments of both solace and inspiration for the increasingly beleaguered indigenous warriors and martyrs was one of the first scripturally based liturgical resources translated into Maori and powerfully embraced by the new believers: the 1662 Book of Common Prayer. Maori have always named this book, *Te Rawiri*, which literally translated, is the name "David."[14] The reverentially affectionate "naming" of this book by Maori is directly attributable to the Maori belief in the authority, or *mana*, of the Psalmist.

For all indigenous peoples for whom the oral tradition is normative, it usually follows that the greater the status of the speaker, the greater the respect given. Treasured friend and colleague, the late Canon Dr. Hone Kaa, once described the early Maori oral tradition accordingly:

> Maori believed that nothing was ever said or sung that could not be attributed to one who had lived. Acknowledgement of their authorship gave you authority to use their words and in that sense to keep them "alive." The acknowledgement also gave the singers or orators direct connection to the person or being from whom the words are said to have come. Their ability to compose, and capture moments in their life became moments in the lives of those who used their songs or uttered

their words. The time, in which they wrote mattered not, it was the events and the actions that were important and they became the actions and events of those repeating them.[15]

For spoken words to have significant meaning, they had to be attributed to a person of authority. David then is seen as *the* figure of authority, as *the* spokesperson of things of great meaning and therefore as a person, a leader of great "power." In spite of contemporary scholarly disputation over authorship, as far as Maori were concerned, the author of *all* of the Psalms was David, or *Rawiri*.

Because the Psalms themselves were among the first biblical resources to be translated into Maori, their significant and enduring influence was assured. When translated, the Psalms assumed a tremendous depth of meaning because the indigenous language of the time was so powerfully evocative of the imagery, symbolism, pain, and beauty inherent in their messages. Maori could find parallels in their experience, particularly with respect to the colonial settlement times when Maori were being systematically relieved of land, language, and resources. It was also during the late nineteenth-century period when diseases against which Maori had no immunity had begun to take their toll.

As the full devastating impact of colonization began to be understood by Maori communities, the Psalms understandably provided solace for Maori suffering. The Psalms inspired, encouraged, and reassured Maori to remain faithful. They provided example after example of "rules" for "right living" in obedience to God in spite of the suffering they were experiencing.

Solace was invoked through the rhythmic chanting of the words of the Psalms. For a people with an oral tradition, the use of chant was a powerful medium for incarnating the Holy Spirit as helper, guardian, defender, protector, refuge, and advocate. The texts of *Rawiri* or David were contextually perfect, for here were found the petitions or pleas of God's people for help, or at least relief, from distress including the physical and emotional experience of suffering, divine affliction (if this were necessary), or liberation and Exodus from persecution.

In retrospect, it is easy to see how the Psalms became such a source of comfort to an increasingly marginalized people. It was the Psalms, which provided extraordinarily beautiful, poignant, poetic hymns, prayers, laments, songs of thanksgiving, liturgies, and instructions for life. The remainder of the Book of Common Prayer provided all of the necessary Orders of Service for the Sacraments, Ordination, and all other Anglican Offices. There are forms of prayer for virtually every occasion. There are hymns for every occasion, calendars, readings, and blessings. In composite then, *Te Rawiri* was and is still regarded by many Maori as being utterly sufficient in itself.[16]

Te Rawiri contains the full range of liturgical resources required to respond in faith and with humility to the sufferings, the joys and the day-to-day challenges experienced by all of God's people in their endeavors to live good lives and to endow those with meaning and purpose according to God's will. The richest form of hermeneutic was here linguistically, literarily, liturgically, and existentially at work.

Throughout the twentieth century, Maori Anglican leaders worked tirelessly in both the political and the church realms seeking justice for Maori. While minor gains were made politically by the establishment of designated Maori seats in Parliament and ecclesially by the appointment of a suffragan Bishop for Maori, the fraught politics of war, of relentless economic hardship and then increasing urbanization, all served to deepen social disenfranchisement of Maori and prevent anything other than token changes being made in either realm.

It was not until well after the mid-twentieth century that the irreversible political movement for social reforms began. By now the church both *establishment* and missionary were but mere vestiges of their former glorious pasts. However, increasingly secular postcolonial New Zealand was no less forcefully propelled into the 1960s and 1970s on the tide of global activism. This tide rightly raised up the universally pressing issues of those times—Black Power, the women's movement, gay rights, anti-war movements, environmental protection, and activism for indigenous rights. Inevitably all of these issues were then being contextualized to the sociopolitical and economic reality of Maori in our homeland of Aotearoa. The intellectual and moral basis for what became a sustained and extraordinarily courageous era of political activism initially by Maori and for Maori, was thus ushered in.

It was this unrelenting and focused activism by young educated Maori, which in turn deeply affected the Maori church leaders of this period. Many reported feeling shamed into action by what they saw as the example of Gospel-based courage and determination being shown by their grandchildren, most of whom had by now completely given up on what they readily described as *"the church of the colonizer."*

Senior Maori church leaders led by the then singular Bishop of Aotearoa or senior Maori Bishop for New Zealand were thus spurred into action. They began to strategize ways of aligning the mission of the Church with the exemplary justice-based pursuits of the young activists. However, in order for the whole Church to be involved, then first the historically anomalous position of the two still essentially racialized streams (albeit by then barely trickles) of church life clearly required attention.

Into such a context was born the radical idea of returning to the Treaty of Waitangi as the nation's founding document for Gospel-based inspiration, for reimagining a new beginning to the relationship between the people of the land and those who came seeking permission to settle. The idea was born of revisioning the Church in Aotearoa New Zealand as a model of Gospel witness where all of the gifts of all of the people were able to be equally deployed in the service of God's mission. Where none of God's people were ever again able to be excluded, devalued, or marginalized.

The idea became a theory for both redemptive justice and political fulfilment, Gospel and law embracing each other. The theory ultimately became both a bilingual and bicultural Revised New Zealand Prayer Book published in 1989, and then the globally unprecedented Constitutional Revision implemented in 1992. Worship was thus intentionally and generously beautifully transformed. Prayers, hymns, liturgy, and the sacraments all now deeply reflected the context of the South Pacific and Maori languages of a fully inclusive Church in Aotearoa New Zealand. Church polity was radically transformed theoretically to reflect treaty-based partnership relationships of mutuality and interdependence originally envisaged by those who drafted and implemented the nation's founding document.

Against this historical background it is entirely understandable how and why both the new New Zealand Prayer Book and the Revised Constitution came to serve as spectacular indicators to the church, to the nation, and to the wider Anglican Communion of the outcomes possible from pursuing redemptive justice within a postcolonial context. Here was the church owning up to its own complicity in the historic injustices inflicted upon indigenous peoples and in particular upon indigenous Anglicans. The church's actions in the 1980s and 1990s were indeed bold, brave, brilliant, and globally unprecedented. Many other mainline churches in Aotearoa New Zealand developed and endeavored to implement similar structural transformations. Secular models of treaty-based partnership were developed for the government sector and some major private sector businesses followed suit.

For a period, the Treaty of Waitangi enjoyed an elevated and much revered new-found status. Sadly however, especially within the church, the halcyon days of basking in the reflected glory of the new Prayer Book, the newly revised Constitution and in particular the partnership relationships known as *tikanga* or rightful ways, were not to last. Within a few short years, inter- and intra-*tikanga* tensions soon became increasingly evident. Tragically, these tensions have not found mutually agreeable release and reconciliation. Instead, they have expanded and escalated, giving impetus to the call for a critical review, which I believe now inevitably confronts us.

Even a cursory appreciation of the history of the Anglican Church in Aotearoa New Zealand would simply serve to confirm that the enduring task of successfully dismantling the persistent and insidious legacies of racism, classism, sexism, and clericalism so deeply embedded in colonialism needed more than a one-off Constitutional Revision and a brilliantly contrived new Prayer Book.

The following are a series of initial considerations with which I consider any adequate review of past intentions, present predicamernts, and future resolutions must wrestle. Even a cursory understanding of race or identity politics would soon reveal the inevitable truth of what George Orwell once famously declared that "those who hold power never ever willingly give it up or share it equitably."[17] To which might be added Lord Acton's reflection that power corrupts . . . even amidst virtue and spirit.

My contention is that instead of the church actually dismantling its historically power-laden, fundamentally unjust, monolingual, and monocultural master's house, it has instead intuitively, without instinctively and wisely leveraging its own Gospel insight and power, opted for the establishment of parallel duplicate power structures.

Each individual *tikanga* orders its life based primarily upon the very same patriarchal and oppressive structures the Constitutional Revision sought to surmount and redeem. Ultimately, this duplicatory project has trebled the weight of patriarchally oppressive leadership and organizational structures, only this time it has done so in the name of postcolonial justice. Essentially, it has been a political adjustment to, rather than a theologically grounded transformation of, what had been a profoundly and undeniably unjust historically established ecclesial structure. A noble undertaking, it has become in its outworking an ignoble confusion and contradiction.

The challenge of maintaining this essentially *racialized* leadership and organizational model has not been easy nor always possible for those charged with senior leadership. Sadly, it has been these internal challenges which have continued unduly and now very unwisely to consume the attention of church leaders and many of its constituents for the past twenty-four years. Inevitably and tragically, the gaze of the church has been distracted from God's pressing missional needs.

In the meantime, the political, cultural, economic, and demographic landscape of Aotearoa New Zealand has also changed dramatically. It is no longer the antipodean backwater postcolonial nation it once was. In 2014, it had one of the highest rates of child abuse and violence against children of any OECD nation in the world. Maori children are disproportionately represented; one in three of our nation's children live (officially) in poverty. Almost half of these are either Maori or Pacific Island children and 63 percent of these children have beneficiary parents. Over 20,000 women sought assistance from Women's Refuge in 2014 and the costs of domestic violence are now estimated at $8 billion annually. Maori and Pacific Island women are disproportionately represented in these domestic abuse statistics. Fifty-eight percent of women in prison are Maori and 51 percent of men. Maori are just 15 percent of the general population of just over 4.1 million. I could readily multiply qualitative data analysis to do with health, education, housing, and any single one of the life chances categories which lead to human flourishing. Furthermore, the statistical reality affecting Maori and Pacific Island people would make for no less harrowing reading.

Tragically, instead of being at the public forefront of prophetic activism now so urgently needed to end such grave social inequity and human suffering, the postcolonial Anglican Church in Aotearoa New Zealand and Polynesia is instead largely preoccupied with its own internal tensions. These arise constantly both within and between *tikanga*. Symptomatic of serious malaise are such phenomena as increasing disaffection among clergy and church leaders over matters of doctrinal difference, and very serious legal battles within *tikanga*.

It is for all of these reasons that I cannot help but to repeatedly and critically reflect, were the rhetorical claims of the Prayer Book able to be more substantively matched by the responses of the Church to the pressing realities of human need, especially among Maori in Aotearoa New Zealand, then this precious liturgical resource *could yet be* a key to the unfinished project of truly reconciling the historically established chasm between indigenous Maori and colonially planted Pakeha Anglicans.

Written in the front cover of the New Zealand Prayer Book are some of the most poignant and beautiful introductory words to any Prayer Book anywhere in the world. "The purpose of liturgy is not to protect particular linguistic forms. It is to enable a community to pray." [18] But I am moved to ask, for whom and for what are we praying given the extent of human suffering now so unavoidably visible in our nation and to which we are largely failing to respond as a church, as the prophetic voice of outrage in the public square, as those accompanying the poor, those in prison, those marginalized by poverty and by social and political injustice?

"Liturgy describes the People of God. Liturgy expresses who we believe we are in the presence of God. Liturgy reveals the God whom we worship. Liturgy reflects our mission. . . ." My question in response is, just what is our publicly articulated mission in these postcolonial times? Has our sense of mission been diverted by the omnipresent challenge of sustaining and protecting our power-laden institutional model for leadership and organization which actually only serves to privilege male domination within three distinctive spheres of racial difference at the expense of the whole church being equipped and enabled to serve the Gospel mandated common good?

"Liturgy isn't primarily what we say, but what we do. . . ."

"If worship is the response of the people of God to the presence of God, then the first function of liturgy is to provide conditions in which that presence may be experienced."

What I have endeavored to do in this chapter is to explore the present populist impressions about worship and liturgy with particular reference to the New Zealand Prayer Book and to ask whether or not the supposedly redemptive postcolonial reality formally constitutionally established by the Church in Aotearoa New Zealand and Polynesia in 1992, is real or illusory?

It is thus a case study and a critique of my own church as I have experienced it first-hand and from a position of leadership privilege over many years. It is the church of my forebears since the time of its arrival in my homeland. I have been raised within the Anglican Church and remain deeply devoted to it. I will work to ensure it becomes once again respected for its previously exemplary commitment to redemptive justice. Its boldness in liturgical development, its courage in supporting radical political activism for justice for all, its openness to innovating for necessary change within its own structures, its commitment to unconditional inclusion and its prioritized commitment to fulfilling God's missional purposes could also continue to bring back to it the global respect it once so deservedly enjoyed.

> God of justice and compassion,
> you give us a work to do
> and a baptism of suffering and resurrection.
> From you comes power to give to others
> the care we have ourselves received
> so that we, and all who love your world,
> may live in harmony and trust.
> Amen.[19]

BIBLIOGRAPHY

Bi-cultural Commission of the Anglican Church on the Treaty of Waitangi. *Te Kaupapa Tikanga Rua*. Auckland, NZ: Provincial Secretary of the Church of the Province of New Zealand, 1992.

Church of the Province of New Zealand. *A New Zealand Prayer Book, He Karakia Mihinare o Aotearoa*. Auchland, NZ: Collins, 1989.

James, Belich. *The New Zealand Wars and the Victorian Interpretation of Racial Conflict*. Auckland, NZ: Auckland University Press, 1986.

Kaa, Hone. "A Personal Understanding of Authority Applied to Scripture and Prayer." DMin. Thesis, Episcopal Divinity School, 2002.

Orwell, George. *1984*. New York: Penguin Books, 1950.

Parr, C. J. "A Missionary Library: Printed Attempts to Instruct the Maori, 1815–1845." *Journal of the Polynesian Society* 70 (1961): 429–50.

Te Paa, Jenny. "From *Te Rawiri* to the New Zealand Prayer Book." In *The Oxford Guide to the Book of Common Prayer: A Worldwide Survey*, edited by Charles Hefling and Cynthia Shattuck, 343–47. Oxford: Oxford University Press, 2008.

NOTES

1. Church of the Province of New Zealand, *A New Zealand Prayer Book, He Karakia Mihinare o Aotearoa* (Auchland, NZ: Collins, 1989).

2. Those known to have written scholarly and or published works in the broad area include Ken Booth, Revs. Alex Czerwonka, John Hebenton, Bosco Peters; Archdeacon Carole Hughes, Bishop George Connor—all of whom are Pakeha New Zealanders.

3. In 1992 the Anglican Church in New Zealand reached beyond its monolingual and monocultural Constitution for the first time in almost 135 years. A carefully and fully revised Constitution was subsequently implemented. The church did so by way of acknowledging the Gospel imperative inherent in the Treaty of Waitangi, the nation's founding document signed in 1840 as a covenantal agreement for peaceful coexistence between indigenous Maori and newcomer/settler Pakeha from colonial Britain. The church therefore established a radically new system of governance based on this treaty-based partnership relationship.

4. See Jenny Te Paa, "From *Te Rawiri* to the New Zealand Prayer Book," in *The Oxford Guide to the Book of Common Prayer: A Worldwide Survey*, ed. Charles Hefling and Cynthia Shattuck (Oxford: Oxford University Press, 2008), 343–47.

5. I do recognize that such an assertion is entirely subjective. I want also to acknowledge unequivocally the sterling work undertaken by the church's official mission and social services agencies. These agencies, however, are fiscally and structurally mandated to do the work they do. The larger body of Christ are, however, also mandated by virtue of our baptism to act with similar Christlike boldness and compassion. It is this readily apparent chasm of indifference to deep and enduring human suffering in twenty-first-century Aotearoa New Zealand to which I am referring.

6. *Tikanga* is the Maori word used specifically by the Anglican Church in Aotearoa New Zealand and Polynesia to describe the distinctive cultural streams established by Constitutional fiat in 1992. The *tikanga* streams are intended to provide organizational autonomy to Pakeha, Maori, and Polynesian Anglicans, enabling each to manage their own affairs in accordance with their cultural preferences, while simultaneously maintaining open and generous collegiality with one another.

7. The 1992 Constitutional Revision drew directly upon the language and symbolism inherent in the wording of the nation's founding document known as the Treaty of Waitangi. See Bi-cultural Commission of the Anglican Church on the Treaty of Waitangi, *Te Kaupapa Tikanga Rua* (Auckland, NZ: Provincial Secretary of the Church of the Province of New Zealand, 1992).

8. The official establishment in 1994 of the Anglican Indigenous Network as one of the official networks of the Anglican Communion has provided a much needed forum for indigenous Anglicans to gather and share their respective "Cross and Crown" histories. Primary among the participating Provinces are New Zealand, Australia, and Canada together with the Diocese of Hawaii and various of the official units within the Episcopal Church which comprise primarily indigenous Episcopalians, for example Province VIII and the Church in Navaholand.

9. See C. J. Parr, "A Missionary Library: Printed Attempts to Instruct the Maori, 1815–1845," *Journal of the Polynesian Society* 70 (1961): 429–50.

10. Even well into the twenty-first century many older Maori Anglicans still self-describe as being of *Te Hahi Mihinare* or the Missionary Church.

11. The first Constitution of the Anglican Church in Aotearoa New Zealand was formally enacted in 1857, the second Revised Constitution in 1992, a gap of 135 years.

12. Formed originally in 1799 by a group of evangelical Christians known for their social activism particularly against slavery, the early Church Missionary Society attracted the likes of William Wilberforce, Henry Thornton, and Thomas Babington.

13. See Belich James, *The New Zealand Wars and the Victorian Interpretation of Racial Conflict* (Auckland, NZ: Auckland University Press, 1986).

14. Part of the discussion of the New Zealand Prayer Book is taken from my essay, "From *Te Rawiri* to the New Zealand Prayer Book."

15. Hone Kaa, "A Personal Understanding of Authority Applied to Scripture and Prayer" (DMin. Thesis, Episcopal Divinity School, 2002).

16. I am grateful to my oral informants, senior Maori Bishop Muru Walters and Archbishop Brown Turei, for providing the details concerning the use of chant and for their descriptions of the ways in which Maori Anglicans deeply treasure *Te Rawiri*.

17. George Orwell, *1984* (New York: Penguin Books, 1950), 263.

18. All of these quotes are taken from the Introduction to *A New Zealand Prayer Book*, x–xv. Used with permission.

19. Ibid., 478.

EIGHT

Church Music in Postcolonial Liturgical Celebration

Lim Swee Hong

In his recent book *Grassroots Asian Theology*, Simon Chan, a well-regarded Asian Pentecostal theologian, observed a significant lack of correlation between Asian Christian theologies and the lived experience of ecclesial communities.[1] In response, he argues for the acceptance of the reality of grassroots Asian Christianity as it draws on a "creative adaptation [of] primal religious contexts" in developing a theology that takes seriously "both sociopolitical and ethnographic contexts."[2] On the surface, this is a commendable stance; it seems to urge that local culture be given due consideration and that lived experiences be reflected in the formation of theological thought.

However, when we look specifically at the field of church music, we are confronted by the reality that local Christian expressions, especially in Asia, are not necessarily derived from creative adaptation or assimilation of local idioms or contexts. More often than not, local congregations are far more passionate about imitating and embracing their western Christian heritage, retaining its empire-based structure and power ideals. From India to Korea, from Kampuchea (Cambodia) to China, grassroots Christian musical expressions continue to demand and appropriate western idioms rather than creatively adapt from their local genus. The latter is typically either ignored or avoided.

In the late twentieth century, the steadfast effort of translating western hymn texts into the local vernacular was superseded by the adaptation of western contemporary worship repertoire. Songs such as Darlene Zschech's "Shout to the Lord" and Chris Tomlin's "How Great Is Our

God" are readily accessible in various tongues such as Thai, Swahili, Arabic and Russian.[3] Without a doubt, church leadership is far more willing to pour resources into acquiring expensive western music instruments and establishing worship teams, which mimic Hillsong United from Australia, rather than cultivating musical expressions that use local instruments and draw on local repertoire. If we were to take seriously the insight of Prosper of Aquitaine, *l egem credendi lex statuat supplicandi*, which can loosely be translated as, "The law of prayer is the law of faith," what would the present music-making efforts in Asian churches say about our Christian spirituality? Do we consider such worship expressions to be grassroots-lived even though they are primarily mimicry of western ethos and expressions? For all intents and purposes, these western-based expressions shape recipients without regard to nurturing local customs or enjoining that indigenous traits be used in Christian worship. More pointedly, what does this say about postcolonial Asian Christian worship and the role of music?

At present, some scholars who work in both theology and music, such as Don Saliers, Edward Foley, and Jeremy Begbie, have asserted that music enables non-music meaning making.[4] In reality—contrary to the hopes of present-day western well-meaning Christians—music making in many parts of the world continues to perpetuate colonial and imperial influences and practices. In their book *Christian Worship: Postcolonial Perspectives*, Michael N. Jagessar and Stephen Burns cite Jeffrey Richards' discussion about musical forms and their correlation to British imperialism.[5] Richards observed that Christian hymns in the nineteenth and twentieth centuries were imbued with themes of militarism and written with imperialistic tones. The expansion of colonial powers is here seemingly fused with the spread of Christianity in its synonymous imperialistic musical expressions. Yet in the twenty-first century, the Church, particularly in Asia, remains unwilling to discard such leanings. Is there a resolution to this tension between the inherited colonial/imperial canon and the emergence of new traditions? How might ecclesial practice be renewed to facilitate methods enabling local cultural heritage to be a key player in formulating a truly grassroots-lived postcolonial Christian worship?

ASSEMBLING THE PIECES

It is crucial to understand that contextual sacred music practices in postcolonial liturgical celebrations are not about simply excising western music influences or seeking to revive "forgotten" indigenous musical vestiges. I contend that church music practices need to remain true to their holy vocation—that is, to be "the excellent gift of God." As Luther asserted, "I would certainly like to praise music with all my heart as the excellent gift of God which it is and to commend it to everyone . . . the gift of language combined with the gift of song was only given to man to let him know that he should praise God with both word and music."[6] Church music is a showcase as well as a conduit of expressions offered by individuals and the corporate assembly who desire to worship God. Yet, it is also important to realize that the practice of church music is much more than a sonic phenomenon or an aural experience. As Jagessar and Burns assert, hymns convey the "sentiments and thoughts" of their creators and "re-inscribe the notions of empire, among other baleful things" to current times.[7]

With that in mind, the role and value of music in liturgical celebration cannot be simply appreciated from a musicological standpoint with description of performance practice or an analysis of scores. Instead, a theological aesthetics paradigm for music making is needed in order to better study the meta-narrative underneath music in its worship context. Such a paradigm will also shed light on the non-musical impetus to consolidate, shape, and enforce the identities of individuals and communities, as well as their interrelationships. Before this can be done, some understanding of these various disciplines and their properties is needed since this paradigm is constructed using the various disciplines in music and theology.

Ethnomusicology

In the mid-twentieth century, scholars in the new field of ethnomusicology began to explore the "outer reaches" of music making beyond the sonic realm framed by traditional musicology, which studied western European art music. This emerging field of study, related to anthropology, was then known as Comparative Musicology. Non-western art music was examined within a specific context that seeks to understand the music-making phenomenon. Such investigation would locate the role of music in the society and study its meaning-making value for the specific cultural location. The field was initiated by luminaries such as Jaap Kunst, Mantle Hood, Alan P. Merriam, and Bruno Nettl.[8] Broadly speaking, its methodology explored the contexts of the sonic events by way of music transcription, ethnographic profiles of the musicians and the community, and organological study of the instruments. All of these are important determinants that support the extra-referential potentiality of music making, which was hitherto viewed with suspicion by the early twentieth-century practice of European musicology. In recent years, ethnomusicology as a field has begun to investigate the contemporary worship music phenomenon. Younger scholars such as Joshua Busman, Monique Ingalls, Deborah Justice, Gerardo Marti, and Anna Nekola are helping to lay the foundation for this work.[9]

Ritual Studies

While not directly focused on music, the neighboring social sciences field of ritual studies with its emphasis on connecting ritual action, identity formation, power, community, and meaning making contribute much to phenomenological research approaches. This in turn offers fresh insight into the study of Christian rituals from sociological and cultural perspectives. The field of Ritual Studies is indebted to the contributions of Arnold van Gennep, Victor Turner, Clifford Geertz, Ronald L. Grimes, Catherine Bell, and others.[10]

Theology

In the theological world, Shoki Coe, Taiwanese missiology scholar and Director of the Theological Education Fund, introduced the term "contextualization" in 1972.[11] Byang H. Kato, presenting at the 1974 Lausanne Congress, wrote,

> We understand the term to mean making concepts or ideals relevant in a given situation. In reference to Christian practices, it is an effort to express the never changing Word of God in ever changing modes of relevance. Since the Gospel message is inspired but the mode of its expression is not, contextualization of the modes of expression is not only right but necessary.[12]

Subsequently, his student I-to Loh harnessed this missiological nomenclature in his investigation of Asian church music making and produced a theological approach for the contextualization of Asian church music that guided his ministry.[13] Others including Stephen Bevans, David Hesselgrave, and Aylward Shorter worked on exploring the parameters of contextualization.[14] They used the Roman Catholic term "inculturation" to function similarly in their approach to examining and transforming liturgy. Riding on the momentum of *aggiornamento*, an ecclesial renewal epitomized by the Second Vatican Council's *Sacrosanctum Concilium* (Constitution on Sacred Liturgy) with its emphasis on revitalization through active participation,[15] Filipino liturgical scholar Anscar Chupungco offered a scholarly understanding of inculturation and its processes in the liturgy.[16] Particularly helpful was his explanation about dynamic equivalence, organic progression, and creative assimilation, and how these processes relate to worship rites, actions, and elements within Roman Catholic liturgical celebration. Scholars such as Michael Amaladoss, Peter C. Phan, Jonathan Tan, and Patrick Chukwudezie Chibuko have investigated the principles of inculturation in their respective contexts.[17]

Coming into the early twenty-first century, liturgical scholars from various ecclesial quarters drew from these fields of ritual and cultural studies to investigate worship and music practices. Scholars like Paul

Bradshaw, Judith Kubicki, Mary McGann, and Tom Driver have significantly influenced the world of worship, church music, and their respective practices with their investigations.[18] Yet as Jagessar and Burns have observed, postcolonial deliberations are nascent when it comes to worship, though they are amply present in the areas of hermeneutics, biblical studies, and feminist and systematic theologies.[19] For music and liturgical studies, postcolonial criticism seems to be expressed in the praxis of contextualization or inculturation.

But as Jagessar and Burns noted, there remains the question of who decides and defines what is contextualized (or inculturated) and what is not. After all—and as Chan asserts—the majority of scholars who argue for contextual theology in Asian Christianity have "ignored the lived theologies from the grassroots."[20] At the same time, we are reminded by postcolonial scholar Musa Dube that power can come from the pen of "the colonized who either collaborate with the dominant forces or yearn for the same power."[21] To that end, how might one understand the term "grassroots"? How might the essence of grassroots-lived expressions be realized so that it can serve as a postcolonial benchmark?

HOW DO WE BEGIN?

Perhaps the way forward is not so much about identifying who has control in determining what cultural expressions are acceptable to the postcolonial church. Rather, consider the alternative of drawing together various fields of knowledge in order to nurture an *aggiornamento* approach, which would in turn inform and transform the current situation. In his essay "Constructing an Asian Theology of Liturgical Inculturation from the Documents of the Federation of Asian Bishops Conferences (FABC)," Jonathan Tan cites Ladislav Nemet who observes, "The process of inculturation is no longer a question of a search for external adaptation to Asian reality and way of living, but a question of an existential nature: being and living in Asia and with Asians, becoming involved in all the aspects of life, collaborating with all the forces which are working actively to build up the Kingdom."[22] In essence, Nemet speaks about the recognizing of a form of consciousness that builds awareness of the many facets of meaning making in being and living; this sense of purpose is harnessed to bring forth change through self-determination. Applied to the practice of music making, this approach would see the community helped by learned leaders who could nurture local expressions for use in Christian worship. Here, the community, shaped by their theological values and socio-cultural context, would determine what constitutes their identity. In this fashion, grassroots-lived expressions are not seduced by the temptation to be exotic to fulfill the desire of outsiders, nor hemmed in by the demand of tradition *potissimum* through insiders seeking to perpetuate the last vestige of colonial power and empire. In my book *Giving Voice to Asian Christians*, I offered a comparative study of two ecclesial communities, the Thai Covenant Church in Thailand and the Methodist Church in Singapore. In these contexts, the process of contextualization is framed within the theological and socio-cultural consciousness of the particular postcolonial communities resulting in different trajectories and music praxis outcomes.[23] In the example of church in Thailand, the interplay of various dynamics brought about overt indigenous expressions in their Christian spirituality. This stands in contrast to the church in Singapore that remains resolute in their use of western idiomatic liturgical resources. Both entities have contextualized in their respective milieu.

Aside from these two examples, a broader research survey to profile liturgical celebration is presently being conducted. This investigation looks at the church music practice in the Indo-China region of Burma (Myanmar), Cambodia (Kampuchea), Thailand, and Vietnam.[24] Early assessment of the data indicates that the state of church music making in this region exhibits a growing awareness of each church's cultural identity. Again, this nascent situation may not necessarily translate into fully realized, localized, Christian liturgical celebration as hoped for by outsiders. I certainly hope that this will come to pass. After all, the current situation is not likely to remain static. And as I have pointed out earlier, the situation is shaped by numerous determinants.

In trying to delineate the grassroots-lived musical corpus, one needs to keep in mind what ethnomusicologist Monique Ingalls noted in her dissertation "Awesome in this Place: Sound, Space, and Identity in Contemporary North American Evangelical Worship," that a people's heart music corpus can be enlarged. This is not only possible but is normative. She writes, "While musical heart language is individual and subjective, it is neither essential nor immutable; rather, it is something that can be learned or experienced through musical conversation through worship. Multi-ethnic worship, that is, worship through the expression of an other, leads to the eventual appropriation of that expression as (partly) one's own."[25] This ethnomusicological understanding underscores the phenomenon in which songs are received and eventually embraced as one's own, even though these resources are culturally *ex situ*. The dimension of transnationalism of songs is an aspect of music making that warrants investigation given its significance in shaping Christian community and given the proliferation and use of western contemporary worship songs and non-western congregational songs by congregations in both western and Global South settings.[26]

With that in mind, what constructs can we use to satisfy the parameters of the various disciplines to frame the practice of church music in a postcolonial liturgical setting? Here I would like to offer a theological aesthetics paradigm for church music that draws from the hermeneutical typology commonly known as the Wesleyan Quadrilateral, proposed by Methodist scholar Albert C. Outler.[27] This preliminary framework served as the methodological approach I took to investigate the Thai Covenant Church in Thailand and the Methodist Church in Singapore mentioned earlier.[28]

The parameters are determined by the communities themselves, along with their leaders, and include embracing the principles of scriptural dogma, drawing on the wider collective wisdom of the Church, and respecting the lived experience of the community in its social cultural context—even as these factors are understood to be within the evolving consciousness of their identity as God's people. Such an effort challenges us to reconsider the assumption that there can only be one contextualization construct, even as it is also akin to putting together the pieces of a jigsaw puzzle! In fact, there are and will be countless varieties, all of them valid in their specific milieu. As Lutheran liturgical scholar Mark Bangert reminds us, "a culture's favored song style reflects and reinforces the kind of behavior considered essential to its work and to its core and prevailing social institutions."[29] Therefore for the practice of church music, having a consciousness of the social and cultural location is critical.

However, such an approach has yet to gain widespread acceptance in academic music circles. For instance, in imbuing the music of J. S. Bach with theological values, well-regarded aesthetics scholar Jeremy Begbie observes that "many Bach scholars are suspicious of theologians who turn their attention to this composer (and for that matter, any Christians eager to uncover the theological dimensions of Bach)."[30] Indeed, more often than not, the scholarship of music and theology tend to develop independently. To address this concern, perhaps the extra-referential nuance in music making can be critically scrutinized and its empire-laden nuance identified so that the concerns of the scholars in the field of music may be addressed. Much work lies ahead in this effort to have a theological aesthetics optic for church music that addresses postcolonial concerns especially regarding the tensions between the merits of indigenous practices and inherited western nuances.

BEYOND THE HORIZON

In recent decades, Christianity has experienced phenomenal growth in the Global South. According to the report *Christianity in Its Global Context*, the bulk of this growth in Asia is through conversion. In 2010, it was estimated that 8.2 percent of the continent's total population were Christians.[31] Despite this impressive growth record, Christianity remains a minority faith tradition in many parts of Asia. This means that Christians have to contend with other *in situ* faith traditions that have successfully grafted themselves to local cultures. How then might Christians locate their social identity in an ambivalent social cultural setting?

Identities, as American sociologist Gust Yep reminds us, are "based on socially constructed differences and social exclusion that create insider/outsider status separating individuals and groups within a hierarchical political system."[32] Therefore it should not be surprising that the current music corpus of many Christian denominations in Asia readily displays western traits, the result of past western influences, as a way of asserting their own particular Christian identity as a minority faith. While Jagessar and Burns might criticize this continued fascination with western nuances as a local appropriation of power which expresses empire, I contend that it is an inevitable phase within the current Asian social cultural milieu.[33] I posit that this phenomenon showcases a grassroots-lived Christian spirituality that is keenly aware of its social-cultural context where Christianity seeks to preserve ecclesial tradition and construct a viable Christian identity in socio-cultural settings that may be ambivalent and sometimes even hostile to Christianity. To that end, I argue that this is a necessary pubescent step of expressions and music making that will lead to further transformation. What is crucial to remember in this process is Heraclitus' reminder that "the only constant is change."

To that end, I offer three examples that demonstrate how recent music making is shaping the future of postcolonial liturgical celebration in tangible ways. First, the forthcoming publication *Let the Asian Church Rejoice!* collects 135 Asian congregational songs that have been sanctioned by several denominations and their affiliated seminaries in the region.[34] The editorial committee of the collection has attempted to take a broadly inclusive approach, a *via media* of lived experience, by not focusing exclusively on indigenous musical expressions. This hospitable approach is a representation of grassroots-lived expressions, even as the collection becomes an avenue that encourages the community to vest their Christian faith with local expressions. The hope is that such an approach will be well received by local constituencies, thus fostering renewed effort of contextualization in liturgical celebrations.

Second, Singapore contemporary worship songwriter, local pastor, and Integrity Asia artist Andrew Yeo invited a dozen emerging songwriters to gather and craft new songs under the banner Jubilee Song Writing Retreat over a two-day period. According to Yeo, the purpose of this event was to create local songs that address the socio-cultural reality of Singapore.[35] At the moment, local expressions are hampered by the lack of support from both ecclesial leadership and the music industry. This venture offers an opportunity for ecclesial affirmation, and music industry support hitherto non-existent for local Christian songwriters.

Finally, the World Association of Chinese Church Music will convene its 2016 conference in Penang, West Malaysia, with the theme, "Great

Commission and Church Music." The conference will feature a workshop on music writing. This is a significant departure from the organization's normative practice, which tended to focus on the adaptation and use of western resources in Chinese Christian communities rather than on nurturing grassroots-lived expressions. It remains to be seen if this significant shift by the organizing committee will heighten interest for the contextualization of church music and the creation of compositions that reflect local sensibilities.

These case studies demonstrate a trajectory of contextualization, an effort to articulate a grassroots-lived spirituality given shape by the sociocultural context and theological consciousness of the community. The case studies attest to the reality that meaning making in liturgical celebration is continually taking place and made visible in music making.

In conclusion, I reiterate that postcolonial liturgical celebration as reflected in the practice of music is not simply about the eradication of western idioms or nuances because they are vestiges of empire. It is also not simply about showcasing indigenous expressions because these challenge colonial power structure. Rather, postcolonial liturgical practices, especially the practice of music, calls for meaning making beyond the reception of its sonic phenomenon. It urges for a narrative that speaks to and for a specific social and cultural context. It is naïve to assume that indigenous music is the only kind of appropriate subaltern expression and hence to be championed as a just cause regardless of its relevance in the socio-cultural reality of the faith communities concerned.

In order for postcolonial liturgical practices to gain traction, a healthy tension needs to be observed between Christian dogma and inheritances and lived experiences within specific social cultural contexts. The decision about the pace for change rightly belongs to the local communities, and ought not to be dictated from outside. However, this does not mean that liturgical scholars should adopt the popular Star Trek's "prime directive" of non-interference. On the contrary, a postcolonial awareness recognizes the paucity of expertise in liturgical revitalization and leadership for the guiding of churches in the Global South through their rapidly changing social-cultural landscape. To that end, the Hippocratic Oath of "doing no harm" seems more appropriate for those providing leadership in liturgical innovation. Competent leadership that is prophetic yet sensitive to the constraints of the faith communities situated in ambivalent social cultural contexts is greatly needed. Vitally important for this approach is an awareness of music's fundamental role in the liturgy; it is a gift of God given to humanity coupled with understanding the dynamics of *lex orandi, lex credendi*.

BIBLIOGRAPHY

Amaladoss, Michael. *Beyond Inculturation: Can the Many Be One?* Delhi: Vidyajyoti Education & Welfare Society, and ISPCK, 1998.

Bangert, Mark Paul. "Dynamics of Liturgy and World Musics: A Methodology for Evaluation." In *Worship and Culture in Dialogue*, edited by S. Anita Stauffer, 183–203. Geneva: Lutheran World Federation, 1994.

Begbie. Jeremy S. *Resounding Truth: Christian Wisdom in the World of Music*. Grand Rapids, MI: Baker Academic, 2007.

———. *Theology, Music and Time*. Cambridge: Cambridge University Press, 2000.

Bell, Catherine. *Ritual Theory, Ritual Practice*, rev. ed. Oxford: Oxford University Press, 2009.

Bevans, Stephen B. *Models of Contextual Theology*, rev. ed. Maryknoll, NY: Orbis Books, 2002.

Bradshaw, Paul, and John Melloh, eds. *Foundations in Ritual Studies: A Reader for Students of Christian Worship*. Grand Rapids, MI: Baker Academic, 2007.

Busman, Joshua Kalin. "Worshipping 'With Everything': Musical Piety Beyond Language in Contemporary Evangelicalism." Paper presented at the Christian Congregational Music Conference, Rippon College, Cuddesdon, Oxford, UK, 2013.

Chan, Simon. *Grassroots Asian Theology: Thinking the Faith from the Ground Up*. Downers Grove, IL: InterVarsity Press, 2014.

Chibuko, Patrick Chukwudezie. *Paschal Mystery of Christ: Foundation for Liturgical Inculturation in Africa*. Frankfurt am Main: P. Lang, 1999.

Chupungco, Anscar. *Cultural Adaptation of the Liturgy*. New York: Paulist Press, 1982.

———. *Liturgical Inculturation: Sacramentals, Religiosity, and Catechesis*. Collegeville, MN: Liturgical Press, 1992.

———. *Liturgies of the Future: The Process and Methods of Inculturation*. New York: Paulist Press, 1989.

Coe, Shoki. "Contextualizing Theology." In *Mission Trends 3: Third World Theologies—Asian, African and Latin American Contributions to a Radical Theological Realignment in the Church*, edited by Gerald H. Anderson and Thomas F. Stransky, 19–24. New York: Paulist Press, 1976.

Driver, Tom F. *Liberating Rites: Understanding the Transformative Power of Ritual*. Charleston, SC: BookSurge Publishing, 2006.

Engle, Richard W. "Contextualization in Missions: A Biblical and Theological Appraisal." *Grace Theological Journal* 4:1 (1983): 85–107. Accessed January 15, 2015, www.biblicalstudies.org.uk/pdf/gtj/04–1_085.pdf.

Foley, Edward. *Ritual Music: Studies in Liturgical Musicology*. Beltsville, MD: Pastoral Press, 1996.

Geertz, Clifford. *The Interpretation of Cultures*. New York, NY: Basic Books, 1977.

Grimes, Ronald L. *Deeply into the Bone: Re-Inventing Rites of Passage*. Oakland, CA: University of California Press, 2002.

Hesselgrave, David J., and Edward Rommen. *Contextualization: Meanings, Methods, and Models*. Pasadena, CA: William Carey Library, 2013.

Hood, Mantle. *The Ethnomusicologist*. New York: McGraw-Hill Inc., 1971.

"How Great Is Our God" in Arabic. youtu.be/BR6wr_Fx450, and in Russian youtu.be/ KKbpfyoyWGk. Accessed on October 29, 2014.

Ingalls, Monique M. "Awesome in This Place: Sound, Space, and Identity in Contemporary North American Evangelical Worship." PhD diss., University of Pennsylvania, 2008.

Jagessar, Michael N., and Stephen Burns. *Christian Worship: Postcolonial Perspectives*. Oakville, CT: Equinox, 2011.

Johnson, Todd M., ed. *Christianity in Its Global Context, 1970–2020*. South Hamilton, MA: Center for the Study of Global Christianity, Gordon-Conwell Theological Seminary, 2013. Accessed January 31, 2015. www.gordonconwell.edu/resources/ documents/2ChristianityinitsGlobalContext.pdf.

Justice, Deborah R. "Sonic Change, Social Change, Sacred Change: Music and the Reconfiguration of American Christianity." PhD diss., Indiana University, 2012.

Kato, Byang H. "The Gospel, Cultural Context and Religious Syncretism." In *Let the Earth Hear His Voice: Official Reference Volume, Papers and Responses of the International Congress on World Evangelization, Lausanne, Switzerland*, ed. J. D. Douglas, 1216–23. Minneapolis: World Wide Publications, 1975.

Kubicki, Judith M. *Liturgical Music as Ritual Symbol: A Case Study of Jacques Berthier's Taizé Music*. Leuven: Peeters Publishers, 1999.

Kunst, Jaap. *Ethnomusicology: A Study of Its Nature, Its Problems, Methods and Representative Personalities to Which Is Added a Bibliography with Supplement*, 3rd ed. Leiden, South Holland: Martinus Nijhof, 1959.

Leaver, Robin A. *Luther's Liturgical Music: Principles and Implications*. Grand Rapids, MI: Eerdmans, 2007.

Lim, Swee Hong. *Giving Voice to Asian Christians: An Appraisal of the Pioneering Work of I-to Loh in the Area of Congregational Song*. Saarbrücken: Verlag Dr. Müller, 2008.

———, and Terry York. *Enactment: Cultivating an Identity for Christian Worship*. Fenton, MO: Morning Star Music Publishing, forthcoming.

Loh, I-to. "亚州教会音乐本社化之趣向：Yazhou jiaohui inyueh bensehua zhi quxiang (Toward Contextualization of Church Music in Asia)." *Theology and the Church*, 17, no. 1 (1986): 57–66.

———, ed. *Let the Asian Church Rejoice!* Singapore: Centre for the Study of Christianity in Asia of Trinity Theological College and Methodist School of Music, 2015.

Marti, Gerardo. *Worship Across the Racial Divide: Religious Music and the Multiracial Congregation*. New York: Oxford University Press, 2012.

McGann, Mary E. *Exploring Music as Worship and Theology: Research in Liturgical Practice*. Collegeville, MN: Liturgical Press, 2004.

Merriam, Alan P. *The Anthropology of Music*. Chicago: Northwestern University Press, 1964.

Nekola, Anna E. "Between This World and the Next: The Musical 'Worship Wars' and Evangelical Ideology in the United States, 1960–2005." PhD diss., University of Wisconsin-Madison, 2009.

Nettl, Bruno. *The Study of Ethnomusicology: Thirty One Issues and Concepts*, expanded ed. Urbana: University of Illinois Press, 2005.

Outler, Albert C. "The Wesleyan Quadrilateral in Wesley." *Wesleyan Theological Journal* 20, no. 1 (Spring 1985): 7–18.

Phan, Peter C. *Mission and Catechesis: Alexandre de Rhodes & Inculturation in Seventeenth-Century Vietnam*. Maryknoll, NY: Orbis Books, 1998.

Richards, Jeffrey. *Imperialism and Music: Britain 1876–1953*. Manchester: Manchester University Press, 2001.

Saliers, Don E. *Music and Theology*. Nashville, TN: Abingdon Press, 2007.

Shorter, Aylward. *Toward a Theology of Inculturation*. Maryknoll, NY: Orbis Books, 1989.

"Shout to the Lord in Thai." youtu.be/WPMlE1zvWTo, and in Swahili youtu.be/ifIDJqDAVZk. Accessed October 29, 2014.

Tan, Jonathan Y. *Christian Mission among the Peoples of Asia*. Maryknoll, NY: Orbis Books, 2014.

———. "Constructing an Asian Theology of Liturgical Inculturation from the Documents of the Federation of Asian Bishops Conferences (FABC). " *East Asian Pastoral Review* 36, no. 4 (1999). Accessed January 31, 2015. www.eapi.org.ph/resources/eapr/east-asian-pastoral-review-1999/volume-36–1999-no-4/constructing-an-asian-theology-of-liturgical-inculturation-from-the-documents-of-the-federation-of-asian-bishops-conferences-fabc/.

Turner, Victor Witter. *The Ritual Process: Structure and Anti-Structure*. Chicago, IL: Aldine Transaction, 1995.

Van Gennep, Arnold. *The Rites of Passage*. Chicago: University of Chicago Press, 1960.

Yep, Gust A. "Approaches to Cultural Identity: Personal Notes from an Autoethno-graphical Journey." In *Communicating Ethnic and Cultural Identity*, ed. Mary Fong and Rueyling Chuang, 69–82. Lanham, MD: Rowman & Littlefield, 2004.

NOTES

1. Simon Chan, *Grassroots Asian Theology: Thinking the Faith from the Ground Up* (Downers Grove, IL: InterVarsity Press, 2014).

2. Ibid., 41.

3. Shout to the Lord in Thai (youtu.be/WPMlE1zvWTo), and in Swahili (http://youtu.be/ifIDJqDAVZk); How Great Is Our God in Arabic (youtu.be/BR6wr_Fx450), and in Russian (youtu.be/KKbpfyoyWGk). These video media files were accessed on October 29, 2014.

4. Don E. Saliers, *Music and Theology* (Nashville, TN: Abingdon Press, 2007); Edward Foley, *Ritual Music: Studies in Liturgical Musicology* (Beltsville, MD: Pastoral Press, 1996); Jeremy S. Begbie, *Resounding Truth: Christian Wisdom in the World of Music* (Grand Rapids, MI: Baker Academic, 2007), 124–30; and Jeremy S. Begbie, *Theology, Music and Time* (Cambridge: Cambridge University Press, 2000).

5. Michael N. Jagessar and Stephen Burns, *Christian Worship: Postcolonial Perspectives* (Oakville, CT: Equinox, 2011), 53; c.f. Jeffrey Richards, *Imperialism and Music: Britain 1876–1953* (Manchester: Manchester University Press, 2001).

6. Martin Luther, *Luther's Works* (St Louis, MO: Concordia Publishing House, 1963), 53:321–23, cited in Robin A. Leaver, *Luther's Liturgical Music: Principles and Implications* (Grand Rapids, MI: Eerdmans, 2007), 70; Preface to Rhau's *Symphoniae* (1538), and *Luthers Werke: Kritische Gesamtausgabe* 50:368, 372.

7. Jagessar and Burns, *Christian Worship*, 56.

8. Jaap Kunst, *Ethnomusicology: A Study of Its Nature, Its Problems, Methods and Representative Personalities to Which Is Added a Bibliography with Supplement*, 3rd ed. (Leiden, South Holland: Martinus Nijhof, 1959); Mantle Hood, *The Ethnomusicologist* (New York: McGraw-Hill Inc., 1971); Alan P. Merriam, *The Anthropology of Music* (Chicago: Northwestern University Press, 1964); Bruno Nettl, *The Study of Ethnomusicology: Thirty One Issues and Concepts*, expanded ed. (Urbana: University of Illinois Press, 2005).

9. Joshua Kalin Busman, "Worshipping 'With Everything': Musical Piety Beyond Language in Contemporary Evangelicalism" (paper presented at the Christian Congregational Music Conference, Rippon College, Cuddesdon, Oxford, UK, 2013); Monique M. Ingalls, "Awesome in This Place: Sound, Space, and Identity in Contemporary North American Evangelical Worship" (PhD diss., University of Pennsylvania, 2008); Deborah R. Justice, "Sonic Change, Social Change, Sacred Change: Music and the Reconfiguration of American Christianity" (PhD diss., Indiana University, 2012); Gerardo Marti, *Worship Across the Racial Divide: Religious Music and the Multiracial Congregation* (New York: Oxford University Press, 2012); Anna E. Nekola, "Between This World and the Next: The Musical 'Worship Wars' and Evangelical Ideology in the United States, 1960–2005" (PhD diss., University of Wisconsin-Madison, 2009).

10. Arnold van Gennep, *The Rites of Passage* (Chicago: University of Chicago Press, 1960); Victor Witter Turner, *The Ritual Process: Structure and Anti-Structure* (Chicago, IL: Aldine Transaction, 1995); Clifford Geertz, *The Interpretation of Cultures* (New York, NY: Basic Books, 1977); Ronald L. Grimes, *Deeply into the Bone: Re-Inventing Rites of Passage* (Oakland, CA: University of California Press, 2002); Catherine Bell, *Ritual Theory, Ritual Practice*, rev. ed. (Oxford: Oxford University Press, 2009).

11. Shoki Coe, "Contextualizing Theology," in *Mission Trends 3: Third World Theologies — Asian, African and Latin American Contributions to a Radical Theological Realignment in the Church*, ed. Gerald H. Anderson and Thomas F. Stransky (New York: Paulist Press, 1976), 21–22. See also, Richard W. Engle, "Contextualization in Missions: A

Biblical and Theological Appraisal" in *Grace Theological Journal* 4:1 (1983): 85–107, accessed January 15, 2015, www.biblicalstudies.org.uk/pdf/gtj/04–1_085.pdf.

12. Byang H. Kato, "The Gospel, Cultural Context and Religious Syncretism," in *Let the Earth Hear His Voice: Official Reference Volume, Papers and Responses of the International Congress on World Evangelization, Lausanne, Switzerland,* ed. J. D. Douglas (Minneapolis: World Wide Publications, 1975), 1217.

13. I-to Loh, "亞州教会音乐本社化之趣向：Yazhou jiaohui inyueh bensehua zhi quxiang (Toward Contextualization of Church Music in Asia)," *Theology and the Church*, 17, no. 1 (1986): 57–66. This initial paradigm was subsequently refined. For further information, refer to Swee Hong Lim, *Giving Voice to Asian Christians: An Appraisal of the Pioneering Work of I-to Loh in the Area of Congregational Song* (Saarbrücken: Verlag Dr. Müller, 2008).

14. Stephen B. Bevans, *Models of Contextual Theology*, rev. ed. (Maryknoll, NY: Orbis Books, 2002); David J. Hesselgrave and Edward Rommen, *Contextualization: Meanings, Methods, and Models* (Pasadena, CA: William Carey Library, 2013); Aylward Shorter, *Toward a Theology of Inculturation* (Maryknoll, NY: Orbis Books, 1989).

15. The concept of *aggiornamento* is suitably explained by Bishop B. C. Butler on this web site, www.vatican2voice.org/3butlerwrites/aggiorna.htm; see the following web site for the complete document of *Sacrosanctum Concilium* as promulgated on December 4, 1963. www.vatican.va/archive/hist_councils/ii_vatican_council/documents/vat-ii_const_19631204_sacrosanctum-concilium_en.html; both sites accessed on January 31, 2015.

16. Anscar Chupungco, *Cultural Adaptation of the Liturgy* (New York: Paulist Press, 1982), *Liturgies of the Future: The Process and Methods of Inculturation* (New York: Paulist Press, 1989), *Liturgical Inculturation: Sacramentals, Religiosity, and Catechesis* (Collegeville, MN: Liturgical Press, 1992),

17. Michael Amaladoss, *Beyond Inculturation: Can the Many Be One?* (Delhi: Vidyajyoti Education & Welfare Society, and ISPCK, 1998); Peter C. Phan, *Mission And Catechesis: Alexandre de Rhodes & Inculturation in Seventeenth-Century Vietnam* (Maryknoll, NY: Orbis Books, 1998); Jonathan Y. Tan, *Christian Mission among the Peoples of Asia* (Maryknoll, NY: Orbis Books, 2014); Patrick Chukwudezie Chibuko, *Paschal Mystery of Christ: Foundation for Liturgical Inculturation in Africa* (Frankfurt am Main: P. Lang, 1999).

18. Paul Bradshaw and John Melloh, eds., *Foundations in Ritual Studies: A Reader for Students of Christian Worship* (Grand Rapids, MI: Baker Academic, 2007); Judith M. Kubicki, *Liturgical Music as Ritual Symbol: A Case Study of Jacques Berthier's Taizé Music* (Leuven: Peeters Publishers, 1999); Mary E. McGann, *Exploring Music as Worship and Theology: Research in Liturgical Practice* (Collegeville, MN: Liturgical Press, 2004); Tom F. Driver, *Liberating Rites: Understanding the Transformative Power of Ritual* (Charleston, SC: BookSurge Publishing, 2006).

19. Jagessar and Burns, *Christian Worship*, 33.

20. Chan, *Grassroots Asian Theology*, 24.

21. Musa Dube, "Reading for Decolonization (John 4:1–42)," in *John and Postcolonialism: Travel, Space, and Power,* ed. Musa Dube and Jeffrey L. Staley (London: Sheffield Academic Press, 2002), 56, cited in Jagessar and Burns, *Christian Worship*, 34.

22. Ladislav Nemet, "Inculturation in the FABC Documents," *East Asian Pastoral Review* 31 (1994): 93; cited in Jonathan Y. Tan, "Constructing an Asian Theology of Liturgical Inculturation from the Documents of the Federation of Asian Bishops Conferences (FABC)," *East Asian Pastoral Review* 36, no. 4 (1999), accessed January 31, 2015, www.eapi.org.ph/resources/eapr/east-asian-pastoral-review-1999/volume-36–1999-no-4/constructing-an-asian-theology-of-liturgical-inculturation-from-the-documents-of-the-federation-of-asian-bishops-conferences-fabc/.

23. Lim, *Giving Voice to Asian Christians*, 176–87.

24. This research will be featured in Swee Hong Lim and Terry York, *Enactment: Cultivating an Identity for Christian Worship* (Fenton, MO: Morning Star Music Publishing, forthcoming).

25. Ingalls, "Awesome in This Place," 300.

26. Becca Whitla and Swee Hong Lim will showcase their investigation of this genre of music at the Third Biennial Conference on Christian Congregational Music: Local and Global Perspective at Rippon College Cuddesdon, Oxford, UK.

27. Albert C. Outler, "The Wesleyan Quadrilateral in Wesley," *Wesleyan Theological Journal* 20, no. 1 (Spring 1985): 7–18.

28. For details of the construct, see Lim, *Giving Voice to Asian Christians,* 165–74.

29. Mark Paul Bangert, "Dynamics of Liturgy and World Musics: A Methodology for Evaluation," in *Worship and Culture in Dialogue,* ed. S. Anita Stauffer (Geneva: Lutheran World Federation, 1994), 195.

30. Begbie, *Resounding Truth,* 121.

31. See Todd M. Johnson, ed. *Christianity in Its Global Context, 1970–2020* (South Hamilton, MA: Center for the Study of Global Christianity, Gordon-Conwell Theological Seminary, 2013), 7, accessed January 31, 2015, www.gordonconwell.edu/resources/documents/2ChristianityinitsGlobalContext.pdf.

32. Gust A. Yep, "Approaches to Cultural Identity: Personal Notes from an Autoethnographic Journey," in *Communicating Ethnic and Cultural Identity,* ed. Mary Fong and Rueyling Chuang (New York: Rowman & Littlefield, 2004), 72.

33. For an in-depth discussion on the question of identity differentiation, see Lim, *Giving Voice to Asian Christians,* 169.

34. I-to Loh, ed. *Let the Asian Church Rejoice!* (Singapore: Centre for the Study of Christianity in Asia of Trinity Theological College and Methodist School of Music, 2015).

35. Email conversation with Pastor Andrew Yeo on February 11, 2015.

NINE

Praying Each Other's Prayers

An Interreligious Dialogue

Cláudio Carvalhaes

The Christian faith cannot be understood without its many ways of praying. Prayer is the very grammar of our faith, the way in which we Christians hear, speak, and understand. As human beings, we cannot escape language, and as Christians we cannot escape prayer. Prayer gives shape to who and what we are. Wittgenstein once said that "the limits of my language mean the limits of my world."[1] In the same way, the limits of our prayers are the limits of our faith. Faith is a complex and interconnected web of personal and collective struggles, hybridisms, behavior codes, voices, random gestures, historical developments, political battles, and the movements of the Spirit of God.

I would say that Christianity stands in between Babel and Pentecost, both in its biblical accounts and its contemporary engagements and enactments across the globe, building societies, dealing with desires and differences between Christians and people of other faiths/wisdom as well. From these ancient and contemporary places we create and recreate our prayers and our identities. In this endless becoming, we are called to expand the traditions of prayers in the history of the church just as we are to expand the limits of our faith and our world.

TRADITIONING OUR PRAYERS

Our prayers are a result of many people's traditions wrestling with the Christian faith in their own times and spaces. Tradition comes from the

Latin *traditio* and the Greek *paradosis*, both of which mean "to hand on." Having received this faith from our ancestors, we are now in charge of shaping it in accordance with our challenges and needs. Frederick Van Fleteren says that "texts from the tradition can legitimately be used as an occasion for entirely new thought."[2] Thus, it is our task, from the location in which we are placed, to engage the sources of our traditions, honor these traditions as they offer possibilities for justice and reshape these traditions according to a new perspective, one that entails both new and old thinking and actions from love. The purpose is not to make it what we want, but rather to bear witness to our people, how people of faith have responded to past challenges and see the ways in which God's love helps us respond to the situations we are living in.

The early church can help us here. It was Prosper of Aquitaine who introduced the saying, *lex orandi lex credendi,* meaning "the law of prayer is the law of belief." Alexander Hwang describes the ways in which Prosper of Aquitaine used it. Interpreting the passage of 1 Timothy 2:4, Prosper sees this passage "as expressed by the prayer of the Church: the 'Prayers of the faithful.' . . . Since the Church prays for the salvation of all people, *ut lex supplicandi statuat legem credendi.* It is the 'law of supplication' that determines the 'law of believing,' thus the theological controversy over the interpretation of this text has been settled by the practice of the Church."[3]

This moment in church history shows how prayer can fundamentally change belief, but also, how the practice of the church can orient life together. In continuing with Prosper of Aquitaine's concern for the prayers of supplication for all, the law of supplication for us today should be for a world without violence, for lives to have a fundamental value even before any sort of religious belief is present, and for the protection and restoration of the ecosystem. Our prayer of supplication must help us realize that we are all the *imago Dei* (image of God), and that we are responsible for each other and for our sons and daughters. Our prayers of supplication for our time are prayers for the survival of every person, especially the poor. In this way, our prayers of supplication done every Sunday and every day must say, "Black lives matter! We offer supplications for them!" Our prayers must say, "We are killing the earth and we need to restore its sources and rhythms of life!" Our prayers must say, "There are people exploiting and subjugating other people, oppressing and killing people of other faiths, and we need salvation for all!"

When we pray these prayers of supplication, we are generating the mutual learning and social sustenance of hope! This work of hope is also a way of engaging our Christian traditions. Orlando Espín talks about traditioning:

> How can Christians tradition their hope without adulterating its subversive challenge? A hope that subverts all that humans regard as de-

finitive has been one of the crucial forces driving the complex of traditioning processes that creates and has sustained the religion we call Christianity.[4]

Against what he calls "Christianity's historical inclination to 'doctrinify' the subversive hope," he proposes that "Christian traditioning can (even as it liberates)—witness interculturally to the subversive hope that lies at the heart of Christianity."[5]

Our commitment is thus not to doctrines, but to our brothers and sisters in need, to the care of the earth, and to brothers and sisters of different faiths living in destitution and fear. Our prayers are a commitment to our neighborhoods, our villages and our communities. Our commitment is to create networks of hope, through prayer, belief and ethical actions, combining the laws of *orandi, credenda et vivendi.*

Our contexts beg for us to recreate the ecumenical connections and relations, moving away from the model of denominational self-sufficiency and distinctive cultural identities, to a model of ecclesio-interconnectedness and intersectionality of identities as if other faiths are to be seen as distinctive instead of deeply engaged. We cannot afford living with one worship book, one prayer book, and one hymnal book. We are called to tradition our worship, prayers, songs, and lives in and through a vast array of identities and sources, so as to be empowered by the Spirit in a multiplicity of God's revelations. Moreover, we are called to connect with our brothers and sisters from different faith and religious traditions, and this chapter seeks to engage the possibilities of that connection.

EXPANDING THE CIRCLES OF TRADITION:
INTERRELIGIOUS PRAYERS

The Dalai Lama once invited Riverside Church of New York for a conversation, and I was part of the group from Union Theological Seminary that created a ritual for his talk. We had art and artists, various symbols and music, but none of them was religious, perhaps because of the fear of superimposing Christian sources upon an already Christian worship space. On the way to the pulpit, the Dalai Lama bowed down to the cross and made a sign of reverence. That was a huge gesture with deep meaning!

On another occasion at Union Theological Seminary, Farid Esack, a Muslim scholar and liberation theologian, recited his Muslim prayers in St. James Chapel in Arabic, and people of different faiths and religious traditions were all there with him. Were we only watching? Were we praying with him by praying through him?

We must ask again: Can we pray each other's prayers? Prayers are the containers of our innermost desires, the treasures of our communication with God, and the beliefs that we hold onto as the source of our identity as Christians. If we are to say somebody else's prayers, are we uttering somebody else's desires and speaking a new tongue? The potentially scary and unsettling feeling between people praying somebody else's prayers is a reality, and the risks are high. Why don't we just leave prayers alone, so that each tradition can say them for themselves? This connection can cause more harm than healing, one might say.

Nonetheless, a possible yes is filled with challenges and apparent impossibilities. In some ways, it might seem impossible, and it might not even be the right thing to do. The main problem for this conversation can be summed up in one word: appropriation. We must be aware of the interconnection of power, history and colonization, and the continuing appropriation and misappropriation of somebody else's theologies, celebrations, and traditions. We must be aware that when we are borrowing, or even making somebody else's prayers our own, we might be continuing the practice of colonial appropriation. So the dangers may be insurmountable, and the perils all around us.

Thus, at the onset of our trajectory of praying together, we must announce in a loud prayer voice (in symbolic and perhaps even concrete ways as well) that when we stand before somebody else from a different religion, we are marked by our inherent inability to access this other religion. Not only are we likely unfamiliar with the core of a particular religion, but we also don't have the practice or the particular life of another religion drenched in its blessings, gifts and demands, all of which we are trying to connect with in some way or another. The irreducibility of somebody else's religion, the unavoidable appropriation of my sister's and brother's prayers and meaning, are always at stake. We must be aware of all of the colonial traces inside of us that want to repeat the trauma, as well as the control, of the colonizing conscious and unconscious process. To avoid this danger, we should search for social gatherings and rituals that will help us pray each other's prayers in each other's presence. Appropriation is the use of somebody else's prayers and stories without the presence of the other, without care for the other, without commitment to the life of somebody else, without engagement in each other's lives. This chapter is exploring the possibility of living together through our prayers.

We must begin by considering that when religious people utter a prayer, they have in mind some sense of their deity, their god, and they are often loyal to this god and to this god alone. Praying somebody else's prayer could mean offering themselves to a different god, being entangled in different religious practices, and this offer and practice could mean betrayal for some religious people. It could also lead to a lack of strong faith and even a commitment to a god and a community that is not their own. That's because the sense/reasoning/understanding of prayer is often marked by an exclusionary commitment to one's own God. Thus, in order to pray each other's prayers, we must assume that there is indeed some sense of disruption, or to use a better word, an expansion of our commitments. Therefore we must ask: Can we keep our oath to Jesus Christ if we pray to Buddha, or Allah, or an orixá? Is the other totally other? Are there possible intersection points between our language and gesture of the divine?

In my Christian upbringing, I was taught to consider people of other religions as the targets of my evangelism. They were all going to hell without knowing it, and I was chosen by God to save them. They were also an obstacle to the conquering Christianity in which I believed, a Christianity that caused me to live in a jumble of compassion, fear, and anger. The binary *they versus us* provided me with the poles that shaped my thinking. It was much later that I learned that people of other religions could also be my brothers and sisters, and that their way to worship God, their God, was to be respected. I even learned I needed to engage in dialogue with them. However, it was only within the last decade that I realized that this dialogue entails a much deeper commitment on my part. In order to engage in dialogue, I had to go a step further and venture into a conversation that demanded not only respect and acceptance, but also presence and a willingness to turn what was foreign to me into something familiar. But how could I do that?

Timothy Wright's book *No Peace without Prayer: Encouraging Muslims and Christians to Pray Together, A Benedictine Approach* can help us here.[6] Wright starts from a Benedictine understanding of spirituality, and engages a Muslim spiritual perspective in order to find common ground between the two. A deep connection emerges out of this dialogue, because the author is not afraid to learn about the Muslim tradition while also exploring a deeper understanding of his own tradition. In this double commitment, Wright brings forth common issues such as healing, remembering God, living in the presence of God, spiritually experiencing God, understanding God's revelation and human responses to it, and finding ways that communities can experience and support each other through a dialogue on spirituality. One very simple way he engages these two religions is through daily prayers. Christians and Muslims pray several times during the day, and each prayer has some specific requirements to be remembered.

Pairing the daily prayers of Christians and Muslims shows that these two forms of faithful practice can be done in such a way that each religion can enlighten, empower, and enrich the other. At the end of the book, Wright says, "This advice offered here from the Christian and Muslim viewpoints is helpful: it starts to build bridges before any dialogue can start. This selected group of themes provides some guidance. At one level, it is the commitment of faith by the participants that will take the dialogue forward."[7]

The key aspect of any interreligious conversation is open engagement with the specificities of each faith. Fear is a monster that keeps us disconnected from each other. We are bombarded daily with news that portrays people who do not look like us as scary and as potential destroyers not only of our faith, but of ourselves and our world. Thus, in order to engage with someone else's faith, one needs to have a more mature personal faith, trusting that God's love is bigger than the differences of one's neighbor. For Christians, it is because we are so loved by God that we can engage in any interreligious dialogue. Also, because this love of God demands that we love our neighbor, we lose the fear of approaching, getting closer, offering ourselves in love and care. This unwavering love and this precious grace received are the ground from which we can go out into the world and work and hope for the restoration of the earth and the empowerment of our neighbors. For love sets us free, gives us freedom to see and realize similarities and differences of our faith in relation to an other.

Any good interreligious dialogue must start with the full affirmation of one's faith. From there, we must find space between us for a(n) un/common ground, a moveable place where we might kneel or dance, praying together.

From this place, we can either pray our own prayers with somebody else, or, if we are able to venture a little further, we might be taught how to pray someone else's prayers. As I try to pray somebody else's prayer, my challenge has to do more with my own trust in my God in this process rather than the fear that somebody else's prayer will do something to me, my relations and my commitments. In the economy of my community's faith, will God still relate to me if I pray to a God who does not have the name of the one to whom I usually pray? The ecos/oikos/house of God in the Christian faith contains a nómos/law that embraces everything. Nothing and nobody are outside of the love/house and nomos of God. In this loving house, we have to strive for peace and mutual dignity and recognize that in this space, the name of our utmost desire will be blessed and anointed.

In this house, my supplications that once were for the salvation of other religious people now include myself. We need each other, and our common prayers of supplication are a sustaining part of this "inescapable network of mutuality," as Martin Luther King Jr. would say.[8] Mutual salvation, collective redemption, common solidarity, one world house for all? Perhaps! We can indeed look at our Christian faith and create the conditions of possibility that would allow this sharing of prayers to happen.

MY EXPERIENCE WITH CANDOMBLÉ AND THE
CHRISTIAN–AFRICAN RELIGIOUS DIALOGUE

In order to wear this garment of mutuality, in order to tradition the hope of the Christian faith, I want to pray with Afro-Brazilians. By doing that, I believe that I, along with others, will be able to honor, love, and restore a word of justice to the black people of my country. Candomblé is a religion that came with Africans to Brazil, and continued to be practiced by them throughout the era of slavery and colonialism. As an oral religion, it was able to survive and continue its practices, even though it has been changed and turned into an indigenous Brazilian religion.

The history of Brazil cannot be told without remembering the history of slavery and the white manufacturing of racism that is so rampant in the country's society today. That history is embedded in the daily lives of people in myriad ways. For instance, I grew up thinking that every African religion (surely made up by black people) was a creation of the devil, and that every one of its practices was infested by demons. I was taught to evangelize its practitioners and cast away their demons. Along with my white Christian religious education from the United States, there was a racist underpinning that gave support to my hatred and deepest fear (of what/whom?). This same hatred and fear has been institutionalized in exclusionary ways within Brazilian society, and new Pentecostal churches' mission goals include the destruction of a certain number of African American houses of worship.

It was in Salvador, Bahia, the Brazilian state with the country's largest black population, that I discovered that this hatred and fear lives in my body, a realization by which I have been forever transformed. While there, I acted as the interpreter for Professor Emilie M. Townes's class from Union Theological Seminary. During our visit, we were supposed to engage with and meet practitioners of Afro-Brazilian religions and in one of these visits, we were scheduled to go to a Candomblé worship service. There, the *mãe de santo* (the mother of the saint) was supposed to throw beads and bring the voices of the Orixás to each student, and I was in charge of translating what the Orixás wanted to tell the person. However, when we were getting into the van, my body froze and I couldn't move. For a couple of minutes, I didn't have any control over my body. One friend, a Brazilian Methodist pastor who was also a member of the Candomblé, told me I was going to be alright. Slowly, my body went back to normal, and I was able to get in the van and go to the worship space. Wondering why my body froze unexpectedly, I realized that while my mind had made the journey from wanting to save this group to desiring to learn with and from them, my body was still dominated by a narrative of fear. My body had learned for so many years that I should fear these people, that they were possessed by demons, and that I could die in their presence. My body was telling me, "I am not going to expose us to this danger!" This experience changed my life, my scholarship, and my way of thinking about interreligious dialogue.

From that day on, I have been challenged to think about interreligious dialogue from the perspective of religious rituals, of presence in practices, and not just from a sociological, theological, or even scriptural viewpoint. It is very difficult to engage varying religious practices, for the spaces in which they occur can be more dangerous due to their religious codes and specificities. For example, in some festivities, if I wear anything black, I can disrupt the movement of the Orixás.

For me to engage in this dialogue is to recover what I have destroyed and to engage in a national movement of recovering the Brazilian soul, honoring African Brazilians (who are more than 50 percent of our population) and protecting not only the Axé people, that is, the people who belong to the Afro-Brazilian religions, but also the perilous lives of Afro-Brazilians in general. This elimination of the black people in Brazil continues. Black boys are being killed every day throughout Brazil. Thus to engage in an inter-religious dialogue has a more expansive way of being in solidarity with the black people.

In a more theoretical perspective, Diego Irarrázaval offers four main points of dialogue within Christian–African religions: (1) to celebrate and to think, meaning that the celebratory ways of African religions are ways of thinking, of constructing their lives, and recreating the world; (2) to identify ourselves and our continent as African-American, calling ourselves Africans so as to help us embrace the life, history, and the religious elements of the African religion as common to us all; (3) to celebrate the mystery of the African way, which is the celebration of the sacred in our bodies, and to realize that the body is a privileged focus/focal point for the revelation of the sacred; and 4) to wrestle with syncretism and belongings.[9] Given Brazil's history of slavery and its pervasive racism, can we provide a space of reconciliation and hospitality through common prayers? We might think about it using a certain common pneumatology.

IT IS THE SPIRIT THAT MAKES US PRAY—HOLY SPIRIT/AXÉ

Every beginning depends upon the Spirit, both for Candomblé and for many Christians.[10] It is the Holy Spirit that initiates God's love in us and prepares and empowers us to live this love in the world. Communal acts of praise and work dedicated to God are always a response to God's love, generosity, and demands. For Candomblé, the Orixás and other entities move the world's energies and make us respond to their calls and demands.

Thus, the very reason for worship in both the Christian and Candomblé faiths is the movement and call of the Spirit/Axé in people's lives. Thus, prayer is an act of praise and gratitude. Because both people depend on the work of the Axé/Holy Spirit, it is to God that people go with petitions.

In both religions, there is common food/common good for the people—that is, Eucharist and food offering—and under the power of the Holy Spirit and Axé, people gather as strangers and become a family. The presence of the Holy Spirit offers forgiveness, healing, and reconciliation through common worship, meal and bath, even if continuously interrupted by fear, hatred, anxiety, injustice, death, and the perils and conflicts of the world. For Candomblé, the presence of Axé also balances the level of bad and good energies in the local communities through offerings and dances.

Since God is the one who manifests Godself where God wants, and makes a covenant with whomever God wants, we are the ones, inspired by the Holy Spirit, to create channels for God's grace to be experienced in ways that we may not yet have been able to experience. Thus, we are trying to find ways in which the covenant of God can be expanded and in which we can offer hospitality to people of other faiths. We are the ones who become channels of God's incarnation.

As practitioners of Candomblé, the communal living out of the faith involves channels of blessings and healings to the community. The dances and offerings are forms of sacrament where the Orixás organize the world of the living, protecting those who are searching to balance their energy and making others pay for the unbalance of the energies brought about by their actions.

In worship, Christians have their Bibles, sing their songs, and pray their prayers, praying "Come Spirit Come." However, in this *dangerous* prayer, since the coming of the Spirit might do something we don't want or like, the Spirit can arrive as the coming of a stranger, a guest, one whom we were not expecting or even desiring. Once we pray "Come Spirit Come," the movement of the Spirit can no longer be controlled. After our prayer, we might have to welcome members of the Candomblé faithful, dressed in their white dresses, dancing and singing, asking for the Orixás to come and move energies through the primal energy, Axé.[11] Once the Holy Spirit takes over, we must follow.

The Holy Spirit and the Axé are the moving forces that establish, shift, and balance the world and all of our respective universes. The Holy Spirit and Axé can transform whatever they want and are the very source of life. Christians and Yorubá are totally dependent on their movement, and they are the sources we tap into so that we can engage each other around the table and be able to expand our religious horizons.

The engagement with Axé and the Holy Spirit can become a vital theological response to the globalized world we live in. The increasing sense of dislocation marked by the growing flow of people around the globe, the hybridity of immigration, the accumulation of capital in the hands of fewer than 500 people around the world, the trafficking of people, brutality against women, shifting labor markets, and the growing diversity of new local neighborhoods are just some of the signs that demand our theologies and communities deal with the constant flow of identities and "mobile personalities."[12] The force, potency, and agency of the Holy Spirit/Axé can help us engage these challenges and dismantle deadly world realities. The Holy Spirit/Axé can also help us find plural identities, not in the de-ritualizing of our religions' rituals, but rather, in the renewing processes of the ritualization (the expansion of our rituals) of our beliefs as we encounter others along the way.

The Spirit of God shows itself through movements of unfolding openness and alterity, movements marked by dis/placements of generosities. The Spirit of God must be seen in my responsibility to myself, but always in relation to somebody else, even if this somebody else throws me into an abyss of inescapable inner and outer workings and challenges. The presence of *somebody else* at the table of Jesus Christ connects me to unexpected obligations toward this other and that person's people, a people that I might not have paid attention to until that moment. Thus, the movement of the Spirit in us can be a call to us to pay attention to somebody else.

From this place of unexpected openness given by the Spirit, Christians can find common ground to welcome practitioners of Candomblé. Common elements for a theology of the Spirit in Christianity and Candomblé include: (1) the Holy Spirit/Axé have a deep connection with the body, and without our bodies there is no community. In both religions, the Spirit/Orixás can possess bodies. (2) The Holy Spirit and the Axé/Orixás help us not only deal with our daily life, our struggles, our wounds, but also give us strength, wisdom and vision to go through life. (3) The Holy Spirit/Axé always engage with a guest or visitor. (4) The Holy Spirit/Axé are deeply connected with creation. (5) It is the Holy Spirit/Axé who create and sustain the gathered communities; and (6) The presence of the Spirit/Axé is manifested in both worship and work.

Candomblé and Christian believers pray to the Holy Spirit and to Orixás for guidance and wisdom in their daily lives. Both groups bless the Spirit, they walk in their daily life in ways pleasing to the Holy Spirit/ entities. Both religions have a deep commitment to the transformation of society through their beliefs and practices. For both religions, God is always doing something through us. Or, using J. Edgar Bruns' words, "God is the doing of something"[13] in our religions.

It is in, under, through and around the Spirit/entities in our diverse bodies and rituals that we can recreate our daily and common life within and among ourselves. In both religions, God/the Orixás are doing something in and through us, and we are also doing something in and through our liturgies/worship, recreating the world, recreating life. As Jaci Maraschin says, "It is in the body that we are spirit especially when our bodies are ready to recreate life. Let us, then, make of our bodies our main instrument of worship."[14] Open to the unknown movements of the Spirit and the Axé, we move along together.

In order to pray together, Christians first need to walk toward adherents of Candomblé, combat the racism that forms most of Brazil, and undo the demonization of the Axé people. This movement is what Derrida calls a *certain pas*, a certain step, moving from one place to another. The movement forward entails working within a given context. In general, in Brazil, depending on the specificities of each local context, this work would entail:

1. Christians starting to pray for Axé people in their own worship services. That they pray not for their salvation but for the continuation of their long history of gifts and blessings to Brazil.
2. Christians surrounding places of Axé worship to protect those inside.
3. Christians visiting the worship places of others and learning how practitioners of Candomblé pray and dance, and what their offerings mean.
4. Christians inviting Axé into their worship spaces to share prayers and common worship celebrations.
5. Christians and Axé getting together for a meal and to share stories.
6. Both Christians and Axé teaching each other daily prayers for comfort, protection, blessings for the house, a new job, a birth, an illness, and other life events.

By loving the Axé people, Christians will learn that love can cast away fear. By loving and creating bridges of connections, dismantling our racism, decolonizing our faith, disrupting our theologies and undoing our fears, we might be able to pray together. Or, by praying together, we might be better equipped to love, and thus, to dismantle our racism, disrupt our theologies and undo our fears. The need for this interreligious dialogue is not for the sake of the dialogue itself. Rather, it must be done for the sake of life together!

CONCLUSION: WORSHIP COMES AFTER

If we are to practice/think/form a ministry that can create possibilities for people to pray somebody else's prayers and to live interreligiously through rituals, we must know that rituals/liturgies never stand alone. Often, rituals are a secondary event in the life of a community. People gather because of friendship, because of a particular issue, because they need to find small forms of social organization. A community gathers because of a need for a place to be, to relate, to search for meaning, to help and to be protected. Thus, it is our mutual responsibility to each other that brings us together. After that comes our rituals and worship, our mutual prayers and singing.

Furthermore, in order to pray together, we need to dance and eat together and get to know each other's lives and faith. We must enter into a common interreligious mystagogical place where we teach and learn together how and what and where to pray. By decentering our religious education, and decolonizing our faith, we will be able to shift the places of trust, and thus the place of God, from structures of power that set us apart to places of mutual confidence in local structures This can be accomplished through the resources we have received and with what we already have in our communities.

Prayer is about getting to know who we are and what our common situation is so that we can offer supplications for each other. Paulo Freire remarks on education—"Things to know, how to know, what to know, for what and who to know and therefore against who and what to know—"[15] can also be said about prayer: "Things to pray, how to pray, what to pray, for what and whom to pray and therefore against whom and what to pray." This is our mission as people of faith!

Releasing our fear, we might begin to see that not only are there points of connections between these two religions, but also fundamental, varied views of the world and gifts of life. Perhaps the Christian catechumenal process could include the stories and the dances and songs of those who practice Candomblé. Perhaps adherents of Candomblé could learn some of the Christian prayers.

Everything starts with the praxis of the people, its challenges and needs. We start with life and friendships. From there, people engage cultural and faith traditions, other important sources, and then move, step beyond themselves toward each other. The place to meet is in the middle, where nobody owns anything and where our prayers can then become a common place of sharing and learning. There must be a certain step beyond ourselves toward somebody else. We are called to cross borders and limits. This step beyond ourselves is a Christian demand, a step that portrays our faith, a movement toward the world and its people.[16]

The step beyond and not beyond is both a step toward somebody and a step of the other toward me; this is a movement toward my life to which I must respond. Alterity is all around us when we pray. My prayers of supplication can be this very step beyond and not beyond, a movement that invites my neighbor and exposes myself to a situation where I am prohibited to shut down, to live in my own bubble. My prayers are a way to care for the world and all that is in it. Shall we pray?

BIBLIOGRAPHY

Betcher, Sharon V. "Take My Yoga upon You: A Spiritual Pli for the Global City." In *Polydoxy: Theology of Multiplicity and Relation*, edited by Catherine Keller and Laurel Schneider, 57–80. New York: Routledge, 2010.

Caputo, John D. *The Prayers and Tears of Jacques Derrida: Religion without Religion.* Bloomington: Indiana University Press, 1997.

Carvalhaes, Cláudio. *Eucharist and Globalization: Redrawing the Borders of Eucharistic Hospitality.* Oregon, OR: Pickwick, 2013.

Derrida, Jacques. *Aporias*, trans. Thomas Dutoit. Stanford: Stanford University Press, 1993.

———. *Parages*, trans. Tom Conley, James Hulbert, and Avital Ronell. Stanford: Stanford University Press, 2010.

———. *Psyche: Inventions of the Other*, trans Catherine Porter. Stanford: Stanford University Press, 2008.

Espín, Orlando O. *Idol and Grace: On Traditioning and Subversive Hope.* Maryknoll, MY: Orbis Books, 2014.

Freire, Paulo. *Cartas À Guiné-Bissau. Registros de uma experiencia em processo.* Coleção O Mundo, Hoje, vol. 22. Rio de Janeiro: Editora Paz e Terra, 1978.

Hwang, Alexander Y. "Prosper, Cassian, and Vincent in the Rule of Faith in the Augustinian Controversy." In *Tradition and the Rule of Faith in the Early Church: Essays in Honor of Joseph T. Lienhard, S.J.*, edited by Ronnie J. Rombs and Alexander Y. Hwang, 68–85. Pittsboro, NC: Catholic University of America Press, 2010.

Irarrázaval, Diego. "Salvação Indígena and Afro-Americana." In *Teologia Pluralista Libertadora Intercontinental*, ASETT, EATWOT, edited by José M. Vigil, Luiza E. Tomita, and Marcelo Barro, 61–88. São Paulo: Paulinas, 2008.

King, Martin Luther, Jr. "Letter from Birmingham Jail." www.uscrossier.org/pullias/wp-content/uploads/2012/06/king.pdf.

Maraschin, Jaci. "The Transient Body: Sensibility and Spirituality." Paper presented at the event "Liturgy and Body," Union Theological Seminary, New York, October 20, 2003.

Prandi, Reginaldo. *Os Candomblés de São Paulo.* São Palo: Hucitec-EDUSP, 1991.

Van Fleteren, Frederick. "Interpretation, Assimilation, Appropriation: Recent Commentators on Augustine and His Tradition." In *Tradition and the Rule of Faith in the Early Church: Essays in Honor of Joseph T. Lienhard, S.J.*, edited by Ronnie J. Rombs and Alexander Y. Hwang, 270–85. Pittsboro, NC: Catholic University of America Press, 2010.

Wittgenstein, Ludwig. *Tractatus Logico-Philosophicus*, trans. C. K. Ogden. New York: Dover Publications, 1998.

Wright, Timothy. *No Peace without Prayer: Encouraging Muslims and Christians to Pray Together, A Benedictine Approach.* Collegeville, MN: Liturgical Press, 2013.

NOTES

1. Ludwig Wittgenstein, *Tractatus Logico-Philosophicus*, trans. C. K. Ogden (New York: Dover Publications, 1998), 5.6., 68.

2. Frederick Van Fleteren, "Interpretation, Assimilation, Appropriation: Recent Commentators on Augustine and His Tradition," in *Tradition and the Rule of Faith in the Early Church: Essays in Honor of Joseph T. Lienhard, S.J.*, ed. Ronnie J. Rombs and Alexander Y. Hwang (Pittsboro, NC: Catholic University of America Press, 2010), 270–85.

3. Alexander Y. Hwang, "Prosper, Cassian, and Vincent in the Rule of Faith in the Augustinian Controversy," in Rombs and Hwang, *Tradition and the Rule of Faith*, 68–85.

4. Orlando O. Espín, *Idol and Grace: On Traditioning and Subversive Hope* (Maryknoll, MY: Orbis Books, 2014), xv.

5. Ibid., xvi.

6. Timothy Wright, *No Peace without Prayer: Encouraging Muslims and Christians to Pray Together, A Benedictine Approach* (Collegeville, MN: Liturgical Press, 2013).

7. Ibid., 312

8. Martin Luther King, Jr., "Letter from Birmingham Jail," www.uscrossier.org/pullias/wp-content/uploads/2012/06/king.pdf.

9. Diego Irarrázaval, "Salvação Indígena and Afro-Americana," in *Teologia Pluralista Libertadora Intercontinental*, ASETT, EATWOT, ed. José M. Vigil, Luiza E. Tomita, and Marcelo Barro (São Paulo: Paulinas, 2008), 69.

10. This part of the chapter is a version of what was first published in my book, Cláudio Carvalhaes, *Eucharist and Globalization: Redrawing the Borders of Eucharistic Hospitality* (Eugene, OR: Pickwick, 2013), 203–41.

11. "Axé is the primal force, life principle, sacred force of the Orixás . . . is power, is charisma, it is the root that comes from the ancestors; we can gain and lose Axé, Axé is a gift from the gods; . . . it is above all, the very house of the Candomblé, the temple, the roça (place where you plant for and with your family) the whole tradition." See Reginaldo Prandi, *Os Candomblés de São Paulo* (São Palo: Hucitec-EDUSP, 1991), 103–4.

12. Sharon V. Betcher, "Take My Yoga upon You: A Spiritual Pli for the Global City," in *Polydoxy: Theology of Multiplicity and Relation*, ed. Catherine Keller and Laurel Schneider (New York: Routledge, 2010), 58.

13. Cited by Betcher, "Take My Yoga upon You," 72.

14. Jaci Maraschin, "The Transient Body: Sensibility and Spirituality," (paper presented at the event "Liturgy and Body," Union Theological Seminary, New York, October 20, 2003).

15. Paulo Freire, *Cartas À Guiné-Bissau. Registros de uma experiencia em processo.* Coleção O Mundo, Hoje, vol. 22 (Rio de Janeiro: Editora Paz e Terra, 1978), carta no 3.

16. Derrida defines this step: "The crossing of borders always announces itself according to the movement of a certain step [*pas*] . . ." This step entails a step beyond and not beyond. John Caputo explains it: "The step not beyond is the necessity and impossibility of approaching the other; it means to approach the inappropriable, to approach without appropriation." Jacques Derrida, *Aporias*, trans. Thomas Dutoit (Stanford: Stanford University Press, 1993), 23. John D. Caputo, *The Prayers and Tears of Jacques Derrida: Religion without Religion* (Bloomington: Indiana University Press, 1997), 84; See also, Jacques Derrida, *Psyche: Inventions of the Other*, trans Catherine Porter (Stanford: Stanford University Press, 2008); Jacques Derrida, *Parages*, trans. Tom Conley, James Hulbert, and Avital Ronell (Stanford: Stanford University Press, 2010).

III

Interfaith Collaboration

TEN

Postcolonial Interreligious Learning

*A Reflection from a North American
Christian Perspective*

Sheryl A. Kujawa-Holbrook

Postcolonialism asserts the right of all peoples to the same material and cultural well-being, argues that the nations of Africa, Asia, and Latin America are in subordination and economic inequality to North America and Europe, and contests this disparity.[1] A key aspect of postcolonial interreligious learning, then, is about implementing strategies that stand against imperialism and critically addressing the colonial biases of religion, the academy, and faith communities with a view to making them more receptive and empowering to global cultures and epistemologies. Indeed, some scholars argue that the terms *religion* and *religions* are constructed categories resultant from the imperial, colonial past, and thus are of limited use as the basis for a creative future.[2] As postcolonial theologian Kwok Pui-lan suggests, "A postcolonial theology of religious difference will also attend to the transformation of religious symbols and institutions in migration, exile, diaspora, and transnationalism."[3] Just as scholars on the margins have long had to do, those engaged in interreligious learning need to take seriously how postcolonial values inform our practices, lest our attempts to foster interreligious learning re-inscribe or intensify inequities between religious groups.

A CHRISTIAN PERSPECTIVE

As a Christian priest, a scholar, and a practitioner of interreligious studies, I enter the conversation as a white, North-American, heterosexual woman, and assume that these social identities influence my work of engaging with those from different traditions and contexts. Christianity is my spiritual home; I am also moved by the beauty of other religious traditions. As a Christian, I believe that it is not only possible to be a disciple of Jesus without disparaging other religions, and I believe it is *integral* to discipleship. As I read Jesus' encounters with religious "others"—Samaritans, the Roman officer, the Syro-phoenician woman, and other marginalized people—I aspire to the example he set for his disciples. Consciously and unconsciously, I have learned my religion, the religion of others, and my perspectives on the world via western schools and faith communities. While I have experienced marginalization mostly due to gender and social class, my life experience is one of privilege, that of the colonizer, rather than the colonized. It is from this social location whereby I reflect on interreligious learning.

For Christians engaged in the postcolonial practice of interreligious learning, a critical understanding of "mission" throughout the centuries is key. Though earlier views of "missions" as sending Christians to far-off lands to convert non-believers and spread civilization have been superseded, there remains a significant lack of clarity among western Christians, in general, about our relationships with the Christian majority in other parts of the world, as well as other religious traditions. "Christian mission has been part of the colonial project of destroying people's culture and self-esteem," writes the late Letty M. Russell, a Christian feminist theologian. "And yet, God's mission of sharing God's love and life calls us in this postcolonial time to "witness to God's justice and care" in every place and for all people."[4] Russell's work also emphasizes that gender inequity and sexual control were part of colonial practice, and thus incompatible with God's mission inclusive of all people.

For those like myself who are western Christians, how far are we prepared to "decolonize" ourselves and our ministries? Postcolonial practices of interreligious learning raise questions about embodied human relationships on the personal, interpersonal, institutional, cultural, and global levels, and questions which ask, "Whose history and experience really counts?" For much of its history, the United States was considered a majority white Protestant country with significant religious diversity. However by the early twenty-first century, the United States moved from being a religiously diverse white Protestant country to being a genuinely pluralistic[5] nation in which no single religious group has a majority.[6] Are we willing to shift our self-perceptions beyond the West to the majority global church? Are we prepared in our formation practices (with all ages) to acknowledge, along with the beauty of our tradition, the injustices perpetrated against some Christians, as well as other religious traditions, in the name of faith? Are we prepared to shift our attention and look at religions from an international perspective, seeing beyond the English-speaking world? Are we able to eliminate outdated frameworks such as "World Religions" and instead recognize the billions of adherents of other religious groups?

The recent fiftieth anniversary of the opening of Vatican II reminds us of the complicated history of the relationship between Christianity and other religious traditions. Given that for centuries Christians maintained that there was no salvation outside of the church and that other religions were seen as obstacles to mission, it is not surprising that potential dialogue partners were skeptical at first. Indeed, given that the slogan for the Edinburgh Missionary Conference in 1910 was "Christianization of the World in this Century," it is amazing that so many interreligious dialogues occurred immediately after Vatican II. Some of those most engaged in interreligious dialogue in the early years were criticized for losing touch with their own faith communities; some Christians maintained a more conservative reaction to the quick pace of changing attitudes toward other religious traditions. The rise in fundamentalism in the twentieth century also contributed to an attitude across religious traditions that positive interreligious relationships and lasting peace were unrealistic dreams.[7]

Here a note on "Christian privilege" is important. The privileging of Christianity within the United States is inextricably linked to colonizing privilege, and thus vital to conceptualizing interreligious learning from a postcolonial perspective. Psychologist Lewis Schlosser adapted Peggy McIntosh's work on white privilege extending it to "Christian privilege," or the advantages inherited by adherents of the dominant religion in the United States. (Although he is careful to point out that all Christians are not treated equally, either.) Like other forms of unearned privilege, Christian privilege also has a negative impact on Christians. The lack of acknowledgment of privilege can make it difficult for some Christians to face negative history and understand how some religious groups view us with mistrust or dread. The sheer variety of Christianities in the United States, while a tribute to the richness of the American religious landscape, are a source of confusion to other religious groups and obfuscate the fact that most Christians do *not* live in North America. Each denominational tradition conveys valuable pieces of the total picture, along with some fairly selective religious history. In her epic poem "On the Pulse of the Morning," Maya Angelou said, "History, despite its wrenching pain, cannot be unlived, but if faced with courage, need not be lived again."[8] Rather than perpetuating outdated models of a mono-religious culture, knowledge about how religions have been authenticated and circulated presents an opportunity to recognize historical divisions between religious groups, as well as working to overcome those divisions.

In recent years, the interreligious scholarship of Fredrick Quinn, an Episcopal priest, scholar, and diplomat, focuses on Anglican contexts and case studies to document responses to other religions in recent decades. Quinn's goal is to make a case to the church that global interreligious contact is a reality and that those of us who are Christians need to intentionally change what we teach and how we practice our faith. He argues that in the years ahead,

> Its [the church's] teaching authority will be more that of advice and guidance in sound scholarship, than a defensive reassertion of ancient dogmatic formulae. Its sacramental life will be more the offer of the unconditional and personal love of God to encourage human flourishing in an equitable and just world, than a hierarchical control of the exclusive means to eternal life. An institutional form will be more one of humble service to the community than of patriarchal dignity and control.[9]

WHAT IS INTERRELIGIOUS LEARNING?

Interreligious learning is an emerging discipline with the aim to help all participants to acquire the knowledge, attitudes, and skills needed to interact, understand, and communicate with persons from diverse religious traditions, and to create democratic communities that work for the common good. Interreligious learning is an interdisciplinary field that draws content, conceptual frameworks, processes, and theories from religious education, religious studies, multicultural education, racial and ethnic studies, women's studies, youth studies, sociology, peace and reconciliation studies, congregational studies, public policy studies, and, as featured in this chapter, postcolonial studies. It also applies, challenges, and interprets insights from these fields to pedagogy and curriculum development in diverse educational settings, including faith communities, schools, and organizations. Power analysis and openness to structural equality and the redistribution of power among diverse groups are key values and skills in interreligious learning. Shared leadership and facilitation is ideal in interreligious encounters, as is the need for democratic space and the expectation that learners are actively engaged in their own learning. Interreligious learning is an antidote to negative conditioning about other religious traditions, and lingering fear about religious differences. For example, many contemporary Buddhists welcome participation in their spiritual practice without encouraging persons to call themselves Buddhists. "We don't need more Buddhists," said His Holiness the Dalai Lama, "what we need are more people practicing compassion."[10]

What then are some concrete practices of postcolonial interreligious learning? The remainder of this chapter will focus on four practices which lie at the heart of postcolonial interreligious learning: sharing personal narratives, religious literacy, forming communities, and critical multiculturalism.

SHARING PERSONAL NARRATIVES

Integral to postcolonial interreligious learning is both the hearing and telling of stories. Jewish philosopher Martin Buber believed that the telling of stories brings healing and is sacred action.[11] Stories have the ability to transform both the storyteller and the listener. It does not matter if a person does not have a formal religious education, or has not studied the Talmud or Torah or Bible or Qur'an. Efforts at interreligious cooperation are empowered by storytelling because stories convey lived religious experiences. Rather than beginning conversations with doctrinal debates or theological abstractions, beginning with personal stories enables people to appreciate each other's human experience. Our personal experience is at the root of how we experience religious differences as well as how we experience God. "Telling my story is not in itself theology but a *basis* for theology," writes theologian Jung Young Lee. "Indeed, the primary context for doing my theology. This is why one cannot do theology for another. If theology is contextual, it must certainly be autobiographical."[12] In postcolonial interreligious learning, empowerment, resistance, and liberation are part of the storytelling process of reflecting, questioning, and inviting diverse participation in mutual learning.

Marc Gopin, the director of the Center for World Religions, Diplomacy, and Conflict Resolution at George Mason University's School for Conflict Analysis and Resolution, writes about the inner lives of Arab and Jewish peacemakers, almost all of whom suffered violence or witnessed it against loved ones. These peacemakers are conscious of their own internal life and struggles, they are prepared to face themselves ethically and spiritually, and they are more ready than the average person to share these stories with others as part of personal growth, as well as an exercise in peacemaking. Gopin writes that self-reflection is a key if individuals and groups are going to overcome violence and despair. He argues that a central source of misery and conflict in families and communities, "is the emotional, cognitive and ethical failure to be self-reflective."[13] Gopin believes that one of the inherent skills of effective storytellers, self-reflection, is also found in the narratives of extraordinary peacemakers. Thus, in postcolonial interreligious learning, self-reflective practices enable learners to break out of religious narratives as they have been traditionally told, written, and interpreted, calling forth the voices not heard and the stories not recorded. Stories "pave a way for intercultural understanding by voicing the violence of systems that bind rather than facilitate creative possibilities of more mutual understanding across differences."[14]

POSTCOLONIAL RELIGIOUS LITERACY

For centuries, colonialism and Christianity worked together to suppress local languages, to disqualify other religions, and to subjugate colonized peoples; and thus, religious education has traditionally served both liberative and oppressive agendas.[15] Within a postcolonial framework, religious literacy is a complex concept, pushing beyond artificially constructed colonial binaries which favor some religions over others, such as "monotheistic" versus "polytheistic," or "written traditions" versus "oral traditions," or "rational religion" versus "religious feeling." Postcolonial interreligious learning builds on and expands the formation of positive and critical religious identities for all ages, including the young, who as "objects of Empire" have been "defined, described, known, and controlled" by adult religious experience.[16] It assumes that adherents are the experts of their own religious experience and have perspectives and information which is of value to others. Interreligious learning strives to first recognize the good in one's own religious tradition and that of others, while at the same time acknowledging that all religious traditions have beauty, as well as limitations, because all are, at best, human interpretations of the Divine.

One of the impacts of Christian privilege in North America is that Christians often have, in fact, a lower degree of religious literacy than their counterparts from other traditions. Theological terms such as "saved" or "scripture" that are taken for granted in Christian vocabulary and affect interreligious relationships cannot be explained with precision by many Christians. Religion scholar and noted pluralist Diana Eck concurs that interreligious learning requires a greater degree of literacy than is now the reality. "I think it is dangerous to live at such close quarters in a society such as ours, with a series of half-baked truths and stereotypes functioning as our guides to the understanding of our religious nature," she writes. "If you ask what my fear is, it's that if our diversity becomes isolated enclaves in which we do not allow ourselves to encounter one another and don't take on the difficult task of creating a positive pluralism in which we have engaged with one another, we may end up with communities that are more isolated."[17] Further, the work of religion scholar Stephen Prothero suggests that the lack of religious literacy is detrimental to participation in civic and political life. Many key issues today, such as immigration, marriage rights, abortion, the environment, euthanasia, poverty, capital punishment, and war, are argued by invoking religion; and thus, religious literacy is needed for people to publicly engage these issues.[18]

FORMING COMMUNITIES

Lucinda Mosher's artful "Faith in the Neighborhood" series grounds interreligious learning in everyday encounters within local communities, as well as within the spiritual needs and connections we share: belonging, praying, grieving. Mosher, an Episcopalian writing for an ecumenical audience, argues that the Ninth Commandment warns us against bearing "false witness" against our neighbors. But how can we be assured that we are not doing that to our neighbors of other religions unless we know about their traditions and practices? If we are commanded to love God and our neighbors, we must "be with" our neighbors, and thus, be equipped with deeper understanding across religious differences. "Christians know that *all* humanity has been created in God's image. . . . We can therefore be of better service—more loving, more respectful of dignity, more likely to establish justice and peace—if we understood how our neighbor 'establishes, maintains, and celebrates a meaningful world,' which is what religion does." [19]

The need to form just communities across religious traditions is a common theme in interreligious learning. Sometimes "hospitality" is used as a buzz word for Christian inclusivism, and hence the concept should be used with caution. Yet, when articulated skillfully as a religious mandate which recognizes the uniqueness and equality of each religious tradition, and when employed as a means to critique exclusion, the idea of interreligious hospitality as a means to forming interreligious communities of justice and peace bears fruit. In such contexts, the idea of hospitality supports the creation of democratic interreligious spaces, less about arguing religious truths or congruence in thought than about shaping opportunities in the interest of human betterment.

For example, English Jesuit Michael Barnes in *Interreligious Learning: Dialogue, Spirituality and the Christian Imagination* argues the importance of interreligious hospitality as an emphasis on difference *and* particularity in the search for meaning. Barnes describes three shifts or "movements" that occur in relationship with the religious other. The first, "meetings," attempts to situate interreligious encounter within the context of theology and history. Here he offers the image of religious traditions as "schools of faith" where teachers and learners can meet and ask the difficult questions about beliefs, actions, prayers and rituals with integrity. The second movement, "crossings," emphasizes the need for people to be translated across cultural boundaries if they are to learn the skills necessary for dialogue. "Imaginings," the third movement, concerns the return back across the threshold of engagement to reflect on how faith is enhanced through interreligious learning and the need to imagine alternative shared futures. Here Barnes' movements are not intended as "fixed" stages, but rather as a way of forming interreligious communities through deep dialogue. "More important than any such logic is the conviction which guides me throughout that, while Christian faith and the beliefs and practices of Jews, Muslims, Hindus, and Buddhists may be saying different things, the very attempt to grapple with difference in a spirit of generous respect can be mutually supportive and illuminating."[20]

Further, the importance of interreligious hospitality as seen through a postcolonial reading of biblical texts is a primary framework for interreligious learning used by evangelical Christian contributors to the field. For example, Pentecostal scholar Amos Yong explores a postcolonial reading of the Pentecost text to conclude that adherents of other religions are not objects for conversion, but rather, religious neighbors to whom hospitality must be equitably extended and received. Using a pneumatological framework, Yong argues that if hospitality played a central role in the Christian theologies of religions today, then the result should not be limited to a set of ideas, but also a correlative set of practices. "Christian mission in a post-modern, pluralistic, and post-9/11 world is constituted by evangelism, social witness, and interreligious dialogue and that evangelism and proclamation always involve social engagements and interreligious dialogues of various kinds," he writes.[21] In essence, Yong argues for a type of postcolonial hospitality among religions, where Christian mission goes beyond traditional boundaries and extends to the need to form communities across religious traditions through mutual respect and social witness.

CRITICAL MULTICULTURALISM

Theologian Fumitaka Matsuoka offers advice to those who hope to support postcolonial interreligious learning: "The starting point is not to find ways of uniting people divided by fear and violence, but to recognize, celebrate, and learn from God's gift of one creation embodied in various cultures, languages, religions, and races. It is to restore moral integrity in the midst of the culture of decay by restoring freedom and dignity to the captives we held."[22]

Human beings are multifaceted. Assuming that individuals and groups inhabit different social identities simultaneously, individuals and faith communities are better prepared for postcolonial interreligious learning when challenged to become critically multicultural. It should be noted here that the term "multiculturalism" has a mixed history of application, at times the term being guilty of essentialism. In the field of education the term "critical multiculturalism" is applied in a way that uses critical pedagogies as a framework which explains all the ways we are connected by intersecting local and global issues. In this way, the term advances the idea of a multi-perspectival understanding of diverse persons engaged in "authentic participation" and shaped by different interacting cultures and ideas.[23] Without an operative understanding of the interlocking relationships between social identities of religion, race, ethnicity, gender, sexual identities, nationality, and culture, there is no foundation upon which to build interreligious learning. In terms of critical multiculturalism, the ability to recognize and respond to varying aspects of cultural differences, including religious differences, and to have the capacity to flourish in relationships across differences is needed for authentic interreligious engagement. Critical multiculturalism is the outcome of engaging a multi-level educational process which enables individuals and groups to learn the following:[24]

1. *Get in touch with one's own religious culture and beliefs, recognizing participation in prejudices and oppression against persons of other religious groups.*

Critical multiculturalism requires each person and each faith community to develop an understanding about how they impact persons and faith communities from different religious traditions. When dealing with cultural and religious differences, feelings of anxiety, fear, awkwardness, and discomfort are natural. Persons often equate religious truth with the experience of childhood; and yet, mature religious formation requires an integration of these early religious experiences with additional layers of experience and ideas. Sometimes there is a feeling that discussing religious differences is wholly negative or that if one lacks a specialized vocabulary it will insult the other group. Biases about other religions are often apparent on a "feeling level" rather than a cognitive level. Here it is important to help people develop their confidence in discussing their own religious histories, cultures, and beliefs through sharing stories. Deep encounters with other religions often challenge and re-invigorate personal belief systems.

2. *Know the difference between religion, race, ethnicity, and culture, and be able to apply this knowledge within local and global contexts.*

Religion is but one of the many different dimensions of culture which constitute the social identities of the people who comprise local and global communities. Other forms of identity, including race, ethnicity, gender, sexual identity, nationality, immigration status, age, and so on, work together and constitute the profiles of members of religious communities. It also means that individuals must understand how colonialism shaped (and to some extent continues to shape) religious identities and how hegemonic Christian culture has an impact on different religious groups.

3. *Challenge the myth that all religions are the same, and uphold their particularities in relationship.*

Critical multiculturalism requires knowledge of one's own religious culture, including the histories, traditions, values, family systems, languages, interpersonal styles, and artistic expressions, as well as of other religions. Postcolonial interreligious learning requires depth beyond colonial labels, such as "exotic" or "polytheistic," and mis-appropriations to understandings of religious cultures beyond their western constructions. While there are *some* similarities among different religious groups, authentic postcolonial interreligious learning is not built on denying the reality or importance of differences, but rather on the acknowledgement of differences and the commitment to form communities with that recognition as a given. Often, well-intentioned people promote the idea that "all religions really are the same" in an effort to encourage cooperation, without realizing the extent to which the denial of deep differences actually impedes authentic interreligious learning.

4. *Recognize that there are multiple centers of truth whose legitimacy is often determined by the amount of power any given perspective may have in a particular context.*

Although there is a human tendency to universalize individual experience, it is important to understand that what we may value as objective truth may be seen quite differently from the perspective of a person from a different religious and cultural background. There is no commonly accepted vision of "unity" among religions; and indeed, many question the efficacy of such a vision. It also means an acknowledgement that all religions do not lead to the same place. In the United States, due to Christian hegemony, people from other religions and the majority world generally know much more about Christianity than vice versa because it is critical to their survival. Linear, dualistic ways of conceptualizing religion commonly accepted in the West are less prevalent in other parts of the world. Postcolonial interreligious learning strives to correct this balance through democratic spaces which allow for sharing the histories and traditions of under-recognized groups.

5. *Understand that the fruits of postcolonial interreligious learning require a long-term commitment.*

As in any change process, building authentic interreligious relationships is a long-term process, fraught with mistakes and frustration as well as joy and celebration. Even in the face of failures, opportunities to deepen interreligious learning expand. When faithful people embrace their religious neighbors in an environment where spiritual, emotional, intellectual, and historical questions and challenges are acknowledged, the quality of the relationships both within and outside the community is enhanced. But the trust needed to overcome centuries of misunderstanding, oppression, privilege, and enmity is not built in short-term situations. Rather, it takes a commitment to go past superficial acquaintances and essentialism to get to core commitments and understanding.

Diana Eck reminds us that that the term *religio* means "to bind." Mahatma Gandhi believed that the purpose of religion was to bring people together and that that purpose was not fulfilled by merely bringing together those of the same tradition or the same culture. He believed that building relationships was at the core of all social action and that intolerance could never survive a transformed relationship. "I am striving to become the best cement between the two communities," he said during the partitioning crisis in his native India. "My longing is to be able to cement the two with my blood, if necessary. But, before I can do so, I must prove to the Muslims that I love them as well as I love the Hindus." Ultimately, according to Gandhi, we are reminded that postcolonial interreligious learning occurs in the depths of real human relationships and is not limited to abstract religious systems. All peoples and all traditions have an equal role to play in this work.[25]

Ultimately, faith communities, the academy, and religious organizations must confront the challenge of envisioning a new way of relating to the religious other, where we not only show hospitality but also seek to share power and privilege. For many religious communities, the first steps of interreligious encounter cause resistance—altering the calendar, changing the food, changing the music, changing the prayers, meeting different people—and they never progress to the stage of rich and mutually fulfilling interreligious learning. Not only do we need to appreciate the diversity of cultures and languages from other religious groups, but we need to share power and decision making with those who have been historically excluded from participation.

Faith communities, the academy, and religious organizations are still far from thinking and acting within postcolonial frameworks by abandoning outmoded and harmful attitudes of superiority. We live in a world where the violence of colonialism and religious hatred is evident every day and continues to disproportionately endanger those living in those regions of the world historically on the receiving end of colonial mission. The time is long overdue to find constructive ways to work with our sisters and brothers of faith (and no faith)[26] to mend the world.

BIBLIOGRAPHY

Angelou, Maya. *On the Pulse of the Morning*. New York: Random House, 1993.

Barnes, Michael. *Interreligious Learning: Dialogue, Spirituality and the Christian Imagination*. Cambridge: Cambridge University Press, 2012.

Buber, Martin. *Werke III*. Basel: Kosel, 1973.

Caldwell, Elizabeth. *God's Big Table: Nurturing Children in a Diverse World*. Cleveland, OH: Pilgrim Press, 2011.

Cannella, Gaile S., and Radhika Viruru, *Childhood and Postcolonialization*. New York: Routledge Falmer, 2004.

Chidester, David. *Empire of Religion: Imperialism and Comparative Religion*. Chicago: University of Chicago Press, 2014.

Eck, Diana L. "Gandhian Guidelines for a World of Religious Difference." In *Gandhi and Christianity*, edited by Robert Ellsberg, 77–90. Maryknoll, NY: Orbis Books, 1991.

Evers, Georg. "Trends and Development in Interreligious Dialogue," *Studies in Interreligious Dialogue* 22, no. 2 (2012): 215–30.

Gyatso, Tenzin (The Dalai Lama). *An Open Heart: Practicing Compassion in Everyday Life*. New York: Little, Brown & Co., 2001.

Gopin, Marc. *Bridges across an Impossible Divide: The Inner Lives of Arab and Jewish Peacemakers*. New York: Oxford University Press, 2012.

Kujawa-Holbrook, Sheryl A. *A House of Prayer for All Peoples: Congregations Building Multi-Racial Community*. Bethesda, MD: Alban Institute, 2002.

Kwok, Pui-lan. *Postcolonial Imagination and Feminist Theology*. Louisville, KY: Westminster John Knox Press, 2005.

Lee, Jung Young. *Marginality: The Key to Multicultural Theology*. Minneapolis: Fortress Press, 1995.

Matsuoka, Fumitaka. *The Color of Faith*. Cleveland, OH: United Church Press, 1998.

Mosher, Lucinda A. *Belonging*. New York: Seabury, 2005.

Mucherera, Tapiwa N. *Meet Me at the Palaver: Narrative Pastoral Counseling in Postcolonial Contexts*. Eugene, OR: Cascade, 2009.

Prothero, Stephen. *Religious Literacy: What Every American Needs to Know—And Doesn't* New York: Harper One, 2007.

Public Religion Research Council, "The End of a White Christian Strategy," pastoralia.org/church/the-end-of-a-white-christian-strategy.

Quinn, Frederick. *Welcoming the Interfaith Future*. New York: Peter Lang, 2012.

Russell, Letty M. "God, Gold, Glory and Gender: A Postcolonial View of Mission." *International Review of Mission* 93, no. 368 (2004): 39–49.

Sharp, Melinda A. McGarrah. "Globalization, Colonialism, and Postcolonialism." In *The Wiley-Blackwell Companion to Practical Theology*, edited by Bonnie J. Miller-McLemore, 422–31. Malden, MA: Wiley-Blackwell, 2012.

———. *Misunderstanding Stories: Toward A Postcolonial Pastoral Theology*. Eugene, OR: Pickwick, 2013.

Yong, Amos. *Hospitality and the Other: Pentecost, Christian Practices, and the Neighbor*. Maryknoll, NY: Orbis Books, 2008.

NOTES

1. Postcolonial theorists contest the dualism in the terms "West" and "East." When the term "West" or "western" are used in this article, they refer to dominant ways of interpreting the world that have been imposed on other parts of the world. The western world view is neither wholly positive nor negative. However, a postcolonial perspective objects to the imposition of a world view on anyone, as well as the inference that western ideas are more advanced, or morally superior.

2. David Chidester, *Empire of Religion: Imperialism and Comparative Religion* (Chicago: University of Chicago Press, 2014), 312–13.

3. Kwok Pui-lan, *Postcolonial Imagination and Feminist Theology* (Louisville, KY: Westminster John Knox Press, 2005), 206.

4. Letty M. Russell, "God, Gold, Glory and Gender: A Postcolonial View of Mission," *International Review of Mission* 93, no. 368 (2004): 41, 44.

5. Scholars have noted that the term "religious pluralism" can have its limitations, especially when it suggests an essentialist approach to religions. However, here it is used to denote the active engagement between members of unique religious groups with each other.

6. Public Religion Research Council, "The End of a White Christian Strategy," pastoralia.org/church/the-end-of-a-white-christian-strategy.

7. Georg Evers, "Trends and Development in Interreligious Dialogue," *Studies in Interreligious Dialogue* 22, no. 2 (2012): 228–29.

8. Maya Angelou, *On the Pulse of the Morning* (New York: Random House, 1993), n.p.

9. Frederick Quinn, *Welcoming the Interfaith Future* (New York: Peter Lang, 2012), 156.

10. Tenzin Gyatso (The Dalai Lama), *An Open Heart: Practicing Compassion in Everyday Life* (New York: Little, Brown & Co., 2001), 12.

11. Martin Buber, *Werke III* (Basel: Kosel, 1973), 71.

12. Jung Young Lee, *Marginality: The Key to Multicultural Theology* (Minneapolis: Fortress Press, 1995), 7.

13. Marc Gopin, *Bridges across an Impossible Divide: The Inner Lives of Arab and Jewish Peacemakers* (New York: Oxford University Press, 2012), 6–7.

14. Melinda A. McGarrah Sharp, *Misunderstanding Stories: Toward A Postcolonial Pastoral Theology* (Eugene, OR: Pickwick, 2013), 183.

15. Tapiwa N. Mucherera, *Meet Me at the Palaver: Narrative Pastoral Counseling in Postcolonial Contexts* (Eugene, OR: Cascade, 2009), 13.

16. Gaile S. Cannella and Radhika Viruru, *Childhood and Postcolonialization* (New York: Routledge Falmer, 2004), 97.

17. Quoted in Elizabeth Caldwell, *God's Big Table: Nurturing Children in a Diverse World* (Cleveland, OH: Pilgrim Press, 2011), 13.

18. Stephen Prothero, *Religious Literacy: What Every American Needs to Know—And Doesn't* (New York: Harper One, 2007).

19. Lucinda A. Mosher, *Belonging* (New York: Seabury, 2005), ix.

20. Michael Barnes, *Interreligious Learning: Dialogue, Spirituality and the Christian Imagination* (Cambridge: Cambridge University Press, 2012), xiii-xiv.

21. Amos Yong, *Hospitality and the Other: Pentecost, Christian Practices, and the Neighbor* (Maryknoll, NY: Orbis Books, 2008), 129.

22. Fumitaka Matsuoka, *The Color of Faith* (Cleveland, OH: United Church Press, 1998), 104.

23. Melinda A. McGarrah Sharp, "Globalization, Colonialism, and Postcolonialism," in *The Wiley-Blackwell Companion to Practical Theology*, ed. Bonnie J. Miller-McLemore (Malden, MA: Wiley-Blackwell, 2012), 424. Here the definition is borrowed from the work of practical theologian Emmanuel Lartey.

24. My work in critical multiculturalism and interreligious learning grew out of earlier work on religion and race. To see the basis of this work, see Sheryl A. Kujawa-Holbrook, *A House of Prayer for All Peoples: Congregations Building Multi-Racial Community* (Lanham, MD: Alban Institute, 2002), 16–19; 29–42.

25. Diana L. Eck, "Gandhian Guidelines for a World of Religious Difference," in *Gandhi and Christianity*, ed. Robert Ellsberg (Maryknoll, NY: Orbis Books, 1991), 88–90.

26. My sister and brother humanists and those from traditions not described as "faith" traditions remind me that they, too, have a stake in interreligious learning and deeply care about the fate of the world.

ELEVEN

Dynamics of Interfaith Collaborations in Postcolonial Asia

Prospects and Opportunities

Jonathan Y. Tan

Contemporary Asia is home to vibrant communities with their ancient cultures, philosophies, and religions. This diversity of communities testifies to Asia's legacy as the birthplace of the ancient great religions of the world, including Hinduism, Buddhism, and Jainism in South Asia, Confucianism and Daoism in East Asia, Zoroastrianism in Central Asia, and Judaism, Christianity, and Islam in West Asia. In the aftermath of the Second World War, decolonization, political independence, and heightened postcolonial consciousness have ushered in not just a resurgence of national pride, but also a revival and growth of traditional religions throughout Asia. The great religions of Asia continue to be deeply embedded and influential at all levels of society across Asia, each practiced and propagated by its many adherents who have brought their ancestral faiths and traditions with them as globalization and ever-widening transnational networks impel them to migrate across the postmodern Asian landscape. India is experiencing a Hindu renaissance. Across the globe, Islam is on the upsurge, making it one of the fastest growing religions in the world. In East and Southeast Asia, Buddhism has a gained a new vitality as new Buddhist movements, which first emerged in the early twentieth century, blossomed in the decades after the Second World War. These religious traditions are very much alive and influential throughout Asia, being intertwined within the sociopolitical and cultural fabric of diverse communities across Asia, and nourishing the present spiritual needs of billions of Asians.

The minority Christian presence across the culturally diverse and religiously pluralistic Asian milieu is challenged by the complex interplay of the forces of postcolonialism, globalization, transnationalism, migration, economic disparities, and political totalitarianism. Confronted with the challenges of rising cultural pride, ethnocentrism, nationalist chauvinism, and religious exclusivism, Asian Christians realize that they are, with few exceptions, minority communities who often experience fear, insecurity, vulnerability, and backlash from their religious majority neighbors for being different from the mainstream. With the exception of the Philippines and Timor-Leste, Asian Christians are not living in a world where Christianity acts as the dominant force that influences and shapes culture, ethics, politics, and society. Instead, the Christian presence in many parts of Asia is characterized by significant minority religious communities in the midst of dominant and resurgent religious majorities who are often very suspicious of them, accusing them of being a threat to "traditional" Asian values. Specifically, Asian Christians have to contend with prejudice, bigotry, chauvinism, and intolerance at the very least, and possibly even experiencing outright harassment and persecution.[1]

CHALLENGES OF RELIGIOUS PLURALISM IN ASIA

According to the Vietnamese American theologian Peter C. Phan, "It is in Asia that the question of religious pluralism is literally a matter of life and death;" and more importantly, "The future of Asian Christianity hangs in balance depending on how religious pluralism is understood and lived out."[2] Phan argues, "The report of the demise of Asian religions was premature and vastly exaggerated." Many parts of Asia have witnessed a vigorous revival of Asian religions; therefore, Asian Christians "must come to terms with the fact that they are destined to remain for the foreseeable future a 'small remnant' who must journey with adherents of other religions toward the eschatological kingdom of God."[3] He further contends that Asian Christians have to "take their Asianness seriously as the context of their being Christian," and respond to the socioeconomic, political, and religious challenges of the contemporary Asian milieu so that they are able to "live their faith in fidelity to the Gospel and the living Christian tradition, here and now, in Asia,"[4] thereby enabling "the Churches *in* Asia [to] become truly *of* Asia."[5]

If Asian Christians take their Asianness seriously as part of their incarnational and embodied Christian faith as Phan suggests above, then they need to acknowledge that the challenges of religious diversity and pluralism are not problems to be overcome, but distinctive characteristics of being Asian and Christian. Asian Christians further realize that the Christian Gospel and their Christian faith cannot be presented as otherworldly, ignoring the daily occurrences of suffering, marginalization, pain, and injustices in their sociopolitical milieu.[6] With its immense religious diversity and plurality, Asia requires a distinctively Asian approach to other religions that acknowledges the fact and reality of religious pluralism in postcolonial Asia not as a dilemma to be eradicated, but as a distinctive characteristic of being Asian and Christian. They know very well that unless they defend religious diversity and pluralism against exclusivist religious chauvinism, there will be no room at all for Christianity on a continent dominated by the great religions of the world. Because Asian Christianity will never dominate Asia to the exclusion and extinction of other religions in the manner of medieval Christendom in Europe, it has to become truly immersed and rooted in the Asian milieu for its survival and growth, as Phan rightly notes.

Moreover, Asian Christians have the daily experiences of being very much "at home" in the pluralistic religious Asian milieu, having been born into and living amid this religious diversity and pluralism. Many of them come from a "mixed" religious background, with extended family members following a variety of religious traditions as a result of interfaith marriages. They live and interact on a daily basis with their family members, relatives, friends, and neighbors from other religious traditions, sharing with them the joys and sufferings as well as blessings and misfortunes of daily living. While many European and North American theologians and church leaders wax lyrical about the practice and achievements of interfaith dialogue in Europe and North America, where the great religions of the world are often viewed as the minority and the exotic "Other" vis-à-vis the dominant position of Christianity, Asian Christians live permanently amid the practitioners of these great religions. And while theologians and church leaders in Europe and North America may invite representatives of these other religions to meet occasionally for dialogue and conversation, Asian Christians engage in a daily dialogue of life witness with these fellow Asian neighbors who are followers of the great religious traditions of Asia.

At the same time, one must also acknowledge the reality that even as Asian Christians interact with fellow Asians who adhere to other religious traditions, those interactions are not always harmonious and peaceful. While Asia is often spoken of as the birthplace of the great religions of the world, including Christianity, many of these world religions are experiencing a resurgence of pride and exclusivist chauvinism in many parts of Asia. Thus, Asian Christians also have firsthand experiences of fanatics and fundamentalists who reject the long history of religious diversity and pluralism in Asia, seeking to impose their vision as normative through coercion and violence, as evident in the simmering Muslim-Christian conflicts in Pakistan and elsewhere, the unwarranted pressure on Indian Christians to renounce Christianity, Hindu violence against Christians in India, and restrictions placed on Christians' freedom of association are imprinted in the consciousness of these Asian Christians.[7]

INTERFAITH COLLABORATIONS AS PARTICIPATION IN THE *MISSIO DEI*

From a theological perspective, when Asian Christians engage in interfaith collaboration with their Asian neighbors, they are, in reality, participating in the *Missio Dei*, a theological concept that was articulated by the International Missionary Conference in Willengen, Germany, in 1952.[8] According to the missiologist David Bosch, the "decisive shift toward understanding mission as God's mission," or *Missio Dei*, marked a profound paradigm shift away from earlier understandings of mission as "saving individuals from eternal damnation," "introducing people from the East and the South to the blessings and privileges of the Christian West," or even "the expansion of the church."[9] Bosch explained that the concept of *Missio Dei* emphasizes three key points: (1) mission as belonging, first and foremost, to God rather than the church; (2) mission as preceding from God reconciling the world through the sending of the Son and the Spirit; and (3) God's mission as God's presence and activity as always present in the created order, beyond the Church, with the goal of bringing about God's reign in the world beyond merely the growth of Christianity and the institutional church.[10]

Hence, when Asian Christians engage in interfaith collaborations as part of their participation in the *Missio Dei*, they are interested not in an Asian Christian presence that is over and against Asian religions and cultures, but rather a presence that is relational and dialogical, recognizing that they are called neither to conquer the postcolonial Asian world in the name of a triumphant Christ nor build a triumphant Christendom on Asian soil. In this vein, the late Angelo Fernandes, Archbishop Emeritus of Delhi, insisted that Asians of other faiths were not to be regarded as "objects of Christian mission," but as "partners in the Asian community, where there must be mutual witness."[11] Archbishop Fernandes explained that the dialogue between the Asian Church and the Asian peoples should be seen as a "manifestation of lived Christianity" with its own integrity that leads toward the Reign of God.[12]

Undergirding Asian Christians' interfaith collaboration with Asians of other religious traditions is the recognition by many Asian Christians that the religious traditions of Asia are neither demonic nor evil, but vehicles of God's salvific encounter with the Asian peoples. This recognition presupposes that other world religions are not Christianity's rivals but potential allies, *collaborating* and *working together* against the real *mutual* enemies of all forms of evil, including attachment to wealth, power, selfishness, and exploitation, as well as the social, cultural, and political structures that support them. In doing so, Asian Christians are able to counter the misconception that Christianity is imported from Europe and North America and therefore not properly "Asian."

COMMITMENT AND SERVICE TO LIFE IN ASIA

More importantly, when Asian Christians engage in interfaith collaboration as part of their participation in the *Missio Dei*, they are also making a commitment to serve Asian peoples in the complexities of their daily life experiences. Making a personal commitment to Asian peoples and their life experiences entails more than mere sympathy or occasional encounters with their daily lives, especially when it comes to people who are poor and marginalized. In other words, this personal commitment is not merely *for* the benefit of the Asian peoples, or *about* the Asian peoples, but *together with* Asian peoples and in solidarity with the fullness of their daily life experiences that also encompass the interfaith dimensions of daily living. As the Indian theologian Felix Wilfred explains, "What we are with the people is more important than what we do for them." [13]

Hence, the call to commitment and service to life in Asia as part of Asian Christians' engagement in interfaith collaboration entails their deep immersion and experiential participation in the lives of their Asian neighbors from various religious communities, not as outsiders who drop by sporadically to visit and then leave, but as insiders who remain bound in solidarity and empathy with them. Such a commitment and service to life may be understood from a twofold perspective—namely, an explicit *epistemological* perspective, which allows one to better understand Asian peoples and their life experiences, and more importantly, an underlying *theological* perspective, which recognizes the presence and workings of God in the daily lives of Asian peoples as part of the *Missio Dei*. This underlying theological perspective is deeply rooted in the incarnation, earthly ministry, death, and resurrection of Jesus, revealing God's solidarity with humanity, especially the poor and marginalized, as well as God's participation in the experiences of pain and suffering in their daily lives.

One could say that the experiences of daily living are the privileged loci where God is to be found and encountered because God has made a deliberate choice to be identified with humanity, especially the poor and marginalized. It is also an acknowledgment of the workings of the Holy Spirit beyond the boundaries of the institutional Church that inspire the deep soteriological underpinnings of Asian religions and philosophies that have inspired multitudes of Asians. In the context of pluri-religious Asia, this is also an acknowledgment that there are many Asians who are inspired by Jesus Christ and his ethical vision for humanity, but choose for various reasons to remain Hindus, Buddhists, Daoists, or Muslims, and who are otherwise excluded from the dialectical setup of present ecclesial structures. As Felix Wilfred explains:

> We have in Asia the phenomenon of a lot [sic] of men and women who are gripped by Jesus, his life and teachings. They are his devotees while they continue to be Hindus, Buddhists, Taoists. What is particularly remarkable is that they can be Hindus, or Buddhists, etc., and devotees of Christ without being syncretistic. Syncretism, they feel, is something which is attributed to them from the outside, while from within, at the level of their consciousness, they experience unity and harmony, and are not assailed by those contradictions and conflicts which may appear to those who look at them from without.[14]

HOSPITALITY AND INTERFAITH COLLABORATIONS

Malaysian-born Chinese American theologian Amos Yong has proposed a theological framework for interfaith collaborations that is rooted in interfaith hospitality which fosters *mutuality* and *reciprocity* between Christianity and other religions.[15] While Yong's main focus is Asian Pentecostal Christianity's response to the workings of the Holy Spirit outside of institutional Christianity, I would like to submit that his insights have broader implications for all Christians in general, and Asian Christians in particular. Specifically, Yong constructs what he calls a pneumatological theology of interfaith hospitality that is rooted in *mutuality* and *reciprocity* between Christianity and other religions.[16] He explains that while Christians cannot be responsible for the actions of others, they can and should take responsibility for their own attitudes and actions in a world where religious believers are becoming more hostile and antagonistic toward those who are different from them.[17]

Like Archbishop Angelo Fernandes, Yong insists that the "religious others" are more than simply the objects of conversion by Asian Christians. Rather, these "religious others" are the guests, friends, and neighbors of Asian Christians, with both sides extending mutual friendship and reciprocal hospitality. Yong further insists that his pneumatological theology of interfaith encounter "not only allows but also obliges us to cultivate different dispositions toward those in other faiths than those traditionally promoted; not only allows but also requires that we look for dialogical situations and opportunities involving religious others; not only allows but also necessitates our establishing friendships and opening our homes for table fellowship with those of other faiths."[18]

Thus, Yong's vision of a pneumatological theology of interfaith hospitality that welcomes believers of other religions in a spirit of friendship and neighborliness undergirds the interfaith collaboration in which Asian Christians engage together with their Asian co-religionists in a shared spirit of hospitality and solidarity for the betterment of their communities. He also reminds us of the importance of the quintessential Asian trait of *dialogue*, which has the potential to bring about opportunities for two or more parties, with their different worldviews, to enter into each other's horizons, thereby creating deeper levels of understanding and friendship.

THE CHALLENGES OF INTERFAITH COLLABORATION IN MALAYSIA

Contemporary Malaysia is a multiethnic, multilingual, multireligious, and multicultural society with a population of 28.3 million, comprising 67.4 percent Malays and other indigenous natives,[19] 24.6 percent Chinese, and 7.3 percent Indians. Around 61.3 percent of the population of Malaysia is Muslim. Malaysian Buddhists comprise the second largest religious community at 19.8 percent. Christians are exclusively non-Malays and comprise around 9.2 percent of the population, followed by Hindus (6.3 percent) and traditional Chinese religions (1.3 percent).[20] At the same time, Malaysia is also a socially and politically volatile society divided by an explosive mix of ethnicity and religion. Although article 3(1) of the Malaysian Federal Constitution specifies that Islam is the official religion of Malaysia and the majority of Malaysians are Muslims, the same article 3(1) also permits other religions "to be practised in peace and harmony in any part of the Federation."[21] Moreover, freedom of religion in Malaysia is guaranteed under article 11(1) of the Malaysian Federal Constitution, which states, "Every person has the right to profess and practise his religion and, subject to Clause (4), to propagate it."[22] However, article 11(4) of the Malaysian Federal Constitution also empowers the federal and state governments to pass laws against the propagation of non-Muslim religions among the Muslims: "State law and in respect of the Federal Territories of Kuala Lumpur, Labuan and Putrajaya, federal law may control or restrict the propagation of any religious doctrine or belief among persons professing the religion of Islam."[23]

Under the British colonial policy of divide and rule, the Malays were given political power while control of trade and economy was given to the Chinese. This political-economic division continued in post-independent Malaysia, engendering much discontent between the Malays and Chinese. Matters came to an explosive clash in the series of violent racial riots, stoked by extremist Malay nationalists against the Chinese community, beginning on May 13, 1969.[24] In the aftermath of these riots, the Malaysian government instituted the New Economic Policy (NEP) to promote national reconciliation and bridge the economic inequality between the Malays and the Chinese in an effort to rebuild a shattered civic society. Unfortunately, the NEP also institutionalized communalism, Malay dominance in nation building, and Malay sovereignty over the other minority communities in all matters political, social, and economic. This resulted in widespread economic inefficiency, corruption scandals, cronyism, and nepotism as a small Malay elite class controlled the political and economic levers of powers to the exclusion of ordinary Malays and people of other races.[25] As the tangible economic benefits of the NEP failed to trickle down to the ordinary Malays in rural communities, the Islamic Parti Islam Se-Malaysia (PAS) emerged to champion Islamization as the alternative to the cronyism and corruption of the NEP. In response to the popularity of PAS's Islamization platform, the ruling political elite adopted a similar policy of Islamization to blunt PAS's tactics.[26]

To say that the Malaysian government's heavy-handed program of Islamization has resulted in increased religious tensions between the majority Muslim and other religious minority communities in Malaysia is an understatement. As a religious minority, Malaysian Christians have found themselves in the direct firing line of legislation and programs aimed at giving Islam a privileged position vis-à-vis the other religious faiths in Malaysia. For example, Malaysian Christians are rankled by state legislation that criminalizes apostasy (*takfir*) by Muslims and the actions of Christians who evangelize their faith to Muslims.[27] The law against apostasy drew international headlines and condemnation in the case of Lina Joy, who filed a suit before the Malaysian Federal Court to compel the Malaysian National Registration Department to record her change of religion from Islam to Christianity on her identity card after her baptism as a Roman Catholic. On May 30, 2007, her appeal was dismissed by a 2–1 majority, and she and her Christian fiancé were forced to leave Malaysia under threats of violence from Malaysian Muslim activists. More importantly, the Malaysian Federal Court ruling further inflamed interfaith tensions as non-Muslim minorities perceive this to be yet another nail in the coffin for the erosion of religious freedom in Malaysia.[28]

Another example of conflict between Malaysian Christians and Muslims is the ongoing controversy over the use of the term "Allah" for God by Malaysian Christians. The issue came to the forefront as a result of the 2007 decision of the Malaysian Ministry of Home Affairs to prohibit the Malaysian Catholic periodical *The Herald* from using the term "Allah" in its Malay language edition. The then–Catholic Archbishop of Kuala Lumpur, Murphy Pakiam, sought a judicial review of the Home Minister's decision.[29] The case wound its way through the Malaysian court system, culminating in the Malaysian Federal Court decision in June 2014 to uphold the 2007 decision of the Malaysian Home Minister and issue a blanket ban against non-Muslims using the term "Allah" under any circumstances.[30]

In response to the pressure from the Malay Muslim majority, the Malaysian Consultative Council of Buddhism,[31] Christianity,[32] Hinduism,[33]

Sikhism,[34] and Taoism[35] (MCCBCHST) was established in 1983 to promote understanding, mutual respect and cooperation among the different religions in Malaysia, resolve interfaith matters, and make representations to the Malaysian government on religious issues.[36] In practice, the MCCBCHST has become an organized channel for interfaith dialogue and engagement between the non-Muslims and the Malaysian government on issues of religious freedom and the impact of encroaching Islamization on the rights of the non-Muslim religious minorities to practice their faith without interference or fear.[37]

The current Catholic Archbishop of Kuala Lumpur, Julian Leow, is insistent on interfaith dialogue and collaboration as the way out of the current tensions and impasse between Muslims and non-Muslims in Malaysia. In his first interview after he was chosen as the new Archbishop of Kuala Lumpur, he spoke of "looking forward to having inter-religious dialogues and fostering closer ties with Malaysians of various races and faiths," explaining that "once dialogue is shut out, there will be a lot of misrepresentation."[38] In his address at his episcopal ordination, Archbishop Leow emphasized, among other things, the need for interfaith dialogue and engagement: "Not only understanding our own faith is important, but to know the faiths of those we live with. Inter-religious dialogue is so crucial in a country like ours. This will dispel misconceptions and create a healthy atmosphere of mutual respect."[39] Moreover, Archbishop Leow's commitment to interfaith engagement is also symbolically represented in his coat of arms by a "tree with religious icons," which depicts "the ability to recognize the Divine in every person we encounter [and] to be open to dialogue and to seek the good of the other."[40]

At the grassroots level, a number of younger Malaysians are seizing the initiative to overcome the sectarian religious divide through the formation of Projek Dialog.[41] Under the leadership of two young Malaysian Muslims, cultural and political studies scholar Ahmad Fuad Rahmat and social media activist Yana Rizal, and advised by Malaysian Muslim political commentator and activist Marina Mahathir and Malaysian Christian theologian Sivin Kit, Projek Dialog seeks to leverage social media to provide a platform for Malaysians from all religious traditions to engage in interfaith and intercultural conversations with the goal of promoting better understanding and collaboration among the diverse ethnic and religious communities in Malaysia. Projek Dialog maintains an active social media presence on Facebook[42] and Twitter[43] to promote an ongoing dialogue on interfaith engagements and collaboration. To date, Projek Dialog has sponsored "interfaith walks" that seek to expose Malaysians to various religious communities and their beliefs and traditions through visits to places of worship and participating in prayer and other ritual activities to promote better understanding, harmony and friendship, and national unity.[44] In collaboration with the London-based human rights non-governmental organization, Article 19,[45] Projek Dialog successfully organized a seminar, "Freedom, Religion, and Social Media: Know Your Rights" on August 24, 2014, to explore the issues surrounding freedom of religion and human rights in the era of social media, as well as provide guidance to young Malaysian activists looking to utilize social media for advocacy on issues of religion and human rights without infringing Malaysian law, in particular the Sedition Act.

CONCLUSION

Asian Christians realize that their life experiences are defined by the fact that for over 2,000 years Christianity has been, at best, a minority religion in Asia, a world that is dominated by the world's ancient great religions. Indeed, these Christians ignore the plurality of ancient religions and spiritual traditions that define the Asian milieu at their peril. They have to contend with the challenges of living and prospering in a pluri-religious milieu that has always been defined by the great religions of the world, recognizing that religious pluralism is an inescapable part of the Asian landscape, a part which is not to be confronted and overcome but accepted and celebrated as a definitive aspect of the Asian world. More specifically, Asian Christians, as a religious minority in many parts of Asia, have no choice but to explore new ways of overcoming the antagonism and chauvinism of the religious majority around them that would take into account the complex and tense relational dynamics between Asian Christians as a religious minority vis-à-vis their religious majority neighbors in the pluralistic Asian milieu.

The Asian Church will always be a "little flock" in the sea of diverse Asian religions and cultures in pluralistic Asia for the future. To be truly Asian and at home in the Asian milieu, Asian Christians are challenged to embrace the religious pluralism of postcolonial Asia, while at the same time prophetically challenging and purifying its oppressive and life-denying elements in the name of the Christian Gospel. In the context of the immense pluralistic Asian *Weltanschauung*, Asian Christians as a religious minority are able to witness to the redemptive power of the Christian Gospel by *not* pouring oil on the fires of religious conflict and violence or engaging in competitive proselytism against the practitioners of other religions. On a continent that is being torn apart by violence and conflicts in the name of exclusivist religious fanaticism, Asian Christians are challenged to break the impasse by going beyond the superficiality of quantitative church growth in favor of a qualitative *prophetic* approach that seeks to critique, transform, and heal the brokenness in Asian realities. They do this by the example of their daily living in companionship, empathy, and solidarity with their neighbors across religious boundaries, working, struggling, and suffering as fellow humans on a common quest for the meaning of life. As religious minority, Asian Christians complain about the majority scapegoating them for social ills and pressurizing them to lose their distinctive ethno-racial or religious features and become fully assimilated in the mainstream of society. They find themselves on the losing end of an "us-versus-them" rhetoric and political manipulations of religious differences by the religious majority that often go down the dangerous path of a power game that politicizes religion and plays off majority and minority communities in the interest of political expediency.

More importantly, the call to witness to the Gospel in pluri-religious Asia through interfaith collaboration goes beyond merely proclaiming abstract doctrines or rational arguments toward rooting the Gospel in the Asian milieu within a framework of hospitality that would enable the Good News to be experienced by the Asian peoples in a spirit of mutuality and relationality. A theology and practice of interfaith collaboration that is rooted and empowered by a spirit of hospitality has the potential to foster thoughtful conversation, attentive listening, mutual dialogue, and mutual collaboration that would witness to the presence of the Reign of God in Asia as part of the *Missio Dei*. Moreover, with the onslaught of migration that is causing great upheavals among different social, ethnic, and religious groups throughout Asia, a theology of hospitality that empowers and undergirds interfaith collaboration is all the more relevant and necessary as an antidote to violence and turbulence, affording opportunities for all Asians, Christians and adherents of Asian religions alike to interact and engage with each other. At the same time, one should also acknowledge the reality that encouraging the majority to move away from reluctant tolerance to mutual trust of, and hospitality toward diverse minority communities is often easier said than done.

Interfaith collaborations represent an opportunity for Asian Christians to promote positive interactions that are grounded in mutual hospitality and mutual relations, breaking down the walls of hostility and division and enabling them to walk together and accompany other Asians in the journey of life in a spirit of love, friendship, and harmony. It seeks to prophetically critique, transform, and heal the brokenness in Asian realities in the name of ushering in God's Reign in Asia. Because Asian Christians participate in the *Missio Dei* to bring about God's reign through their life witness, they are called to contribute to the common good and promote peace, harmony, and the well-being of their racial-ethnic, cultural, and religious communities and societies, even if they do not become institutionally Christian. Without a doubt, dialogue as a source of reconciliation can only arise from genuine relations of mutuality and solidarity between majority and minority communities at the grassroots level. In turn, dialogue could pave the way for conversion, forgiveness, and healing. The common good is promoted at all levels when barriers are broken down, the fires of hatred are quenched, bridges are built between majority and minority communities, and goodwill is promoted at grassroots levels to foster reconciliation and harmony, thereby breaking the vicious cycle of hate, fear, mistrust, and violence.

BIBLIOGRAPHY

Bosch, David J. *Transforming Mission: Paradigm Shifts in Theology of Mission.* Maryknoll, NY: Orbis Books, 1991.

Camilleri, Rita. "Religious Pluralism in Malaysia: The Journey of Three Prime Ministers." *Islam and Christian-Muslim Relations* 24 no. 2 (2013): 225–40.

Chin, James. "The Malaysian Chinese Dilemma: The Never Ending Policy (NEP)." *Chinese Southern Diaspora Studies* 3 (2009): 167–82.

"Coat of Arms of Most Rev. Julian Leow." Accessed October 10, 2014. www.archkl.org/index.php/archbishop/coat-of-arms.

Comber, Leon. *13 May 1969: A Historical Survey of Sino-Malay Relations.* Kuala Lumpur: Heinemann Asia, 1983.

Crowe, Jerome. *From Jerusalem to Antioch: The Gospel Across Cultures.* Collegeville, MN: Liturgical Press, 1997.

Department of Statistics, Malaysia. "Population Distribution and Basic Demographic Characteristics." Accessed October 10, 2014. www.statistics.gov.my/portal/index.php?option=com_content&id=1215 and www.statistics.gov.my/portal/download_Population/download.php?file=census2010/Taburan_Penduduk_dan_Ciri-ciri_Asas_Demografi.pdf.

Federal Constitution of Malaysia, 2010 Reprint. Kuala Lumpur: The Commissioner of Law Revision, 2010.

Fernandes, Angelo. "Dialogue in the Context of Asian Realities." *Vidyajyoti Journal of Theological Reflection* 55 (1991): 545–60.

Goh, Cheng Teik. *The May Thirteenth Incident and Democracy in Malaysia.* Kuala Lumpur: Oxford University Press, 1971.

Kahn, Joel S., and Francis Loh Kok Wah, eds. *Fragmented Vision: Culture and Politics in Contemporary Malaysia.* Honolulu: University of Hawaii Press, 1992.

Leow, Archbishop Julian. "Speech for Episcopal Ordination." October 8, 2014. Accessed October 10, 2014. www.archkl.org/index.php/what-s-happening/press-news/784-speech-for-episcopal-ordination.

"Malaysia's Highest Court Dismisses Divisive 'Allah' Case." Accessed October 10, 2014. www.abc.net.au/news/2014–06–23/top-malaysian-court-dismisses-divisive-religious-case/5544324.

Murad, Dina. "Father Julian Leow Is New Archbishop of Kuala Lumpur." *The Star Online,* July 3, 2014. Accessed October 10, 2014. www.thestar.com.my/News/Nation/2014/07/03/father-julian-leow-new-archbishop-of-kuala-lumpur/.

Pak, Jennifer. "The Man Behind Malaysia's Interfaith Tours," BBC News. October 22, 2013. Accessed October 10, 2014. www.bbc.com/news/world-asia-24583935.

Phan, Peter C. "*Ecclesia in Asia*: Challenges for Asian Christianity." *East Asian Pastoral Review* 37 (2000): 215–32.

———. Review of *Introducing Theologies of Religion,* by Paul F. Knitter. *Horizons* 30 (2003): 113–17.

Phan, Peter C., and Jonathan Y. Tan. "Interreligious Majority-Minority Dynamics." In *Understanding Interreligious Relations,* edited by David Cheetham, Douglas Pratt, and David Thomas, 218–40. Oxford: Oxford University Press, 2013.

Rizal, Yana, and Ahmad Fuad Rahmat on BFM 89.9 "Social Media and Human Rights." Recorded August 19, 2014. Accessed October 10, 2014. www.bfm.my/social-media-human-rights-yana-rizal-ahmad-fuad-rahmat.html.

Tan, Chee Ing Paul, and Theresa Ee. "Introduction." in Tunku Abdul Rahman Putra et al, *Contemporary Issues on Malaysian Religions*, 5–15. Petaling Jaya: Pelanduk Publications, 1984.

Walters, Albert Sundaraj. "Issues in Christian-Muslim Relations: A Malaysian Christian Perspective." *Islam and Christian-Muslim Relations* 18 no. 1 (2007): 67–83.

Wilfred, Felix. "Inculturation as a Hermeneutical Question." *Vidyajyoti Journal of Theological Reflection* 52 (1988): 422–36.

—————. "What the Spirit Says to the Churches (Rev 2:7)." *Vidyajyoti Journal of Theological Reflection* 62 (1998): 124–33.

Yong, Amos."The Spirit of Hospitality: Pentecostal Perspectives toward a Performative Theology of Interreligious Encounter." *Missiology* 35 (2007): 55–73.

NOTES

1. On the implications of Asian Christians as minority communities, see Peter C. Phan and Jonathan Y. Tan, "Interreligious Majority-Minority Dynamics," in *Understanding Interreligious Relations*, ed. David Cheetham, Douglas Pratt, and David Thomas (Oxford: Oxford University Press, 2013), 218–40.

2. Peter C. Phan, review of *Introducing Theologies of Religion*, by Paul Knitter, *Horizons* 30 (2003): 117.

3. Peter C. Phan, "*Ecclesia in Asia*: Challenges for Asian Christianity," *East Asian Pastoral Review* 37 (2000): 224.

4. Ibid., 218.

5. Ibid., 219.

6. As Jerome Crowe explained succinctly, "The gospel can only be experienced and communicated in the form of a particular human culture. There is no such thing as a 'pure' gospel, untainted by incorporation into a human culture, because the gospel is not a system of divine truths existing somewhere outside this world and untouched by human feeling, language, and customs but God's self-involvement in the concrete circumstances of a people's history and culture." See Jerome Crowe, *From Jerusalem to Antioch: The Gospel Across Cultures* (Collegeville, MN: Liturgical Press, 1997), 153–54.

7. For a more in-depth discussion, see Phan and Tan, "Interreligious Majority-Minority Dynamics."

8. David J. Bosch, *Transforming Mission: Paradigm Shifts in Theology of Mission* (Maryknoll, NY: Orbis Books, 1991), 389–93.

9. Ibid., 389–90.

10. Ibid., 389–91.

11. Angelo Fernandes, "Dialogue in the Context of Asian Realities," *Vidyajyoti Journal of Theological Reflection* 55 (1991): 548.

12. Ibid., 548.

13. Felix Wilfred, "What the Spirit Says to the Churches (Rev 2:7)," *Vidyajyoti Journal of Theological Reflection* 62 (1998): 132.

14. Felix Wilfred, "Inculturation as a Hermeneutical Question," *Vidyajyoti Journal of Theological Reflection* 52 (1988): 429.

15. Amos Yong, "The Spirit of Hospitality: Pentecostal Perspectives toward a Performative Theology of Interreligious Encounter," *Missiology* 35 (2007): 55–73.

16. Ibid., 65.

17. Ibid., 66.

18. Ibid., 66.

19. The Malays and other indigenous natives of Malaysia are collectively classified as "Bumiputeras" by the Malaysian government.

20. The figures cited here are from the 2010 Population and Housing Census of Malaysia. See Department of Statistics, Malaysia, "Population Distribution and Basic Demographic Characteristics," www.statistics.gov.my/portal/index.php?option=com

_content&id=1215 and www.statistics.gov.my/portal/download_Population/download.php?file=census2010/Taburan_Penduduk_dan_Ciri-ciri_Asas_Demografi.pdf (both accessed: October 10, 2014).

21. *Federal Constitution of Malaysia,* 2010 Reprint (Kuala Lumpur: The Commissioner of Law Revision, 2010), 20.

22. Ibid., 25.

23. Ibid., 26.

24. For critical discussions of the race riots of May 13th, 1969, see Goh Cheng Teik, *The May Thirteenth Incident and Democracy in Malaysia* (Kuala Lumpur: Oxford University Press, 1971) and Leon Comber, *13 May 1969: A Historical Survey of Sino-Malay Relations* (Kuala Lumpur: Heinemann Asia, 1983).

25. On the impact of the NEP on the Malaysian Chinese, see James Chin, "The Malaysian Chinese Dilemma: The Never Ending Policy (NEP)," *Chinese Southern Diaspora Studies* 3 (2009): 167–82.

26. This issue is explored in greater detail in Joel S. Kahn and Francis Loh Kok Wah, eds., *Fragmented Vision: Culture and Politics in Contemporary Malaysia* (Honolulu: University of Hawaii Press, 1992).

27. Rita Camilleri, "Religious Pluralism in Malaysia: The Journey of Three Prime Ministers," *Islam and Christian-Muslim Relations* 24 no. 2 (2013): 225–40. Camilleri explains that apostasy from Islam (*takfir*) is a criminal offense in the states of Pahang, Perak, Melaka, Sabah, and Terengganu (Camilleri, "Religious Pluralism in Malaysia," 231).

28. For a discussion of the Lina Joy case and its implications for Muslim-Christian relations in Malaysia, see Albert Sundaraj Walters, "Issues in Christian-Muslim Relations: A Malaysian Christian Perspective," *Islam and Christian-Muslim Relations* 18 no. 1 (2007): 67–83.

29. *Titular Roman Catholic Archbishop of Kuala Lumpur v. Menteri Dalam Negeri.*

30. "Malaysia's Highest Court Dismisses Divisive 'Allah' Case," accessed October 10, 2014, www.abc.net.au/news/2014–06–23/top-malaysian-court-dismisses-divisive-religious-case/5544324.

31. The Buddhist representatives are the Malaysian Buddhist Association (MBA), Buddhist Missionary Society Malaysia (BMSM), and Sasana Abhiwurdhi Wardhana Society (SAWS).

32. Malaysian Christians are represented by the Christian Federation of Malaysia (CFM), which comprises the Catholic Bishops Conference of Malaysia (CBCM), Council of Churches of Malaysia (CCM), and National Evangelical Christian Fellowship (NECF).

33. The Malaysia Hindu Sangam (MHS) represents Malaysian Hindus on this council.

34. The Sikh representatives are the Malaysian Gurdwaras Council (MGC), Khalsa Diwan Malaysia (KDM), and Sikh Naujawan Sabha Malaysia (SNSM).

35. The Taoist representatives are the Federation of Taoist Associations Malaysia (FTAM).

36. Paul Tan Chee Ing and Theresa Ee, "Introduction," in Tunku Abdul Rahman et al, *Contemporary Issues on Malaysian Religions* (Petaling Jaya: Pelanduk Publications, 1984), 13.

37. For current information on the MCCBCHS, its outreach, projects, and other activities, see harmonymalaysia.wordpress.com/.

38. Dina Murad, "Father Julian Leow Is New Archbishop of Kuala Lumpur," *The Star Online,* July 3, 2014, accessed October 10, 2014, www.thestar.com.my/News/Nation/2014/07/03/father-julian-leow-new-archbishop-of-kuala-lumpur/.

39. Archbishop Julian Leow, "Speech for Episcopal Ordination," October 8, 2014, accessed October 10, 2014, www.archkl.org/index.php/what-s-happening/press-news/784-speech-for-episcopal-ordination.

40. "Coat of Arms of Most Rev. Julian Leow," accessed October 10, 2014, www.archkl.org/index.php/archbishop/coat-of-arms.

41. The background information on Projek Dialog in this paragraph is taken from its website, www.projekdialog.com (accessed October 10, 2014) and the podcast interview of Yana Rizal and Ahmad Fuad Rahmat on BFM 89.9 "Social Media and Human Rights," recorded August 19, 2014, accessed October 10, 2014, www.bfm.my/social-media-human-rights-yana-rizal-ahmad-fuad-rahmat.html.

42. https://www.facebook.com/projekdialog.

43. https://twitter.com/ProjekDialog.

44. Jennifer Pak, "The Man Behind Malaysia's Interfaith Tours," BBC News, October 22, 2013, accessed October 10, 2014 at www.bbc.com/news/world-asia-24583935.

45. For more information on Article 19, as well as its objectives and activities, visit www.article19.org.

TWELVE

Postcolonializing "Mission-Shaped Church"

The Church of England and Postcolonial Diversity

Jenny Daggers

The Anglican Communion is a postcolonial legacy of British imperialism. However, in the white British mind, empire is too easily consigned to a closed chapter of history, rather than being seen as a persistent legacy that actively shapes the present. Such blindness is itself a significant mark of a colonizer heritage. The postcolonial diversity of contemporary British life—where people of colonized and colonizer descent live alongside as neighbors—is also a legacy of empire. In discerning its mission today, the Church of England needs to be mindful of this. Undoubtedly the 2004 Church of England report *Mission-Shaped Church* marked a significant turning point for the English church, ushering in a renewed urgency for mission.[1] Yet it appears that postcolonial diversity has been given insufficient attention in both report and subsequent Church of England policy.

This chapter argues there is an urgent need for the Church of England to respond to a clear agenda set by postcolonial theologians of colonized heritage, and that this response must radically impact on notions of mission in twenty-first century England. This postcolonial agenda is named within the wider Anglican Communion but rarely heeded within the English church. Clearly stated, white British Anglicans of colonizer heritage need to decolonize our minds. This decolonizing process involves dismantling attitudes that are testaments to the continuing legacy of empire. It is simultaneously a means of "postcolonializing" in the sense of ushering in a truly post-colonial order, where colonizing attitudes are no more. White British Anglicans of colonizer descent need to decolonize our minds if we are to renew the commitment of the Church of England to work for the common good of English society in its contemporary configuration. An implication of ethnic and religious diversity for the Church of England as an aspiring "mission-shaped" national church is that closer attention needs to be given to ecumenical and interfaith aspects of mission among people of colonized heritage, both Christians and those of other faiths.

The chapter is in three parts. First, the continuing impact of *Mission-Shaped Church* is assessed by reviewing General Synod reports that set the agenda for the current quinquennium. Then the term "postcolonializing" is clarified to draw out its implications for the Church of England in contemporary English life. Finally, this postcolonializing perspective is brought to bear on the drive toward mission-shaped church in order to indicate the decolonizing work that is still to be done.

RENEWED MISSION IN THE CHURCH OF ENGLAND

Recent General Synod reports show that the Church of England is living through a period of rapid change, albeit uneven in its effects at parish level. In a church which has been accustomed to leaving mission to its evangelical congregations, a shift is occurring across the spectrum toward more visible witness by an outgoing church. The movements of "emerging Church" and "fresh expressions" are reaching out to the unchurched. Clergy who have experienced ordination training since the publication of *Mission-Shaped Church* bring a new priority to the task of re-engaging the Church within the local parish. The term "mission-shaped church" has caught the attention of English Anglicans. While there were significant mission initiatives in the post-war decades of the twentieth century,[2] it was the 2004 report with its documenting of church-planting and fresh expressions that brought mission into a stronger contemporary focus.[3]

While this has created tension and sometimes polarization with the traditional received forms of Church of England liturgical practice, epitomized in the stand-off between *Mission-Shaped Church* and *For the Parish*,[4] there are also signs of the emergence of a more "generous ecclesiology."[5] In Ian Mobsby's words, this charitable commitment seeks a path beyond a created binary "between the two great theologies of the Christian faith," namely redemptive versus incarnational theologies, as represented respectively in the low/protestant/evangelical and high/sacramental/catholic traditions in the Church of England.[6] In this sense, the aspiration to be a "mission-shaped church" goes beyond the specific forms of fresh expressions and emerging Church.

The context for these Church of England struggles is postmodern and postsecular. It is also postcolonial; but this is less clear to the majority of white British Anglicans, whose theological grappling is too often fully immersed in our local Eurocentric concerns, where postmodernity and postsecularity dominate. All too easily we forget our whiteness and overlook the undone task of postcolonializing, given that a full appreciation of our postcolonial location is sorely lacking in white British consciousness. Our positioning within world Christianity and the wider Anglican Communion and our national diversity in ethnic heritage and faith traditions provide us with invaluable contexts for learning about our whiteness and the continuing effects of our colonizer heritage. We need to recognize and value these opportunities to decolonize and postcolonialize our national church.

A survey of papers considered at the General Synod in February 2015 shows a renewed missional urgency within the Church of England.[7] The need for a more "intentional evangelism" had been identified and an Archbishops' Task Group established to pursue this aim in November 2013.[8] When this theme is developed in GS1977, "Developing Discipleship," preoccupation with postmodern and postsecular issues is evident in the claim: "As the Church of England in 2015 we face the challenge of calling one another afresh to follow Christ in the face of a global, secularised, materialistic culture."[9] This wording shows that the term "global" assumes the extension of western consumer culture; in contrast, a critical postcolonial perspective puts into question such unexamined global neoliberalism.

This uncritical reference to the "global" supports my claim that white British Eurocentrism obscures pressing postcolonial issues. Similarly, in addressing our local issues of de-churched postmodernity, *Mission-Shaped Church* made fresh analysis of patterns of life in the United Kingdom, an analysis which draws on contemporary sociological analysis and adopts a twenty-first century tone. However, while it is mindful of technological change and globalization, it ignores both the colonial era that facilitated these developments and the postcolonial and multireligious immigration that has come in its wake.[10] It appears that mission is tacitly directed to the detraditioned white British population alone.

Important questions arise. What sense can we make of the phrase "discipleship of the whole people of God" in our postcolonial British context?[11] How does this theological notion work out in British society which is not only detraditioned and postmodern, so inviting re-evangelization, but which also in its postcolonial variety indicates the need for "receptive ecumenism"[12] with postcolonial diasporic churches, and equally receptive interfaith hospitality with other postcolonial faith communities?

A possible way forward is suggested by the recent synod documents. In defining goals for the current quinquennium, clear expression is given to the need to balance growth in the church with working for the common good. [13] GS1917 refers to the Anglican Communion's "five marks of mission," which place three other missional priorities alongside the evangelistic tasks of proclamation of the good news, baptism, and nurture of new disciples. These three other missional priorities are service; justice, peace and reconciliation; and the integrity of creation. [14] The document reiterates the theme of "contributing as a national church to the common good." [15] GS1982 goes a step further when it explicitly includes within the remit of the common good the building of partnerships with other Christians and those of other faiths. [16] Assertion of this wider missional remit is promising for the postcolonializing of the mission-shaped church. I will return to this point in the closing pages of this chapter.

While the term "postcolonial" will be familiar to many readers of this volume, for those who come for the first time to the task of "postcolonializing," it will be helpful to clarify what is at stake and to engage with the body of work that has built up in this area, albeit without a great deal of attention within the Church of England. In the following part of the chapter we turn to the writings on this question from within the Anglican Communion and more broadly. The aim is to shape a critical lens for viewing the English mission-shaped church.

POSTCOLONIALIZING: WHAT? WHO? HOW?

The term "postcolonial" can be used simply to suggest we now live in a time "after" the colonial era, a time marked by reverse migration from former colonies into the British metropole, so creating the rich ethnic and religious diversity of the contemporary United Kingdom. However, critical perspectives insist that colonialism persists in deeply embedded political practices and in colonized minds, minds of both colonizer and colonized heritage. In this sense, (neo)colonialism is perpetuated and repeatedly reinscribed in an apparently postcolonial era; the postcolonializing move seeks to dis-embed, and so overcome, these ongoing practices. This chapter considers how the Church of England may respond to this critical challenge to "decolonize" and "postcolonialize." In theological perspective, as Emmanuel Y. Lartey insists, this human enterprise reflects a postcolonializing God who "acts to decolonize, diversify and promote counter-hegemonic conditions." [17]

By the 1990s, the big three postcolonial theorists Edward Said, Gayatri Spivak, and Homi Bhabha had burst on the western academic scene, jostling for attention with the high postmodern theory that also peaked during this decade. Of more direct relevance to this chapter is the emergence from the 1990s of postcolonial biblical criticism, pioneered in the work of R. S. Sugirtharajah and developed by other biblical scholars, including Musa Dube. From this body of work, the term "postcolonial" acquires a critical meaning that goes beyond the simple sense of "after colonialism." Mission, past and present, is deeply implicated in the colonial. Mission today is likely to perpetuate (neo)colonialism unless it wrestles with the radical implications of postcolonial perspectives. This question is directly relevant to the Church of England as an aspirational mission-shaped church. In the wider Anglican Communion, valuable insights on this issue are on offer in the work of postcolonial theologians who resist neo-colonialism and support the emergence of postcolonial forms of Church.

By 1998, the year when the dominant white western identity of the Anglican Communion was to be forcefully challenged at the decennial Lambeth Conference, a colloquium on "Anglicanism in a Post-Colonial World" was convened at Episcopal Divinity School in Cambridge, Massachusetts, leading to a landmark publication, *Beyond Colonial Anglicanism*.[18] The conference was a timely attempt to "imagine an Anglican Communion for the twenty-first century . . . beyond the colonial legacy."[19] When Glauco S. de Lima adjudicates, "For those of us who believe that the church is a sign and foretaste of the reign of God in the world, the task of undoing colonialism in our mission is urgent,"[20] his sentiment is of direct relevance not only to the wider Anglican Communion but equally to the Church of England. In similar vein, Kwok Pui-lan's challenge that "the Anglican Communion must determine whether it will be a relic of the colonial past, or a bridge to the postcolonial future"[21] applies directly to the English church.

Anglican women theologians bring their own perspectives to the future of the Anglican Communion. However, for indigenous and two-thirds world Anglican women, access to theological education is problematic and this impedes their coming to voice. An important step forward was the inauguration of the Global Anglican Theological Academy (GATA) as an outcome of the work of the Archbishop of Canterbury's Commission on Theological Education for the Anglican Communion (TEAC). GATA was formed in Canterbury in 2009, at a gathering of thirty-five women from across the Anglican Communion facilitated by TEAC.

The collection *Anglican Women on Church and Mission* emerged from a series of similar meetings.[22] As co-editor of *Anglican Women* and co-founder of GATA, Jenny Te Paa Daniel is informed in her writings by her role as the former Principal of St. John's College, Auckland, New Zealand, and by her service on Anglican and World Council of Churches working groups and commissions. Te Paa Daniel writes with passion and insight into the implications of women's near absence from leadership in the provinces of the Anglican Communion, and on strategies for mentoring potential leaders drawn from indigenous Anglican women of color.[23]

Te Paa Daniel gives powerful testimony from her own lived experience as an indigenous Anglican woman theological educator and leader in a communion marked by "deeply embedded patriarchal preferences and practices."[24] Te Paa Daniel's own exceptional position arose in the reordering of the Anglican Church in Aotearoa, in response to indigenous political protest over the legacy of colonial injustice to the Maori peoples.[25] However, received Anglican traditions assumed male leadership, and this pattern has largely persisted in the Anglican Communion to exclude women. As Te Paa Daniel puts it, obstacles to women's leadership are "hidden behind the veil of attitudinally and institutionally mired gender injustice."[26]

She brings into view the complexity of Anglicanism after colonialism. Being of colonized heritage is insufficient to ensure a commitment to postcolonializing. Te Paa Daniel, with her Aoteraoan experience of the transformative potential within postcolonial Anglicanism, speaks powerfully of the double impact of excluding the voices of the marginalized—indigenous, women, and gay—and of the ignorance of Anglican ecclesiology and missiology on the part of a number of global Anglican leaders. The effect is seen in domination by unrepresentative male leadership in the interminable debates on sexuality in the Anglican Communion, and the further muting of women's voices within these debates.[27] These actions utterly fail to meet Lartey's criteria for human activities that reflect a postcolonializing God: actions need to be decolonizing and diversifying, as well as countering hegemony.

It is encouraging to note Te Paa Daniel's confidence in the transformative potential of Anglican ecclesiology and missiology. With her endorsement firmly in view, the final section of the chapter returns to the Church of England.

POSTCOLONIALIZING A MISSION-SHAPED CHURCH OF ENGLAND

As a feminist theologian more accustomed to engaging with systematic theology, I was privileged to be invited to the colloquium on "Postcolonial Practice of Ministry" at Episcopal Divinity School in November 2014. I found myself drawn into a rich engagement with a vibrant community of practical theologians, and it was in this setting that I met for the first time the leading black British theologian, Michael Jagessar. This encounter led me to reflect on how it was possible for me to have overlooked the rich vein of black British theology in my fifteen-year theological passage.[28] On returning to the United Kingdom, I set about correcting this deficit.

My anecdote is of direct relevance to the task of postcolonializing the Church of England as it morphs into a mission-shaped church. On reading black British theology, including some Anglican works, I find a clear analysis of racism within British society, and its effects on the life of black British Christians. As a white British Anglican who takes seriously the aspiration of the Church of England to work for the common good of the population of England today, I need to keep this analysis firmly in view.

As Kwok Pui-lan has observed, "To participate in weaving the common tapestry, European and Euro-American women must first decolonize their minds and save themselves from the state of unknowing."[29] Yet, decolonizing is a relational task: left to ourselves, it is not an agenda we easily address. Racism is a direct effect of a still-colonized mind. I have come to recognize that if postcolonializing is to be more than an unrealized good intention, I need the perspective of those who can make visible to me what is currently invisible. In this, I seek to share this conviction with my fellow white British Anglicans.

If we are to be mindful of our whiteness, and of the postcolonializing imperative, we need to learn from the postcolonial perspectives of fellow Christians elsewhere, from Christians of colonized heritage. As Christians within world Christianity, we need to resituate our received European traditions, with all their Eurocentrism, within the changed global pattern of Christianity. It is conceivable that in facing our local dilemmas, our still-cherished colonial Christ may become remade in postcolonial forms; but this will never happen through the initiative of white theologians, ministers, and lay people alone. It may happen if we white Christians learn an unaccustomed receptivity toward the perspectives of those who can detect our continuing racism and imperialism. Receptivity goes beyond a polite inclusion of voices different to our own as a brief interruption before we return to our own pressing concerns. Rather, receptivity implies a willingness to change what is revealed about us when we hear what is spoken by these voices.

When we turn outward from our own concerns, how can we address the inherent risk that we will reinscribe imperial and colonizing attitudes? Given that European modernity was accompanied by a colonial expansion beyond European borders, part of the colonizer heritage is an assumed entitlement to travel where one chooses on one's own terms, rather than on the terms of those encountered in this outward move. Unexamined assumptions of white supremacy— itself a creation of European colonialism—are embedded within our received imperial and colonizing attitudes. This is the seed bed for ongoing racism, which may be at odds with our self-perception, but all too evident to people of color in their encounter with us. What, then, can be learned from black British theologians of colonized heritage?

It is not possible within the scope of this chapter to do justice to the rich vein of theology represented in the British-founded journal *Black Theology* and other substantial writings. British theology is enriched by the work of Robert Beckford, Michael Jagessar, Anthony Reddie and Kate Coleman[30] within the wider field of British black theology. For the current discussion, I draw insight from two Anglican theologians, David Isiorho and Mukti Barton.

From Isiorho, I learn that to deal with racism and the racializing process, we white English people need to erode concepts of superiority "that centuries of aggressive colonialism have embedded deep within the national psyche."[31] His comments are based on careful analysis of Church of England reports from the 1980s and 1990s, noting and stripping away their underlying complacency. His analysis offers hard lessons. Isiorho identifies a deep Anglicanism that looks back to the past of the English church, combining "theism and English ethnicity." Institutional racial discrimination in the Church of England originates in "values located within English ethnicity."[32] Strategic appointments of black clergy are not enough to redress this. Further, Isiorho urges that "personal contrition" is needed; merely spotting institutional racism is insufficient.[33]

Running through his article is a future-oriented eschatological perspective that beckons the church into a new present; if the Church of England is to work for the common good, it needs to heed Isiorho's call "to rediscover what it means to be English in this third millennium."[34] This can only happen through personal contrition for our still-colonized minds, requiring us to make our whiteness visible to ourselves. It is conceivable that this transformation will open a rich new chapter in the life of Church of England that is beyond the grasp of our still-colonized imaginings.

Bangladeshi-British theologian Mukti Barton's testimony challenges me to recognize the enduring effects of my colonizer heritage. Barton draws on her own life experience to shape her powerful critique of white feminist theology in the British context. She refers to the work of the Tunisian writer, Albert Memmi, who, Barton says, "has detected something immutable about the relationship that was established between the colonizer and the colonized in the colonial era."[35] Memmi's comment is troubling for those of us who seek to decolonize our minds.

Barton finds a closer affinity not only with postcolonial feminist and womanist theologies, but with all people of color, men as well as women, than she finds with white feminism. In the context of recent bombings in Afghanistan and Iraq, she states, "when we are bombed, we die not with white women, but with our men of colour."[36] Conversely, she analyzes western foreign policies in terms of Gayatri Spivak's pithy critique of the use of feminist language to establish western hegemony, as "white men saving brown women from brown men."[37] For Barton, imperial patriarchy continues the project of saving black/brown women from black/brown men.[38] White Christians, including white feminists, are all too easily drawn into endorsing this venture.

Identifying herself with the biblical figure of Hagar, Barton speaks of the barriers to forming a solid sisterhood with white feminists, who she identifies with Sarah/Sarai. In comparison with the feminist solidarity she had experienced in Bangladesh, Barton found that white British women in women's groups "unconsciously collude with imperial patriarchy," and that in our all-white groups we are also unconscious of our racism.[39] For Barton, when in contact with white feminist groups, "the past British imperialism was always an unseen guest making me feel, to some extent isolated from my peers."[40] Barton therefore finds a greater affinity with postcolonial feminist and womanist theologies than with white feminist theology.[41] For white Anglican Christians, including Anglican feminist theologians, she sets an agenda of receptivity toward her postcolonializing insights, so that we may recognize our still-imperial collusions. Barton has indicated a path for postcolonializing white Anglican congregations.

In their different ways, Isiorho and Barton make visible what would otherwise remain invisible to white British Anglicans within the Church of England, namely, our unacknowledged racism and our reinscription of colonial patterns. The closing discussion brings this postcolonializing perspective to bear on Church of England aspirations to be a mission-shaped Church.

The Anglican "five marks of mission" can usefully be placed in the context of broadened understandings of Christian mission since the formation of the World Council of Churches and subsequently the Second Vatican Council. While notions of mission as service, rather than solely as evangelism, were already well developed in pre-Vatican II twentieth century mission theology, a stronger multidimensional notion of mission as including witness and ecumenical and interfaith dialogue has grown in significance over the past half century.[42] This is reflected in the "five marks" of mission. Although as I showed in the opening discussion, overall aims of the Church of England reflect this breadth and reiterate the importance of ecumenical and interfaith engagement, mission-shaped church is at risk of severing intentional evangelism from these wider aims.

Church of England thinking reflects a wider problem in linking recent missional wisdom to western contexts. Thus the multireligious setting of mission is clearly recognized in guidelines set out in the ecumenical document *Christian Witness in a Multi-Religious World: Recommendations for Conduct*.[43] Yet, when introduced by Ron Wallace, it remains ambiguous as to whether mission within multireligious western nations is included in the frame of this global document.[44] On review of available Euro-American literature on mission and ministry, it is striking that scant attention is paid to either the presence of other faith traditions within western nations, or to working out the missional implications of this multireligious reality.[45]

One exception to this oversight is the reader, *The Gospel among Religions: Christian Ministry, Theology, and Spirituality in a Multifaith World*.[46] The book is a valuable resource for practical theologians, educators and ministers, as it makes accessible a range of relevant historical and contemporary writings on interreligious attitudes and engagement. The editors' introductions are helpful in mapping the material, but readers are largely left to make their own sense of its varied contents. Further and in parallel with recent Church of England synod documents, the term "globalization" is invoked in a solely Euro-American perspective of global awareness in a global village,[47] but without any discussion of inherent postcolonial power relations.[48]

With regard to the United Kingdom, some excellent work in interfaith dialogue is carried out within the Church of England.[49] However, the multidimensional models of mission forged in ecumenical debate were not deployed in *Mission-Shaped Church*. Given the danger of this omission being carried forward into "intentional evangelism," reflections on postcolonial mission will inform intentional evangelism that promotes the common good of contemporary multiethnic and multireligious English society.

A postcolonial missional approach recognizes the neocolonialist tendency to impose cultural forms on those who are missionized. Instead, postcolonial mission is receptive to learning from the missionized. Thus Joerg Rieger warns that neocolonialism is invisible to most westerners, then distinguishes colonial mission as "outreach" from postcolonial mission as "inreach."[50] Receptivity enables inreach, which is defined as learning about the ill effects of colonizing attitudes and practices and growing more conscious of white western complicity in neocolonialism. For Rieger, this inreach model ensures that the source of energy is with other people and with the *Missio Dei*, the divine Other "whose mission meets us in unexpected ways and transforms the way things are."[51] In these terms, the invaluable insights of British black theologians appear as inreach into white British Anglicanism.

Sathianathan Clarke's constructive argument for postcolonial mission in the context of world Christianity is also helpful. Clarke presents a considered alternative to the western narrative of economic and cultural globalization.[52] Recommending a postcolonial hybridity between contrasting evangelical and liberal "platforms" of international mission, Clarke discerns four shared and postcolonial characteristics, namely the prominence of the Global South in generating mission, critique of the former alliance of western missionaries with imperial and colonial regimes, a preferential option to empower the marginalized, and commitment to probe and dismantle present neocolonial forces.[53]

In this perspective, the mission-shaped Church of England is invited to perceive itself as one local church within the scope of world Christianity, while addressing its ongoing neocolonialist tendencies. If the postcolonializing imperative is accepted, then mission in the United Kingdom might be perceived as postcolonializing mission, receptive to perspectives arising in the Global South. In the perspective offered by Clarke, mission equips local communities to participate collaboratively in God's project of the coming kingdom.[54] There are resonances with this kingdom-seeking in the quinquennial aims of the Church of England. However, as Richard Kuuia Baawobr argues, "dialogue is not optional in mission today. It is part and parcel of it."[55] Thus alongside the commitment to intentional evangelism, the words of Ghaleb Moussa Bader, Archbishop of Algiers, have as much pertinence in the United Kingdom as in Africa and Asia:

> The coexistence of cultures and interreligious dialogue are no longer a choice but a *fait accompli*. . . . We are called to live together. We do not have a choice . . . the other may think differently, . . . the other may belong to another religion. My duty as a Christian is to tell everyone that the human person is God's creation: the Christian person, the Muslim person, the Buddhist person, but also the non-believer.[56]

As Marion Grau puts it, "We can opt for the friction of polydox mutual mission."[57] By postcolonializing our practices and choosing Grau's option, we will work for the common good.

CONCLUSION

This chapter has investigated the quinquennial commitment of the Church of England toward both intentional evangelism and promoting the common good. Postcolonial perspectives require white British Anglicanism to decolonize, so that evangelism may find its place within the church's wider mission to work for the common good of contemporary English society. Mission as inreach and mutual mission are to be welcomed as opportunities to transform the English church through learning from those who are missionized, from wider ecumenical relations inclusive of diasporic Christian churches, and from continued interfaith dialogue and hospitality. Postcolonial diversity is a gift to white British Anglicans. In learning to be transformed, rather than to transform, we are enabled to decolonize both our minds and the received tradition of our beloved English church.

BIBLIOGRAPHY

Baawobr, Richard Kuuia. "Change and Its Effect on Mission and Church Relationship: A Roman Catholic Perspective." *International Review of Mission* 101, no. 2 (2012): 393–403.

Bakker, Janet Kragt. "The Sister Church Phenomenon: A Case Study of the Restructuring of American Christianity against the Backdrop of Globalization," *International Bulletin of Missionary Research* 36, no. 3 (July 2012): 129–34.

Barton, Mukti. "Wrestling with Imperial Patriarchy." *Feminist Theology* 21, no. 1 (2012): 7–25.

Beckford, Robert. *Jesus Is Dread*. London: DLT, 1998.

Brockman, David R., and Ruben L. F. Habito, eds. *The Gospel among Religions: Christian Ministry, Theology, and Spirituality in a Multifaith World*. Maryknoll, NY: Orbis Books, 2010.

"Challenges for the Quinquennium: Intentional Evangelism." General Synod of the Church of England, 2013, Paper GS1917, November 2013. Accessed March 9, 2015, https://www.churchofengland.org/media/1872415/gs%201917%20-%20intention-al%20evangelism.pdf.

Clarke, Sathianathan. "World Christianity and Postcolonial Mission: A Path Forward for the Twentieth Century." *Theology Today* 7, no. 2 (2014): 192–206.

Coleman, Kate. "Black Theology and Black Liberation: A Womanist Perspective." *Black Theology* 1 (1998): 59–69.

Davison, Andrew, and Alison Milbank. *For the Parish: A Critique of Fresh Expressions.* London: SCM Press, 2010.

Douglas, Ian T., and Kwok Pui-lan, eds. *Beyond Colonial Anglicanism: The Anglican Communion in the Twenty-first Century.* New York: Church Publishing, 2001.

Gittoes, Julie, Brutus Green, and James Heard, eds. *A Generous Ecclesiology: Church, World and the Kingdom of God.* London: SCM Press, 2013.

Graham Cray, ed. *Mission-Shaped Church: Church Planting and Fresh Expressions of Church in a Changing Context.* London: Church House Publishing, 2004. Accessed October 20, 2014, www.chpublishing.co.uk/uploads/documents/0715140132.pdf.

Grau, Marion. *Rethinking Mission in the Postcolony: Salvation, Society, and Subversion.* London: T. & T. Clark, 2011.

Isiorho, David. "Black Theology in Urban Shadow: Combating Racism in the Church of England." *Black Theology* 1, no. 1 (2002): 29–48.

Jagessar, Michael N., and Anthony E. Reddie. *Postcolonial Black British Theology: New Textures and Themes.* Peterborough: Epworth, 2007.

Kwok, Pui-lan. "Unbinding Our Feet: Saving Brown Women and Feminist Religious Discourse." In *Postcolonialism, Feminism, and Religious Discourse*, edited by Laura E. Donaldson and Kwok Pui-lan, 62–81. London: Routledge, 2002.

———, Judith A. Berling, and Jenny Plane Te Paa, eds. *Anglican Women on Church and Mission.* London: Canterbury Press, 2013.

Lartey, Emmanuel Y. *Postcolonializing God: An African Practical Theology.* London: SCM Press, 2013.

Mobsby, Ian. "Afterword: The World and the Church." in *A Generous Ecclesiology: Church, World and the Kingdom of God*, edited by Julie Gittoes, Brutus Green, and James Heard, 170–74. London: SCM Press, 2013.

Murray, Paul. "Introducing Receptive Ecumenism." *The Ecumenist* 51, no. 2 (Spring 2014): 1–8.

Reddie, Anthony. "Black Theology in Britain." In *The Cambridge Companion to Black Theology*, edited by Dwight N. Hopkins and Edward D. Antonio, 234–44. Cambridge: Cambridge University Press, 2012.

Richardson, Rick. "Emerging Missional Movements: An Overview and Assessment of Some Implications for Mission(s)." *International Bulletin of Missionary Research* 37, no. 3 (July 2013): 131–36.

Rieger, Joerg. "Theology and Mission between Neocolonialism and Postcolonialism." *Mission Studies* 21, no. 2 (2004): 201–27.

Te Paa, Jenny Plane. "Leadership Formation for a New World: An Emergent Indigenous Anglican Theological College." In *Beyond Colonial Anglicanism: The Anglican Communion in the Twenty-first Century*, edited by Ian T. Douglas and Kwok Pui-lan, 270–96, New York: Church Publishing, 2001.

———. "Women's Leadership Development for the Anglican Communion: Oh Lord, How Long Must We Wait . . . ?" In *Anglican Women on Church and Mission*, edited by Kwok Pui-lan, Judith A. Berling, and Jenny Plane Te Paa, 77–93. London: Canterbury Press, 2013.

Wallace, Ron. "Introducing Evangelism in the New Affirmation." *International Review of Mission* 101, no. 2 (2012): 376–80.

World Council of Churches, the Pontifical Council for Interreligious Dialogue and the World Evangelical Alliance. *Christian Witness in a Multi-Religious World: Recommendations for Conduct* (2011). Accessed October 28, 2014. www.oikoumene.org/en/re-

sources/documents/wcc-programmes/interreligious-dialogue-and-cooperation/
christian-identity-in-pluralistic-societies/christian-witness-in-a-multi-religious-
world.html.

NOTES

1. Graham Cray, ed., *Mission-Shaped Church: Church Planting and Fresh Expressions of Church in a Changing Context* (London: Church House Publishing, 2004), accessed October 20, 2014, www.chpublishing.co.uk/documents/0715140132.pdf.

2. The 1945 Church Assembly Report, *Towards the Conversion of England*, and the Decade of Evangelism, 1988–1998, cited in GS 1917, para 34, p. 8 and para 37, p. 9. See "Challenges for the Quinquennium: Intentional Evangelism," General Synod of the Church of England, 2013, Paper GS1917, November 2013, accessed March 9, 2015, https://www.churchofengland.org/media/1872415/gs%201917%20-%20intentional%20evangelism.pdf.

3. The recent appointment of Bishop David Kings as Mission Theologian at University of Durham also gives testament to renewed interest in mission. Archbishop of Canterbury, Durham University and CMS press release, "Mission Theologian in the Anglican Communion," accessed March 9, 2015, www.missiontheologyangcom.org/.

4. Cray, *Mission-Shaped Church*; Andrew Davison and Alison Milbank, *For the Parish: A Critique of Fresh Expressions* (London: SCM Press, 2010).

5. Julie Gittoes, Brutus Green, and James Heard, eds., *A Generous Ecclesiology: Church, World and the Kingdom of God* (London: SCM Press, 2013).

6. Ian Mobsby, "Afterword: The World and the Church," in Gittoes, Green, and Heard, *A Generous Ecclesiology*, 170–171.

7. The relevant papers are: GS1976 "In Each Generation: a Programme for Reform and Renewal"; GS1977 "Developing Discipleship"; GS1978 "Report on the Task Force on Resourcing the Future of the Church of England"; GS1979 "Resourcing Ministerial Education in the Church of England"; GS1980 "Report of the Simplification Task Group"; GS1981 "Church Commissioners' Funds and Inter-Generational Equity"; GS 1982 "Discerning and Nurturing Senior Leaders." All available at https://www.churchofengland.org/about-us/structure/general-synod/agendas-and-papers, accessed March 9, 2015.

8. "Challenges for the Quinquennium: Intentional Evangelism" GS1917, November 2013, p. 1. This paper informs the subsequent paper, "Developing Discipleship" GS1977, prepared for the February 2015 synod. The Archbishops' Task Group on Evangelism is yet to report to General Synod.

9. GS1977, para 30, p. 6.

10. Cray, *Mission-Shaped Church*. Vincent Donovan's approach in mission to the Masai in Kenya is cited as an example of inculturation (91–92), but this reinscribes the white missionary/African convert trope without reflecting on its implications for the contemporary Church of England.

11. GS 1977, para 39, p. 8.

12. Paul Murray, "Introducing Receptive Ecumenism," *The Ecumenist* 51, no. 2 (Spring 2014): 1–8.

13. See for example: GS1917, para 24, p. 6; GS 1982, para 31, pp. 9–10. Also see GS1815 (2011). A third priority of re-imagining ministry is also identified.

14. GS1917, para 23, p. 6.

15. GS1815 (2011), cited in GS1917 para 46. p. 11.

16. GS1982., para 32, p.10.

17. Emmanuel Y. Lartey, *Postcolonializing God: An African Practical Theology* (London: SCM Press, 2013), xiii.

18. Ian T. Douglas and Kwok Pui-lan, eds., *Beyond Colonial Anglicanism: The Anglican Communion in the Twenty-first Century* (New York: Church Publishing, 2001).

19. Glauco S. de Lima, "Preface," in Douglas and Kwok, *Beyond Colonial Anglicanism*, 1.

20. Ibid., 4–5.

21. Kwok Pui-lan, "The Legacy of Cultural Hegemony," in Douglas and Kwok, *Beyond Colonial Anglicanism*, 66.

22. Kwok Pui-lan, Judith A. Berling, and Jenny Plane Te Paa, eds., *Anglican Women on Church and Mission* (London: Canterbury Press, 2013).

23. Jenny Plane Te Paa, "Women's Leadership Development for the Anglican Communion: Oh Lord, How Long Must We Wait . . . ?" in Kwok, Berling, and Te Paa, *Anglican Women*, 77–93.

24. Ibid., 81.

25. See Jenny Plane Te Paa, "Leadership Formation for a New World: An Emergent Indigenous Anglican Theological College," in Douglas and Kwok, *Beyond Colonial Anglicanism*, 270–96, for a full account.

26. Te Paa, "Women's Leadership Development," 78.

27. Ibid., 85–86.

28. Black British theologians make a strong contribution to practical theology, but their work is not confined to this area of theology.

29. Kwok Pui-lan, "Unbinding Our Feet: Saving Brown Women and Feminist Religious Discourse," in *Postcolonialism, Feminism, and Religious Discourse*, ed. Laura E. Donaldson and Kwok Pui-lan (London: Routledge, 2002), 79.

30. Robert Beckford writes from a Pentecostal perspective, Jagessar from a United Reform Church, Reddie from a Methodist, and Kate Coleman from a Baptist. See, for example, Robert Beckford, *Jesus Is Dread* (London: DLT, 1998), noting his critique of racism within the Church of England, 51–54 and 108–110; Kate Coleman, "Black Theology and Black Liberation: A Womanist Perspective," *Black Theology* 1 (1998): 59–69. Also Michael N. Jagessar and Anthony E. Reddie, *Postcolonial Black British Theology: New Textures and Themes* (Peterborough: Epworth, 2007); Anthony Reddie, "Black Theology in Britain," in *The Cambridge Companion to Black Theology*, ed. Dwight N. Hopkins and Edward D. Antonio (Cambridge: Cambridge University Press, 2012), 240, where he makes pertinent criticism of "the unreconstructed whiteness and colonially informed norms of inherited ecclesial practices and liturgical formations."

31. David Isiorho, "Black Theology in Urban Shadow: Combating Racism in the Church of England," *Black Theology* 1, no. 1 (2002): 47.

32. Ibid.,46.

33. Ibid.

34. Ibid., 48.

35. Mukti Barton, "Wrestling with Imperial Patriarchy," *Feminist Theology* 21, no. 1 (2012): 12.

36. Ibid.

37. Gayatri Spivak, "Can the Subaltern Speak?" cited in Barton, ibid.,13.

38. Ibid., 14.

39. Ibid., 11.

40. Ibid.

41. Ibid., 12.

42. See Richard Kuuia Baawobr "Change and Its Effect on Mission and Church Relationship: A Roman Catholic Perspective," *International Review of Mission* 101, no. 2 (2012): 393–403, for a useful discussion of the outworking in his own North African missional context of "six essential components of mission"—derived from an ecumenical synthesis made by Stephen Bevans and Eleanor Doidge.

43. World Council of Churches, the Pontifical Council for Interreligious Dialogue and the World Evangelical Alliance, *Christian Witness in a Multi-Religious World: Recommendations for Conduct* (2011), accessed October 28, 2014, www.oikoumene.org/en/resources/documents/wcc-programmes/interreligious-dialogue-and-cooperation/christian-identity-in-pluralistic-societies/christian-witness-in-a-multi-religious-world.html.

44. Ron Wallace, "Introducing Evangelism in the New Affirmation," *International Review of Mission* 101, no. 2 (2012): 376–80.

45. See Rick Richardson, "Emerging Missional Movements: An Overview and Assessment of Some Implications for Mission(s)," *International Bulletin of Missionary Research* 37, no. 3 (July 2013): 131–36, for a discussion of mission in the US setting, which also fails to take into account multireligious realities.

46. David R. Brockman and Ruben L. F. Habito, eds., *The Gospel among Religions: Christian Ministry, Theology, and Spirituality in a Multifaith World* (Maryknoll, NY: Orbis Books, 2010).

47. Ibid., 2–5.

48. This is true also of the fascinating study conducted by Janet Kragt Bakker of "sister churches" established between local US congregations and African partners. (See "The Sister Church Phenomenon: A Case Study of the Restructuring of American Christianity Against the Backdrop of Globalization," *International Bulletin of Missionary Research* 36, no. 3 (July 2012): 129–34.)

49. See for example, Andrew Wingate, "Mission as Dialogue: A Contextual Study from Leicester, UK," in Brockman and Habito, *The Gospel among Religions*, 153–67.

50. Joerg Rieger, "Theology and Mission Between Neocolonialism and Postcolonialism," *Mission Studies* 21, no. 2 (2004): 201–27.

51. Ibid., 224. Rieger contrasts this approach with the assumption that the energy comes from our own missional commitment in the outreach model.

52. Sathianathan Clarke, "World Christianity and Postcolonial Mission: A Path Forward for the Twentieth Century," *Theology Today* 7, no. 2 (2014): 195.

53. Ibid., 197–98. Clarke cites as key players the (evangelical) Lausanne Movement and the (liberal) Commission on World Mission and Evangelism.

54. Ibid., 199.

55. Baawobr, "Change and Its Effect," 400.

56. Ghaleb Moussa Bader cited in Baawobr, "Change and Its Effect," 400.

57. Marion Grau, *Rethinking Mission in the Postcolony: Salvation, Society, and Subversion* (London: T. & T. Clark, 2011), 280.

THIRTEEN

Womanist Interfaith Dialogue

Inter, Intra, and All the Spaces in Between

Melanie L. Harris

Womanist is inherently interfaith. The contours and depth of the definition and dialogue about the various theological perspectives, historical
and life experiences, religious beliefs, and ethical mores of women of
African descent necessitate an interfaith mode of engagement. Black
women and their belief systems are not monolithic. Contrary to the fantastic hegemonic imagination and other essentialist myths, African,
African American, and/or black women's identities and religious identities are sacredly diverse.[1] According to third wave womanist approaches that include attention to interdisciplinary methods, analysis of
intersections between gender, globalization and peace building, and an
interreligious landscape, women of African descent embody a variety of
religiosities, ethical worldviews, and political ideologies that create a
beautiful array of complex subjectivity and ways of living in community
with the earth.[2]

One word that describes the sense of agency and choice that womanists have in self-naming and embracing their religious identity or spirituality is lifesystem. This term is explained best by Layli Maparyan and is
inclusive of a variety of religious, indigenous, and faith traditions, as well
as mystical and metaphysical belief systems. She writes that the use of the
term helps to distinguish religion from spirituality, an important distinc-
tion to make for womanist religious thought in that one refers to a culturally organized framework (religion) and the other acknowledges relationship with the divine realm (spirituality). Maparyan explains that both

are important: "Historically, religion has been the province of institution-alized structures, while spirituality as such has been the province of mys-ticism and metaphysics. Yet the two are connected and interpenetrating in ways that, again, require new language."[3] The new term, "lifesystem," is important in that it offers a model of womanist ingenuity and agency to produce "new language that fits us" in the same way and in the same spirit that Alice Walker coined the term "womanist" separate and apart from feminist, and in the way that Katie G. Cannon, Delores S. Williams, and other womanist scholars have created new language to explain the multivocal nature of black women's religiosities and theological perspec-tives.[4] Lifesystem is also innovative and in keeping with third wave womanist perspectives; it reaches "beyond womanism"[5] past the use of traditional religious Christian-centered theological categories used in the discourse, and provides a term that "allows Hinduism, Judaism, Zoroas-trianism, Buddhism, Christianity, Islam, the Baha'i faith, and all other 'institutionalized' religions to be on equal footing with African tradition-al and African-derived religions, Native American religious traditions, Aboriginal religious traditions, and all other 'indigenous' spiritual sys-tems."[6] This equal footing that Maparyan suggests opens up the dialogue of womanist religious thought to be more inclusive of new language and new categories necessary for interfaith and interreligious dialogue.

Like Walker's creative and scholarly development of the new word "womanist" in the late 1970s, Mapayran's introduction of the term "life-systems" to womanist discourse helps point to the positive nature of difference expressed in the definition of womanist. Just as there are di-verse embodiments of color recognized in the various shades and skin tones of women in womanist communities, so too are the religious lives of women of African descent throughout the diaspora varied and beauti-ful with "every color . . . represented."[7] When we examine more closely the definition of womanist by Walker we find "more room in it for changes"[8] and an openness to religious spiritual practices and interpreta-tions of "Spirit" as this is defined as an important aspect of a womanist life and perspective.[9] Womanist religious thought also gives celebratory and positive attention to the various particularities in religious life. Rec-ognized as a theory and praxis, womanist religious thought examines the plethora of religious ideas, practices, ethical ideals, sacred texts (and more) that shape the religious perspectives and spiritual practices of women of African descent.

WOMANIST ROOTS

Emerging out of a (mostly) North American context focusing on the lives of African Americans and later reaching out to the wider African diaspo-ra, "womanist" was defined by literary artist and Pulitzer Prize–winning author Alice Walker, and then took root as a method and a movement. In intellectual circles, academic and activist realms, scholars and thinkers began adopting Walker's term "womanist" as a descriptor of the socioanalytical method used to highlight the complex subjectivity of black women. Their use of race-class-gender analysis in social movements of the 1960s placed attention on the importance of civil rights, gender, and economic equality for black women. In these social movement settings, womanism emerged out of dialogue with those in the "mainstream" (read: white) feminist movement who exposed sexism and the unfair advantage of men over women in the United States and globally. These feminists (often white), pointed out gender disparities from everything from access to education, job salary equity, women's bodily rights and health care, but regularly neglected race as a category to examine when looking at these same issues and their impact on women of color.

Regarding civil rights, many African American women leaders and activists participated deeply in the struggle for the rights of African Americans and other peoples of color to have the right to vote and for the dismantling of the Jim Crow system, an oppressive system that legalized brutal acts of racial violence such as lynchings and segregation. A focus on gender and race, as well as economic justice, framed a "tripartite" analytical frame that guided activists, leaders, teachers, and everyday black women and men to push for political social action, policy change, and equal rights. This kind of race-class-gender analytical frame became a foundational theoretical base for womanist and (later) feminist thinkers.[10]

WOMANISM IS POSTCOLONIAL

It is important to note that womanism emerged out of an insistence that this kind of tripartite focus be taken seriously in *all* social justice action and interrogation of theoretical development. This methodological move to use race-class-gender analysis as an embedded part of a womanist lens is also a postcolonial move. In sync with an impulse to self-define even in the midst of a colonial myth about the self or community, womanist analysis is postcolonial because it insists that a lens be developed and used that "demystifies" inaccurate cultural representations of black women. These representations are designed to rob women themselves of power and agency. Breaking from traditional Eurocentric lenses that historically view black women as victims lacking in moral character and self-respect, womanist analysis pushes beyond notions of western aesthetics. Instead, the focus is on the beauty and complexity of black women's lives and the depth of sheer wisdom that comes from black women who daily navigate and survive shifting oppressive systems. Naming structural racism, classism, and sexism as oppressive systems, womanism exposes the underside of colonialism and its impact historically on the lives of black women as well as the lack of access to opportunity they have experienced. The field of womanist ethics particularly reflects post-colonial theory and practice in that it mines the moral systems and ethical values of black women by validating women's voices, experience, and story as valid epistemology. Shifting the power of the production of knowledge, womanist religious thought (and especially womanist ethics) critiques traditional western logic wherein black women are rarely considered fully human, and problematizes the use of value hierarchal dualisms. Finally, rather than using a sole category of analysis through which to examine black women's lives, theological interpretations, or religious ideas, womanist analysis necessitates a combination of lenses be used to re-humanize black women, debunk a logic of domination, and circumvent that logic by placing epistemological privilege on black women's voices, stories, and experiences. This connection between theory and praxis in womanist religious thought is key in both the intellectual development of womanist thought and in womanist activism.

Within activist circles in the Civil Rights movement, figures like Fannie Lou Hamer, Ella Baker, and Diane Nash arose as some of the most prominent voices that consistently pointed out the connections between gender, economics, and racial disenfranchisement.[11] In the feminist movement, other voices emerged including bell hooks, Audre Lorde, and Alice Walker; each pointed out the flaws in feminist thinking to attempt to universalize all women's justice concerns according to a paradigm based on the life experience of middle- to upper-class white women. As formative leaders and thinkers, hooks, Lorde and Walker's very embodiment as racial, gendered, and sexual selves fighting for economic, gender, and sexual justice and racial equality was itself a message to and from the movement. There was often a disconnect between white women involved in the early feminist movement and black, Latina, Asian and Native American women who refused to lay down their racial identity or their communities to "fit" within white feminism.

bell hooks writes explicitly about these tensions within the feminist movement in the early years:

> they [white women] entered the movement erasing and denying difference, not playing race alongside gender, but eliminating race from the picture. Foregrounding gender meant that white women could take center stage, could claim the movement as theirs, even as they called on all women to join. The utopian vision of sisterhood evoked in a feminist movement that initially did not take racial difference or anti-racist struggle seriously did not capture the imagination of most black women/women of color.[12]

Pushing the boundaries of the feminist movement to be inclusive of race, two primary discourses grew out of this struggle, black feminism and womanism. As previously mentioned, the term "womanist" was coined by Alice Walker to distinguish the complex subjectivity of black women and to help explain why their insistence of the acceptance of their *whole* selves (racial, economic, gender identities and more) was imperative to acknowledge if true social justice was to be achieved. She coined the term in the late 1970s in an essay entitled, "Coming Apart" and later publicized the term in the form of a four-part definition in her non-fiction collection of essays, *In Search of Our Mothers' Gardens: Womanist Prose*. In later conversation with Audre Lorde and others, Walker expanded the meaning of the term to be inclusive of women's sexuality and political ideology.[13]

HOME: WOMANIST EPISTEMOLOGY AND INTERFAITH WOMANIST DIALOGUE

Scholars and religious leaders working in the discipline of religion also adopted the term "womanist." In 1985, the landmark essay, "The Emergence of Black Feminist Consciousness," written by Katie G. Cannon was published. The essay ignited a firestorm in the world of theology and ethics. Suddenly marginalized voices of African American women were shifting themselves to the center and arguing that the entire discourse of theology was incomplete without hearing the voices of women, and women of African descent. Arguments from every angle began to take shape for the emergence of womanist religious thought. There were those who like Cannon provided black feminist methodology as a base from which to grow womanist "gardens" and praxis and scholarship. There were also scholars who rooted the heart of womanism in black women's interpretation of the bible (Renita Weems), and still others who argued that different theological categories were necessary to examine if in fact black women's voices were to be heard in Christian theology (Delores S. Williams and Jacquelyn Grant). Responding "yes" to the invitation to engage theology from the heart of their own womanist identity, these women adopted the term "womanist" by Alice Walker, giving special attention to the phrase in the definition, a womanist "*Loves* the Spirit."[14]

In my previous work, *Gifts of Virtue: Alice Walker and Womanist Ethics*, I have argued that the term "womanist" and its acknowledgment of "Spirit" opened wide the door for theological and religious inquiry for all those who chose to be womanist.[15] That is, even as the term was often problematized and questioned, it was indeed adopted by several womanist religious scholars in the 1980s. Some from a more evangelical branch of Christianity argued that the inclusion of the reference to "spirit" in the definition was not *Christian* enough and did not point toward Christian roots or origins. There was deep concern expressed by Cheryl Sanders that the definition of womanist was inclusive of lesbian, gay, bisexual, transgender persons and for her, this was not in keeping with the community of Christ. Still, other scholars in these first wave womanist debates argued that methodologically, the term fit the larger goals and scholarly direction that womanist theology and ethics was moving.

THE WOMANIST DANCING MIND, METHOD, AND INTERFAITH WOMANIST DIALOGUE

As first wave debates opened the door for new discourse in the second and third waves of womanist scholarship, scholars such as Emilie M. Townes began to develop important methods to uncover and understand African life and religion. In regard to interfaith dialogue, Townes offers an exceptional method that opens and expands the discourse. There is a remarkable religious plurality alive in the African diaspora which speaks to the richness of African tradition and heritage. As a religious scholar and womanist ethicist with a scholarly eye toward justice and hope, she points to the value of this heritage as womanist and African American epistemology and argues that a specialized approach with attention to the vastness of the particular be used when studying the interreligious contours of womanist religious and African American religious thought.

Shaping a method to do this kind of work, Townes moves away from modes of destructive criticism (similar to those in most literary and academic discourses) and moves toward constructive criticism. Making a classic womanist methodological turn,[16] she chooses African American women's literature to shed light on the construction of a womanist scholarly method. She cites the work of Toni Morrison and the dancing mind: "There is a certain kind of peace that is not merely the absence of war. . . . The peace I am thinking of is the dance of an open mind when it engages another equally open one—an activity that occurs most naturally, most often in the reading/writing world we live in."[17]

Toni Morrison's concept of the dancing mind can be summarized as the creation and tending to of an embodied space of peace in which minds meet and dance in openness with one another. Absent of harsh criticism and judgment so often associated with religious dialogue in which one tradition is attempting to convert the other, the dancing mind is a kind of mutually enhancing engagement of thought. Creatively writing in a style that is reflective of this kind of mutuality, Townes responds to Morrison's idea:

> It is in the dancing mind that many of us meet each other more often than not. . . . It is in this dancing mind—where we tease through the possibilities and the realities, the hopes, the dreams, the nightmares, the terrors, the critique, the analysis, the plea, the witness—that womanist work is done in the academy, in the classroom, in the religious gatherings of our various communities, in those quiet and not so quiet

times in which we try to reflect on the ways in which we know and see and feel and do. . . . This womanist dancing mind is one that comes from a particular community of communities yearning for a common fire banked by the billows of justice and hope. As such, this particularity marks us with indelible ink. My task is to explore the twists and turns of the communities from which we spring and have our very life and breath. It is to be particular about the particular—and explore the vastness of it. [18]

The "vastness" of the particular that Townes is addressing here is both the geographical and religious plurality alive in the communal religious practices and people of the African diaspora. In this sense, Townes' concept of the womanist dancing mind is both art and method. It informs the theory and practice of doing interreligious and interfaith work. Here, she describes how the womanist method is being used in an interreligious context:

The womanist dancing mind—the one what weaves in and out of Africa, the Caribbean, Brazil, the United States (South, North, East and West); the Christian, the Jewish, the Muslim, the Condomblé, the Santeria, the Vodun, the Native American, the caste of color, the sexuality, the sexual orientation, the socioeconomic class, the age, the body image, the environment, the pedagogies, the academy—has before it an enormous communal task. One in which we are trying to understand the assortments of African American life. If I do this task well, I will realize the ways in which Black life is not my life alone, but a compendium of conscious and unconscious coalitions with others whose lives are not lived solely in the Black face of United States life. . . . I am interested in exploring the depths of African American life—female and male. For it is in exploring these depths, in taking seriously my particularity—not as a form of essentialism, but as epistemology—where I can meet and greet others for we are intricately and intimately interwoven in our postmodern culture. [19]

The method of the womanist dancing mind recognizes the complexities of a globalized world and its impacts on the lives of women of African descent. It highlights the importance of interdisciplinary (religiosocial-literary) approaches and especially signals that fresh attention be made to the interreligious nature of African, African American, and black religious life. Furthermore, the method is undergirded with an ethical frame reflective of its connection with the history of black intellectual thought where life itself sparks a fire in the hearts of those committed to uncovering the retentions of African life and moral and religious principles such as peace, harmony with the earth, and justice; these are all aims of interfaith dialogue.

Townes' method of the womanist dancing mind is hopeful and useful in determining the best ways to promote interfaith dialogue and recognize the importance of interreligious realities in the heart of womanist religious thought.[20] Womanist epistemology embodies a unique beauty that simultaneously honors and embodies interreligious and, in some cases, intrareligious dialogue and practice.[21]

EYES TOWARD JUSTICE: THE VALUE OF INTERDISCIPLINARY APPROACHES AND GLOBAL LINKS IN WOMANIST INTERFAITH DIALOGUE

The emphasis on justice in womanist religious thought and the accompanying political nature of womanist interfaith dialogue cannot be overlooked. I now turn toward some of the other important sociological and politically based social justice discourses that play a role in the establishment of interfaith womanism.

Postmodern approaches in womanist religious thought will point to the importance of teaching the varieties of religion alive in communities of African peoples for many reasons. One of the most important is the emphasis on the history of African peoples to survive and find a quality of life, especially in the North American context where the will to live was tested daily. Religion served as a tool for hope, meaning making, and survival for enslaved African peoples forced to breed, provide free labor, and build the economic base for the United States.

Taking a historical look beyond the discourse that illuminates the rich history and practice of African indigenous religious traditions, Egyptian Coptic Christianity and the history of Islam on the continent of Africa, the debates between sociologists Melville Jean Herskovits and E. Franklin Frazier provide an important and interdisciplinary entry into the dialogue of interfaith womanism. First published in 1941, Herskovits' landmark book, *The Myth of the Negro Past*, argued against accepted claims of the time (such as Frazier's), which offered a negative portrayal of Africa. This shift was exemplified in the writings of eighteenth-century poet and pioneering African American woman writer, Phyllis Wheatley. Rejecting the enforced shame and denial of Africa, Herskovits disagreed with arguments that the Middle Passage and enslavement of African peoples permanently damaged any cultural memory that Africans had linking them to their past heritage. Instead, he argued that there were many cultural retentions (Africanisms) that survived the traumatic journey and history of African Americans. Herskovits' scholarship laid the groundwork for later African American literary scholars and anthropoligists such as Zora Neale Hurston, and contemporary scholars such as Donald Matthews to investigate the retention of African story telling rites and religious rituals that make obvious the connection between African American religious communities and a host of other African communities across the diaspora.[22] The uncovering of Africanisms, especially through the practice of religion, can be described as a multiple-edged sword in that it cuts through the myths and dynamic movement of the fantastic hegemonic imagination. That is, it provides truth regarding African peoples' connection and cultural remnants that establish a link to African culture and also a recognition of the explosion of African retentions (religious and cultural) that spread like fire, even as the horrific and violent act of the transatlantic slave trade was taking place. Interreligious, intrareligious, and interfaith African American and specifically, womanist religious thought (global in its approach) are examples of this cultural and historical explosion.

Although often overlooked, the writings of anthropologist Zora Neale Hurston are scholarly sources that help support an argument for religious plurality within the African disaporic context. By placing African and African American peoples' religious history and political demand for rights at the center of discourse, Hurston's research on the retentions of African rites and rituals, and Caribbean religious expression and culture suggested that black religious lives matter and are a crucial part of the project of understanding religion. In addition to writing about voodoo and hoodoo in the deep southern United States, Hurston's work also took a kind of interfaith turn as she researched the religious lives of women and their communities in Haiti and Jamaica. As such, her work also paves a path for contemporary religious scholars to take up the proven existence of religious plurality and global links in African diasporic and especially African American religious life.[23] This reality of religious plurality, in the context of mainstream scholarly pluralist (versus exclusivist or inclusivist) approaches to religion suggest that interfaith dialogue is not only a part of womanist religious thought, but a foundation of the discourse.

INTERFAITH, INTERRELIGIOUS, AND INTRARELIGIOUS WOMANISM

Interfaith and interreligious womanism acknowledges a rich diversity of religious orientations, lifesystems, and spiritualties practiced by women of African descent and others who identify as womanist and apply womanist teachings and approaches to their justice work. In keeping with the three hallmarks of third-wave womanist approaches that I have articulated in my previous work,[24] interfaith womanism (1) explores the interreligious landscape of African diasporic perspectives through the use of comparative religious and interfaith approaches; (2) uses interdisciplinary methods and approaches to find strategies of justice keeping and peace building;[25] and (3) examines the impact of globalization and links across the African diaspora. In part, these hallmarks help to focus a path toward uncovering similar and distinct ethical imperatives for justice in a variety of religious traditions and spiritual practices.

For the sake of clarity, this section will describe the distinctions between interfaith, interreligious, and intrareligous from a womanist perspective.

Interfaith Womanist Dialogue

Delores S. Williams, a founding mother in womanist theology, explains the heart of womanism and the purpose of the discourse best in
her book, *Sisters in the Wilderness: The Challenge of Womanist God Talk*.[26]
She states, "womanist theology especially concerns itself with the faith,
survival and freedom-struggle of African-American women" and explains why it is so important to express the particularity of African
American women's faith perspectives, theologies, and religious worldviews. The reason for this is in part because theses perspectives are too
often overlooked or underappreciated by normative religious discourse.
While maintaining a liberationist frame that "challenges all oppressive
forces impeding black women's struggle for survival and for the development of a positive, productive quality of life conducive to women's and
the family's freedom and well-being . . . (and) opposes all oppression
based on race, sex, class, sexual preference, physical disability and caste,"
Williams insists that womanist theology goes even further than this.[27]

Perhaps one of the most inspiring aspects of Williams' articulation of
womanist theology (within the first wave of womanist theology) is its
insistence on transformation through dialogue. An important step in
Williams' method and her understanding of womanist opens the door for
interfaith dialogue and collaboration. While Williams grounds her own
perspective of womanist theology from the lens of Christian liberation
theology, I argue that her words can be interpreted to encourage us to
open the door of womanist discourse beyond this perspective. Regarding
the importance of dialogue, she writes:

> Womanist theology is usually non-separatist and dialogical. It wel-
> comes discourse with a variety of theological voices—liberation, white
> feminist, Mujerista, Jewish, Asian, African, classical and contemporary
> "male-stream," as well as non-feminist, non-womanist female voices.
> Womanist theology considers one of its primary tasks to dialogue with
> the church and with other disciplines.[28]

Taking this challenge seriously and building it alongside the hallmarks of
third-wave womanists, we see a frame for interfaith womanist dialogue.

The term and reflective practice of interfaith dialogue began after Vatican II. While many scholars argue that religious faiths certainly had
encounters with each other centuries before, Vatican II shifted the theological orientation to non-Christians. Instead of holding missionizing and
evangelizing approaches as the sole ways to engage persons of various
religious orientations, Vatican II promoted reflection upon the sacred

truths in various religions. Documenting this history, Kwok Pui-lan describes interfaith dialogue as "sustained reflection on dialogue and religious plurality."[29] The discourse widens the door for people of different faiths to creatively and critically engage each other's faiths and supports them "working together to address shared problems of a local community or wider concerns."[30] Since social justice issues and the impact of globalization are key hallmarks to third-wave womanism, this understanding of interfaith fits well with the practice of interfaith communities in womanist communities.

Interreligious Womanist Dialogue

The emphasis on dialogue mentioned in Williams' method and understanding of womanist theology is also a key factor in interreligious womanist dialogue. Often used interchangeably, in fact interreligious conversations can have a different starting point than interfaith dialogue. The former often dives into the depth of difference between doctrine, dogma, and theology, but can also give attention to reflection on religious experiences from a different tradition, and faith encounters wherein one's own "home" faith is deepened or reflected upon differently as a result of sustained critical engagement with another faith tradition.[31] For womanist religious thought, interreligious might also take on another dimension whereby practitioners share an ethical worldview such as the moral imperative for earth justice that arises from a shared African cosmological outlook that connects divine, nature, and human realms.[32] As previously discussed, shared racial, ethnic, or cultural identities that peoples of African descent have across the diaspora can also have an impact on interreligious dialogue. There is often a link between people's experiences of having to defend their own humanity in a context that is controlled by white supremacy. Whether these experiences of survival emerge from persons of African descent enduring racism in America or surviving British or European colonialism, the experiences and religious reflection upon them can serve as an important link that connects these peoples who may practice and be guided by different religious worldviews.[33]

Depending on the setting, these connections can at times transcend religious differences for the sake of thinking together and finding answers to global social problems. One example of this is a gathering I attended in Ghana, West Africa, in July 2012. The "African and African Diasporan Women in Religion and Theology Conference" was hosted by African feminist theologian Mercy Amba Oduyoye at Trinity Theological Seminary's Talitha Qumi Institute of African Women in Religion and Culture in Legon, Ghana. The focus of the conference was finding practical solutions, theological sources, and methods that would help end violence against women and girls of African descent. Participants came from various African cultures and religious traditions including Islam, Christianity, and several African indigenous religions. In large and small group discussions, there was a genuine sense of interfaith community developed in part because the emphasis was finding a solution to an ethical problem. At one point, I recall a woman leader and teacher in Islam having conversation with a Christian participant who posed a question about the value of women's bodies in religion. What unfolded was an extraordinary exchange about interpretations of the story of Esther as told in narratives and sacred stories from Islam and how these truths might open up Christian readings of Esther. While this discussion did not involve critical comparison of language, source of literature, and doctrinal differences, the interreligious dialogue that occurred was central to sharing religious viewpoints of how to create and sometimes rediscover woman-affirming narratives from religious texts and interreligious dialogue.

Intrareligious Womanist Dialogue

As more and more millennials describe themselves as "spiritual but not religious," scholars, religious practitioners, and faith leaders have begun to ask questions regarding the context in which this generation has learned about religion. Globalization, quick and easy access to information about sacred truths held by people and religious communities all over the planet, and a rise in an interest that many millennials have in social action are some of the factors that scholars believe influence their decisions about religious identity.

At the same time, it has also been observed that millennials, as well as many in older generations, see the world of religion as a cornucopia of choices and religion itself as a place of agency and self-naming. That is, many find that their own choice to be or identify as religious or not, embrace multiple religious belongings, or to become intrareligious are all agency-producing choices. From a womanist perspective, this is not surprising. Considering the impact of the black church and African American religious life has had on social movements and the agency-inspiring empowerment of African and African American communities (from the Civil Rights movement to the movement to eradicate mass incarceration),[34] there is more acceptance of the right to choose one's religion and practice than one might think.

Intrareligious womanist spirituality examines ways in which many women of African descent combine aspects of a variety of religions to shape a spiritual path that empowers them to overcome oppressions, name themselves, and create wholeness for their own lives and for the whole earth community. Similar to the articulation of intrareligious by Raimon Panikkar, this form of religious practice relies heavily on self-reflection regarding various religious experiences, theological shifts and transformations that occur as a result of encountering more than one religion simultaneously. The "inner dialogue" that occurs in intrareligous reflection can be seen as another aspect of the womanist directive: dialogue.[35] Similar to the ways in which nineteenth-century Shaker Eldress woman Rebecca Jackson called upon and trusted her "inner wisdom" and spirit to guide her through the terrors of losing credibility as a preacher woman in her denomination and being forced to make a risky decision to leave her church, home, and family in order to resist patriarchy, so too does intrareligious dialogue take on a sacred sharing within.[36]

Celebrating the work of first-wave womanist religious scholars and building upon the methodologies articulated by the second wave, one of the primary hallmarks of third-wave womanist scholarship is the expansion of comparative religious and interreligious dialogue featuring the religiously pluralistic perspectives embodied by women of African descent across the globe.[37] Interfaith womanism acknowledges the wide variety of religious orientations, life systems and spiritualties practiced by women of African descent or others who identify as womanist in their pursuit of justice work. Methods emerging from interreligious womanism explore the interreligious landscape of African diasporic religious traditions and use comparative religious and interfaith approaches while reflecting upon issues of social justice (racial, gender, sexual, earth, economic). In addition, interfaith womanist approaches give special attention to developing interdisciplinary methods to find ethical imperatives for justice that exist in a variety of religious and spiritual practices, examining the impact of globalization and links across the African diaspora, as well as identifying strategies of justice keeping and peace building.

The expansive nature of the term "womanist" coined by Alice Walker and its reference to black women's spirituality is read positively by many scholars, as is made evident in the work of Emilie M. Townes.[38] In widening womanist discourse, the emphasis on dialogue and inner dialogue continues to be a central component of womanist interfaith and interreligious dialogue. The web-like openness of the definition of womanist was written by Walker to have "more room in it for changes,"[39] thus allowing womanist spirituality to take on a more fluid characteristic and not be burdened by ties to particular religious doctrine or dogma. This freedom of black women to express their spirituality in a variety of ways has become a foundation of womanist religious thought and a crucial point from which to argue against the systems of patriarchy, sexism, classism, racism, homophobia, and anthropocentrism in society and religions. Womanist interfaith dialogue helps women of African descent come to voice and offer reverence to "spirit" in ways that clearly identify womanist wisdom, mutuality, inner sanctity, freedom, and community as values worth sharing.

BIBLIOGRAPHY

Alexander, Michele. *The New Jim Crow: Mass Incarceration in the Age of Colorblindness.* New York: The New Press, 2010.

Harris, Melanie L. "Buddhist Resources of Womanist Reflection." *Buddhist-Christian Studies* 34 (2014): 107–14.

———. "An Ecowomanist Vision." In *Ethics That Matters: African, Caribbean and African American Sources,* edited by James Logan and Marcia Y. Riggs, 189–93. Minneapolis: Fortress Press, 2012.

———. *Gifts of Virtue, Alice Walker and Womanist Ethics.* New York: Palgrave Macmillan, 2010.

———. "Womanist Humanism: A Deeper Look." *Crosscurrents* 57, no. 3 (2007): 391–403.

Hurston, Zora Neale. *Mules and Men.* New York: J. P. Lippincott Inc., 1935.

———. *Tell My Horse: Voodoo and Life in Haiti and Jamaica.* New York: J. P. Lippincott Inc., 1938.

hooks, bell. *Feminism Is for Everybody.* Cambridge, MA: South End Press, 2000.

Knitter, Paul F. *Without Buddha I Could Not Be a Christian.* Oxford: Oneworld Press, 2009.

Kwok, Pui-lan. *Globalization, Gender and Peacebuilding: The Future of Interfaith Dialogue.* New York: Paulist Press, 2012.

Maprayan, Layli. *The Womanist Idea.* New York: Routeledge, 2012.

Matthews, Donald. *Honoring the Ancestors: An African Cultural Interpretation of Black Religion.* New York: Oxford University Press, 1998.

Morrison, Toni. *The Dancing Mind.* New York: Alfred A. Knopf, 1996.

Ross, Rosetta. *Witnessing and Testifying: Black Women, Religion, and Civil Rights.* Minneapolis: Fortress Press, 2003.

Simancikova, Karla. *To Live Fully, Here and Now: The Healing Vision in the Works of Alice Walker.* New York: Lexington Books, 2007.

Townes, Emilie M. *In a Blaze of Glory: Womanist Spirituality as Social Witness.* Nashville, TN: Abington Press, 1995.

———. *Womanist Ethics and the Cultural Production of Evil.* New York: Palgrave Macmillan, 2006.

Walker, Alice. *Anything We Love Can Be Saved: A Writer's Activism.* New York: Ballantine Books, 1995.

———. "Democratic Womanism: A Poem." Alice Walker Official Site (October 2012). Accessed March 15, 2015. alicewalkersgarden.com/2012/10/article-i-will-not-vote-for-evil-i-want-a-different-system/.

———. *In Search Of Our Mothers' Gardens: Womanist Prose.* New York: Harcourt Brace and Jovanovich, 1983.

Williams, Delores S. *Sisters in the Wilderness: The Challenge of Womanist God-Talk.* Maryknoll, NY: Orbis Books, 1993.

NOTES

1. Emilie M. Townes, *Womanist Ethics and the Cultural Production of Evil* (New York: Palgrave Macmillan, 2006).

2. Melanie L. Harris, *Gifts of Virtue, Alice Walker and Womanist Ethics* (New York: Palgrave Macmillan, 2010).

3. Ibid., 5.

4. See Alice Walker's explanation of why and how the term "womanist" was distinct from feminism in her essay "Audre's Voice" in *Anything We Love Can Be Saved: A Writer's Activism* (New York: Ballantine Books, 1995), 80.

5. Karla Simcikova, *To Live Fully, Here and Now: The Healing Vision in the Works of Alice Walker* (New York: Lexington Books, 2007).

6. Layli Maprayan, *The Womanist Idea* (New York: Routeledge, 2012), 5.

7. Alice Walker, "Womanist" in *In Search Of Our Mothers' Gardens: Womanist Prose* (New York: Harcourt Brace and Jovanovich, 1983), xi.

8. Walker, "Audre's Voice," 80.

9. Womanist scholar Layli Maparayan argues in *The Womanist Idea* that this connection to "spirit" in its various manifestations is one of the aspects of womanism that makes it unique, and different from traditional black feminism.

10. For more on the engagement with race in early feminist thought see the work of bell hooks, *Feminism Is for Everybody* (Cambridge, MA: South End Press, 2000) and Melanie L. Harris, "Womanist Humanism: A Deeper Look," *Crosscurrents* 57, no. 3 (2007): 391–403.

11. See Rosetta Ross, *Witnessing and Testifying: Black Women, Religion, and Civil Rights* (Minneapolis: Fortress Press, 2003).

12. hooks, *Feminism is for Everybody*, 56.

13. See Walker, "Audre's Voice," 79–82. Also see, Alice Walker's "Democratic Womanism: A Poem," Alice Walker Official Site (October 2012), accessed March 15, 2015, alicewalkersgarden.com/2012/10/article-i-will-not-vote-for-evil-i-want-a-different-system/

14. Walker, *In Search of Our Mothers' Gardens*, xii.

15. Harris, *Gifts of Virtue*.

16. See Melanie L. Harris's analysis of Katie G. Cannon's methodological step to incorporate African American and African American women's literature as a primary source for womanist thought in "A Path Set Before Us: Womanist Virtue Method" in *Gifts of Virtue*, 49–59.

17. Toni Morrison, *The Dancing Mind* (New York: Alfred A. Knopf, 1996), 7–8.

18. Townes, *Womanist Ethics and the Cultural Production of Evil*, 1–2.

19. Ibid., 2.

20. And even more specifically in the heart of womanist spirituality which is interreligious by nature, that helps to shape a method for peace building, social and earth justice.

21. I have found Raimon Panikkar's understanding and interpretation of intrareligious dialogue most helpful in explaining the experience that many African American women have as they explore religious practices that are healing for their self esteem and value systems, that are sometimes outside of the faith traditions that they were born into. For more discussion on these realities, see my discussion of fluid and hybrid womanist spiritualities in *Gifts of Virtue*, where I write, "One of the hallmarks of third-wave womanism is to be more inclusive of various religious perspectives held by women of African descent across the Diaspora . . . and I argue that Townes' work is a model out of which third-wave womanist approaches find grounding. . . . Building upon Townes' work, third-wave womanist approaches examine the ways in which many women of African descent combine aspects of a variety of religions to shape a spiritual path that empowers them to overcome oppressions." (136). Also, see "Buddhist Resources of Womanist Reflection" *Buddhist-Christian Studies* 34 (2014): 107–14.

22. Donald Matthews, *Honoring the Ancestors: An African Cultural Interpretation of Black Religion* (New York: Oxford University Press, 1998).

23. Zora Neale Hurston, *Tell My Horse: Voodoo and Life in Haiti and Jamaica* (New York: J. P. Lippincott Inc., 1938). Also see her *Mules and Men* (New York: J. P. Lippincott Inc., 1935).

24. Melanie L. Harris "Third-Wave Womanism: Expanding Womanist Discourse, Making Room for Our Children" in *Gifts of Virtue*, 125–38.

25. Ibid.

26. Delores S. Williams, *Sisters in the Wilderness: The Challenge of Womanist God-Talk* (Maryknoll, NY: Orbis Books, 1993), xiv–xv.

27. One might note the similar tone and broad reach of Williams' articulation here and bell hooks's often quoted and inclusive definition of feminism, "Feminism is a movement to end sexism, sexist exploitation, and oppression" in *Feminism is for Everybody*, xiii.

28. Ibid., xiv–xv.

29. Kwok Pui-lan, *Globalization, Gender and Peacebuilding: The Future of Interfaith Dialogue* (New York: Paulist Press, 2012), 22.

30. Ibid.

31. See the work of Paul F. Knitter, *Without Buddha I Could Not Be a Christian* (Oxford: Oneworld Press, 2009).

32. See Melanie L. Harris, "An Ecowomanist Vision," in *Ethics That Matters: African, Caribbean and African American Sources*, ed. James Logan and Marcia Y. Riggs (Minneapolis: Fortress Press, 2012), 189–93.

33. Of course these points of similarities can also operate as points of difference. Just as Kwok Pui-lan's book *Globalization, Gender and Peacebuilding* points out, it is important to note the multiple layers of privileged, religious, economic, and otherwise (western, capitalistic, colorism, or internalized sexism or racism etc.) that can also work against mutual sharing and trust necessary for interreligious dialogue. Being aware of these points of privilege and forming a method that immediately attends to these in an effort to create honest mutuality is very important for successful interreligious dialogue.

34. See Michele Alexander, *The New Jim Crow: Mass Incarceration in the Age of Colorblindness* (New York: The New Press, 2010).

35. Harris, *Gifts of Virtue*, 118–19.

36. This might also be connected to Howard Thurman's idea of the inward journey.

37. For more on distinctions between the waves in womanist thought, see Harris, *Gifts of Virtue*.

38. Emilie M. Townes, *In a Blaze of Glory: Womanist Spirituality as Social Witness* (Nashville, TN: Abington Press, 1995).

39. See Walker, "Audre's Voice," 80.

Epilogue

Kwok Pui-lan

In the mid-1990s, postcolonial studies was introduced to biblical studies and in the early 2000s to theology. In recent years, several pastoral and practical theologians have begun to apply postcolonial insights to the fields of pastoral care and counseling, worship and preaching, music, religious education, and mission studies. I had the privilege of being involved in several meetings in which scholars in the practical fields gathered to explore the implications of postcolonial theory. In April 2013, the conference of the International Academy of Practical Theologians held at Toronto had the theme "Complex Identities in a Shifting World: One God, Many Stories." It included my plenary address and several papers on changing identities, activism, and congregational song from postcolonial perspectives.[1] In October 2014, the Center for Practical Theology at the Boston University School of Theology sponsored a consultation on "Preaching and Postcolonial Theology." The faculty and doctoral students gathered had animated discussions on this under-researched topic, and the papers were subsequently published in the journal *Homiletics*.[2] One month later, the conference on "Challenging the Church: Postcolonial Practice of Ministry" was held at the Episcopal Divinity School, out of which this anthology emerged. In November 2015, at the annual meeting of the American Academy of Religion in Atlanta, Georgia, I responded to a panel on "Postcolonializing Practical Theology," which drew a diverse audience and enthusiastic responses.[3]

The growing interest in postcolonial studies in practical theology and the practice of ministry reflects a collective consciousness of the limitations of colonial Christianity and its models of ministry to address the needs in our world. Michael Hardt and Antonio Negri have argued that the old form of imperial European dominance has been replaced by a form of Empire, with a new political power of globalization that knows no limits and boundaries.[4] This new global order is dominated by multinational corporations and financial agencies controlled by a rising transnational capitalist class, which amasses a significant amount of income and wealth. According to Oxfam, an organization that fights poverty, the top one percent of the world holds a staggering 48 percent of the world's wealth.[5] In the United States, the top one percent owns 35.6 percent of all private wealth, more than the bottom 95 percent combined.[6] Such gross economic inequality has caused not only economic insecurity and widespread poverty, but also contributed to racial tensions, religious and ethnic conflicts, devastating wars, growing gender violence, and global migration and refugee crises.

At the same time, Christian demographic has shifted to the Global South with the emergence of new ecclesial forms and practices. By 2025, about one-half of the world's 2.6 billion Christians will live in Latin America and Africa, and another 18 percent in Asia. At this rate, non-Hispanic whites will make up only one-fifth of the world's 3.2 billion Christians by 2050.[7] With the influx of immigrants into Europe and North America, the immigrant, ethnic, and multiethnic churches are flourishing, while membership in white mainline denominations continues to decline. With social and ecclesial changes happening globally, models of ministry defined largely by European or Euro-American theological understanding and cultural experience will no longer be adequate. We have to ask whether the colonial trappings of the church—such as western-style vestments, songs and hymns from a missionary era, liturgies rooted in European cultures, and hierarchal and clerical church structures—would be able to galvanize and equip faith communities in the Global South in the struggle for justice, when they have lost much appeal in the Global North.

In this book, contributors reimagine what the practice of ministry will look like in the twenty-first century. They find postcolonial theory valuable in offering insights, language, and analytical tools to critique lingering colonial legacies in the churches, as well as to envision new and emergent possibilities. First, postcolonial theory debunks rigid and binary constructions of the world, challenges cultural essentialism, and confronts political and religious ideologies that legitimate the status quo. Postcolonial scholars argue that the old ways of conceptualizing identity based on religion, nation, race, gender, class, or sexuality are no longer tenable, because cultural boundaries and social markers are shifting. Eleazar Fernandez describes the transnational world in which we live as one characterized by "global complexity, geographic/geopolitical deterritorization and reterritorialization, border crossings, threshold dwelling, transnationality, fluidity, and hybridity."[8] This is seen in the increasing cultural and religious diversity in the Global North and complex negotiations of tradition and modernity as well as the local and the global in the Global South. Emmanuel Y. Lartey describes the postcolonial communities in Sub-Saharan Africa as heterogeneous and multilayered, with competing claims from plurality of discourses and divergent truths. In the church and society, there is the resurrection of the conventional, dominated by western doctrines and cultural forms, as well as the urge for reinvigorating indigenous cultures, religions, and knowledge. The competition between indigeneity and globality is no less intense in Asia, especially after decolonization and rapid economic growth in recent decades. Jonathan Tan observes that there is a resurgence of traditional religions throughout Asia, and in some places religious fundamentalism has led to intolerance and bloody conflicts. In the past, Christianity could be associated with colonial privilege, but today it may be seen in some contexts as a threat to "Asian values." Contributors from the United Kingdom and the United States describe their societies as increasingly pluralistic, with racial and ethnic minorities and immigrants bringing new elements into the culture. Sheryl Kujawa-Holbrook notes that "by the early twenty-first century, the United States moved from being a religiously diverse white Protestant country to being a genuinely pluralistic nation in which no single religious group has a majority."[9]

Facing such changes, postcolonial pastoral leadership requires the capacity to live in ambiguities, transverse diverse cultural terrains, and translate and interpret for different groups in the Christian community. For Lartey, such leadership is counter-hegemonic, and requires dynamism and creativity in using disparate elements to produce "new forms of being, institutions, and practices in the church, community, and world."[10] Speaking from the North American context, Melinda McGarrah Sharp emphasizes the need for future pastoral leaders to be able to read diverse cultural contexts and facilitate intercultural human encounters. The reading of diverse contexts is not linear or straightforward, for it involves the arduous work of listening, mis-hearing, and commitment to listening again. She says pastoral leaders must be prepared to challenge one's established assumptions and be self-reflective of one's ministry. She describes some of the best practices of postcolonial practices as "careful navigation of boundaries accountable to the ever-present risk of abuse of power; recognition of misunderstanding stories; cultivation of listening practices that privilege reinterpretation; advocacy for reading as a human right; and continuous participation in opportunities for courage and risk."[11]

Second, postcolonial theory enables new theoretical connections to be made and encourages the interrogation of social identities and related systems of oppression or discrimination intersectionally. Although Asian American and Hispanic/Latino theologians have published works on postcolonial theology,[12] there are not many contributions from African American scholars,[13] and even fewer from womanists. This anthology is unique in featuring two chapters by womanist scholars. Stephanie Mitchem's chapter stages a multidimensional conversation between womanist pastoral theology and postcolonial thought. She writes, "The inclusion of black women in the United States in postcolonial conversations alters the framework of their oppression discussions, opening to re-encounter the global reach of colonization."[14] At the same time, she is vigilant that postcolonial theory would not become another master narrative shaping the conversation between women of color, Africans in diaspora, and

Africans on the continent. Her chapter makes the connection between the work of Maori scholar Linda Tuhiwai Smith on decolonizing methodologies and the work on black womanist leadership, ministry, and knowledge production. Melanie L. Harris's chapter incorporates postcolonial insights in her investigation of womanist interfaith dialogue. Specifically, she challenges Eurocentric cultural representation of black women, explores the intersectionality of various kinds of oppression, and reclaims black women's moral and intellectual agency. She attends to the multiple layers of black women's faith traditions, including the influences of African religious traditions, and explores the inter-, intra-, and all the spaces in between in which dialogue can happen. These two chapters expand womanist pastoral theology and interfaith dialogue in the wider context of global colonization, and at the same time provide insights on postcolonial theory through womanist perspectives.

If Mitchem and Harris explore the intersections among race, gender, and postcolonial theory, Mona West focuses on the intersection between postcolonialism, queer theory, and pastoral theology in the Metropolitan Community Church (MCC). West finds postcolonial discussions on otherness, hybridity, and third space helpful for the discussion of queer experience. She notes that in the church and wider society, lesbian, gay, bisexual, and transgender persons are often treated as "the other," and relegated to the margin. Within the queer community, there is tremendous diversity in terms of hybrid identities and family arrangements. Because of their marginalization, queer Christians often need to create a third space to meet and try out transgressive actions. As the MCC has become a global movement with membership in different countries, postcolonial theory will help the MCC to avoid privileging churches in the Global North and to develop pastoral practices that place gender identity and sexual orientation in the larger matrices of race, class, religion, and other systems of oppression.

Third, postcolonial theory helps us to debunk Eurocentric liturgies and explore new horizons in liturgical and bodily practices. Liturgy, as the work of the people, is a public act of remembrance, proclamation, and celebration. Liturgy and rituals can be used to reinforce social control and solidify ecclesial power, or as subversive sites for counter-memory and resistance. Let me use the celebration of Eucharist as an example. HyeRan Kim-Cragg reminds us of the diverse and localized Eucharistic practices in the early church, in which not only wine and bread, but also fruits, vegetables, milk and oil could be shared. But gradually the pluralistic and divergent Eucharistic practices have become patriarchal, colonial, and even market-driven, as the production of "altar breads" has become a transnational business. Using a postcolonial optic, she reimagines Eucharist as a site of resistance, which can take place both inside or outside the church. In the Occupy Movement, for example, the chaplains celebrated Eucharist in the campsites, where the people gathered in public spaces. Kim-Cragg emphasizes the performative aspects of Eucharist and the subversive potentials of remembering the death and resurrection of Christ in public to counteract violence and injustice toward the innocent. She gives the examples of how poor people have gathered and used their own words to celebrate Eucharist and of women priests who claim the right to preside in challenging male authority.

Michael Jagessar's chapter offers food for thought because he situates the Eucharist in the cultural discourse of eating, drinking, and table habits, and in such a way connects Eucharist with what we do in our daily lives and in community. Using the metaphor of *Pelau*, a Trinidad meal with mixed ingredients that can be cooked in different ethnic styles, he invites us to rethink Eucharist as an open table that welcomes ambiguity, creolization, and the encounter of multiple identities. When examining different Eucharistic theologies, he asks us to ponder what kind of table habits — rules of eating and drinking and conversations — are encouraged. Colonial table habits tend to reinforce the colonial class structure, such that those on the lower rung of society would be excluded or made to feel unwelcome. In contrast, Jagessar points out that Jesus' table ministry welcomed all kinds of people, pushed social hierarchy and boundaries, and created new spaces in the interest of God's kingdom. In our postcolonial world in which cultures collide and peoples comingle, the Eucharist should not be a ritual to safeguard doctrinal and cultural purity, but a symbolic act that welcomes hybridity, difference, and liminality. Jagessar also finds the metaphor of the third or in-between space helpful in understanding the mystery of the sacrament of Eucharist. In the exchange in the in-between space of the table, he says, the spirit is at work "to produce mutual inconveniencing, transformation, and new creation with regard to identities and belonging."[15]

Fourth, postcolonial theory challenges colonial constructions of religious boundaries and stimulates scholars to find new models of interreligious learning and collaboration. As Tomoko Masuzawa has pointed out, the construction of Buddhism, Islam, Daoism, Confucianism, and Hinduism as "world religions" in nineteenth-century European thought was not meant to celebrate multiculturalism or religious diversity, but to reinforce the hierarchal ordering that treated Christianity as the highest stage of religious development.[16] In the colonial setting, Christian missionaries taught indigenous Christians to believe that their religious traditions were superstitious and idolatrous. Such teachings continue to have long-lasting impacts on interreligious relationships and ecclesial practices, and in some cases contribute to conflicts between Christians and people of other faiths. In order to promote religious peacebuilding, Jonathan Tan says that Christian witness cannot simply mean the proclamation of abstract doctrines and rational arguments, but must be rooted in the spirit of hospitality, such that the Good News can be experienced in mutuality. Living as religious minorities in Asia, Asian Christians can do this "by the example of their daily living in companionship, empathy, and solidarity with their neighbors across religious boundaries, working, struggling, and suffering as fellow humans on a common quest for the meaning of life."[17]

Living as religious neighbors when different kinds of fundamentalisms, xenophobia, and the "war on terrorism" are promoted for political gains is not easy. Kujawa-Holbrook's chapter provides some concrete suggestions and steps for interreligious learning, including sharing personal narratives, deepening postcolonial literacy, and forming just communities across religious boundaries. A moving testimony of such learning is provided by Cláudio Carvalhaes, who describes his experience of accompanying a Christian group to visit a Candomblé worship service in Brazil. Candomblé is a religion that came to Brazil with the Africans and continues to be practiced among the Afro-Brazilians. As a white Brazilian, Carvalhaes has grown up thinking that the African religious practices were demonic and Christians have to reject them and cast out the demons. Thus, before Carvalhaes got into the van to go to the Candomblé worship place, his body froze. The incident provided him with the embodied insight that interreligious dialogue must go beyond doctrinal arguments and sympathetic understanding to include the possibilities of religious rituals and presence in practices. His chapter describes interfaith dialogue through praying each other's prayers, an idea that has seldom been explored.

In a number of ways, the discussion in the book has already gone beyond criticizing western models and begun offering new ideas about postcolonial practice of ministry. It also pushes us to reflect on the relation between practice and theology, especially from a postcolonial lens. Postcolonial theology is not simply about the study of past doctrines or abstract theological reasoning, but is socially engaged and committed to the transformation of the world. Serene Jones says that "doing systematic theology is itself a practice—a form of engaged knowing, a disciplined habit of body and mind, a patterned action, a way of embracing the world that is as embodied and ritualized and traditioned and improvisational as any of the other forms of 'practical know-how.'"[18] Doing postcolonial theology, for me, involves cultivating a habit of decolonizing the mind, resurrecting suppressed theological knowledge, and taking part in social praxis to contest empire and change the world. Postcolonial theology will only be words if it is not embodied in alternate forms of faith communities and ecclesial practices. The practices suggested in this book offer us helpful hints and pointers to think about postcolonial ecclesiology in action: Eucharistic table habits, ways of listening, contextual music making, confronting oppression intersectionally, hospitality for religious neighbors, and mutual mission. The postcolonial church is not a cozy and secure place reinforcing the status quo and what we already know. It is a messy, in-between space such that God's grace, beyond human understanding, can be made known.

BIBLIOGRAPHY

Choi, Hee An. *A Postcolonial Self: Korean Immigrant Theology and Church*. Albany: State University of New York Press, 2015.

Couture, Pamela, Robert Mager, Pamela McCarroll, and Natalie Wigg-Stevenson, eds. *Complex Identities in a Shifting World: Practical Theological Perspectives*. Zürick: LIT, 2015.

"Facts and Figures in 99 to 1." Inequality.org, Accessed February 19, 2016. inequality.org/99to1/facts-figures.

Fernandez, Eleazar S. "The Geopolitical and the Glocal: Situating Global Theological Voices in Theological Education." In *Teaching Global Theologies: Power and Praxis*, edited by Kwok Pui-lan, Cecelia González-Andrieu, and Dwight N. Hopkins, 163–76. Waco, TX: Baylor University Press, 2015.

Hardt, Michael, and Antonio Negri, Empire. Cambridge, MA: Harvard University Press, 2000.

Jenkins, Philip. *The Next Christendom: The Coming of Global Christianity*, 3rd ed. Oxford: Oxford University Press, 2011.

Joh, Wonhee Anne. *Heart of the Cross; A Postcolonial Christology*. Louisville, KY: Westminster John Knox Press, 2006.

Jones, Serene. "Practical Theology in Two Modes." In *For Life Abundant: Practical Theology, Theological Education, and Christian Ministry*, edited by Dorothy C. Bass and Craig Dykstra, 195–212. Grand Rapids, MI: Eerdmans, 2008.

Hill, Johnny Bernard. *Prophetic Rage: A Postcolonial Theology of Liberation* (Grand Rapids, MI: Eerdmans, 2013.

Masuzawa, Tomoko. *The Invention of World Religions: Or, How European Universalism Was Preserved in the Language of Pluralism*. Chicago: University of Chicago Press, 2005.

Rivera, Mayra. *The Touch of Transcendence: A Postcolonial Theology of God*. Louisville, KY: Westminster John Knox Press, 2007.

Slater, Jon. "Richest 1% Will Own More than All the Rest by 2016." Oxfam Blogs, January 19, 2015. Accessed February 19, 2016. www.oxfam.org.uk/blogs/2015/01/richest-1-per-cent-will-own-more-than-all-the-rest-by-2016.

NOTES

1. See the section on "Postcolonialism" in *Complex Identities in a Shifting World: Practical Theological Perspectives*, ed. Pamela Couture, Robert Mager, Pamela McCarroll, and Natalie Wigg-Stevenson (Zürick: LIT, 2015), 115–65.

2. See the articles in *Homiletics* 40: 1 (2015): 3–62.

3. Panelists included Hee-Kyu Heidi Park, Emmanuel Lartey, Fulgence Nyengele, Melinda McGarrah Sharp, and Cedric Johnson.

4. Michael Hardt and Antonio Negri, *Empire* (Cambridge, MA: Harvard University Press, 2000).

5. Jon Slater, "Richest 1% Will Own More than All the Rest by 2016," Oxfam Blogs, January 19, 2015, accessed February 19, 2016, www.oxfam.org.uk/blogs/2015/01/richest-1-per-cent-will-own-more-than-all-the-rest-by-2016.

6. "Facts and Figures in 99 to 1," Inequality.org, accessed February 19, 2016, inequality.org/99to1/facts-figures.

7. Philip Jenkins, *The Next Christendom: The Coming of Global Christianity*, 3rd ed. (Oxford: Oxford University Press, 2011), 2–3.

8. Eleazar S. Fernandez, "The Geopolitical and the Glocal: Situating Global Theological Voices in Theological Education," in *Teaching Global Theologies: Power and Praxis,* ed. Kwok Pui-lan, Cecelia González-Andrieu, and Dwight N. Hopkins (Waco, TX: Baylor University Press, 2015), 173.

9. Sheryl Kujawa-Holbrook, chapter 10 in this volume, 000.

10. Emmanuel Y. Lartey, chapter 1 in this volume, 000.

11. Melinda McGarrah Sharp, chapter 2 in this volume, 000.

12. For example, Wonhee Anne Joh, *Heart of the Cross; A Postcolonial Christology* (Louisville, KY: Westminster John Knox Press, 2006); Hee Ann Choi, *A Postcolonial Self: Korean Immigrant Theology and Church* (Albany: State University of New York Press, 2015); and Mayra Rivera, *The Touch of Transcendence: A Postcolonial Theology of God* (Louisville, KY: Westminster John Knox Press, 2007).

13. Johnny Bernard Hill, *Prophetic Rage: A Postcolonial Theology of Liberation* (Grand Rapids, MI: Eerdmans, 2013).

14. Stephanie Mitchem, chapter 4 in this volume, 000.

15. Michael Jagessar, chapter 6 in this volume, 000.

16. Tomoko Masuzawa, *The Invention of World Religions: Or, How European Universalism Was Preserved in the Language of Pluralism* (Chicago: University of Chicago Press, 2005).

17. Joanthan Tan, chapter 11 in this volume, 000.

18. Serene Jones, "Practical Theology in Two Modes," in *For Life Abundant: Practical Theology, Theological Education, and Christian Ministry,* ed. Dorothy C. Bass and Craig Dykstra (Grand Rapids, MI: Eerdmans, 2008), 199.

Index

Contributors

Stephen BURNS (PhD, Durham University) is Stewart Distinguished Lecturer in Liturgical and Practical Theology, Co-coordinator of Ministerial Formation, and Associate Dean of Trinity College Theological School, University of Melbourne, Australia. He has also taught in the USA and United Kingdom. A British-Australian citizen, he is a presbyter in the orders of the Church of England. His many publications include *Worship in Context: Liturgical Theology, Children and the City* (Epworth Press, 2006); *Christian Worship: Postcolonial Perspectives* (co-author with Michael N. Jagessar; Equinox/Routledge, 2011); *Worship and Ministry: Shaped Towards God* (Mosaic Press, 2012); and *Pastoral Theology for Public Ministry* (Church Publishing, 2015).

Cláudio CARVALHAES (PhD, Union Theological Seminary, New York) is Associate Professor of Worship at Union Theological Seminary in New York, USA. He is from Brazil and is a pastor of the Independent Presbyterian Church of Brazil. His publications include *Eucharist and Globalization: Redrawing the Borders of Eucharistic Hospitality* (Wipf and Stock, 2013) and *Liturgy in Postcolonial Perspectives: Only One Is Holy* (editor; Palgrave, 2015), as well as three books in Portuguese.

Jenny DAGGERS (PhD, Manchester University) is Associate Professor in Christian Theology at Liverpool Hope University, UK. A British citizen, she is a lay Anglican. Her publications include *The British Christian Women's Movement: a Rehabilitation of Eve* (Ashgate, 2002), *Gendering Christian Ethics* (editor; Cambridge Scholars Press, 2012); *Postcolonial Theology of Religions: Particularism and Pluralism in World Christianity* (Routledge, 2013). She also co-edited with Grace Ji-Sun Kim, *Reimagining with Christian Doctrines: Responding to Global Gender Injustices* (Palgrave, 2014), and *Christian Doctrines for Global Gender Justice* (Palgrave, 2015).

Melanie L. HARRIS (PhD, Union Theological Seminary, New York) is Associate Professor of Religion and Ethics at Texas Christian University, Fort Worth, Texas, USA. A former broadcast journalist, Dr. Harris worked as a television news producer and news writer for ABC, CBS and NBC news affiliates in Atlanta and Denver. A US citizen, she is an ordained minister in the African Methodist Episcopal Church. Her publications include several articles and books including *Gifts of Virtue, Alice*

Walker, and Womanist Ethics (Palgrave, 2010) and *Faith, Feminism and Scholarship: The Next Generation* (co-editor with Kate M. Ott; Palgrave, 2011).

Michael N. JAGESSAR (PhD, Utrecht University) was Assembly Moderator, and serves as Secretary for Racial Justice and Intercultural Ministry in the United Reformed Church, is responsible for Global and Intercultural Ministries in the United Reformed Church, and is an independent researcher. He is from Guyana and serves as a pastor in the United Reformed Church. His many publications include *Full Life for All: The Work and Theology of Philip A. Potter* (Peter Lang, 1998), *Black British Postcolonial Theology: New Textures and Themes* (co-editor with Anthony Reddie; Epworth Press, 2007), *Christian Worship: Postcolonial Perspectives* (co-author with Stephen Burns; Equinox, 2011), *At Home with God and the World: A Philip Potter Reader* (co-editor with Andrea Froechtling et al; World Council of Churches, 2013).

HyeRan KIM-CRAGG (ThD, University of Toronto) is Lydia Gruchy Professor of Pastoral Studies at St. Andrew's College in the University of Saskatchewan in Saskatoon, Saskatchewan, Canada. A Korean-Canadian, she is pastor in the Presbyterian Church of the Republic of Korea. Her publications include *Story and Song: A Postcolonial Interplay between Christian Education and Worship* (Peter Lang, 2012), *The Encounters: Retelling the Bible from Migration and Intercultural Perspectives* (co-author with Eun-Young Choi; Daejanggan Press, 2013), *Hebrews* (co-author with Mary Ann Beavis, Liturgical Press, 2015), *The Authority and Interpretation of Scripture in the United Church of Canada* (co-author with Don Schweitzer, Daejanggan Press, 2016), and *2 Thessalonians* (co-author with Mary Ann Beavis, Liturgical Press, 2016).

Sheryl A. KUJAWA-HOLBROOK (PhD, Boston College, Ed.D, Columbia University) is Professor of Practical Theology and Religious Education and Vice-President for Academic Affairs at Claremont School of Theology in Los Angeles, California, USA. A Polish-American citizen, she is a priest of the Episcopal Church. Her many publications include *Born of Water, Born of Spirit: Supporting the Ministry of the Baptized in Small Congregations* (co-author with Fredrica Harris Thompsett; Alban Institute, 2010), *Injustice and the Care of Souls: Taking Oppression Seriously in Pastoral Care* (co-editor with Karen Montagno; Fortress Press, 2010), *Pilgrimage, The Sacred Art: Journey to the Center of the Heart* (SkyLight Paths, 2013), and *God Beyond Borders: Interreligious Learning among Faith Communities* (Cascade, 2014).

KWOK Pui-lan (ThD, Harvard University) is William F. Cole Professor of Christian Theology and Spirituality at Episcopal Divinity School in

Cambridge, Massachusetts, USA and has taught at Chung Chi College in the Chinese University of Hong Kong. She is a past president of the American Academy of Religion (2011). Her many publications include *Discovering the Bible in the Non-Biblical World* (Orbis Books, 1995); *Postcolonial Imagination and Feminist Theology* (Westminster John Knox, 2005); *Hope Abundant: Third World and Indigenous Women's Theology* (editor, Orbis Books, 2010); and *Occupy Religion: Theology of the Multitude* (co-author with Joerg Rieger, Rowman and Littlefield, 2012).

Emmanuel Y. LARTEY (PhD, Birmingham University) is L. Bevel Jones III Professor of Pastoral Theology, Care, and Counseling at the Candler School of Theology, Emory University, Atlanta, Georgia, USA. He comes from Ghana and is a minister of the Methodist Church. His book publications include *Pastoral Counselling in Intercultural Perspective* (Peter Lang, 1987); *In Living Color: An Intercultural Approach to Pastoral Care and Counseling* (Jessica Kingsley, 2003); *Pastoral Theology in an Intercultural World* (Chalice Press, 2006) and *Postcolonializing God: An African Practical Theology* (SCM Press, 2013).

LIM Swee Hong (PhD, Drew University) is Deer Park Assistant Professor of Sacred Music and Master Sacred Music Program Director at Emmanuel College of Victoria University in the University of Toronto, Ontario, Canada. Born in Singapore, he has taught at Trinity Theological College, Singapore and Baylor University, Texas. His publications include *Giving Voice to Asian Christians: An Appraisal of the Pioneering Work of I-To Loh in the Area of Congregational Song* (VDM Verlag, 2008) and his compositions are included in many hymnals. He serves as the Director of Research for the Hymn Society in the USA and Canada and was the Co-Moderator of the Worship Committee of the World Council of Churches 10th Assembly in Busan, Korea.

Stephanie Y. MITCHEM (PhD, Northwestern University) is Professor of Religious Studies at the University of South Carolina, Columbia, South Carolina, USA. A US citizen and a womanist scholar, she teaches contemporary theology and women's studies. Her publications include *Introducing Womanist Theology* (Orbis Books, 2002), *African American Women Tapping Power and Spiritual Wellness* (Pilgrim Press, 2004), *African American Folk Healing* (New York University Press, 2007) and *Name It and Claim It?: Prosperity Preaching in the Black Church* (Pilgrim Press, 2007).

Melinda A. McGarrah SHARP (PhD, Vanderbilt University) is Assistant Professor of Pastoral Theology and Ethics at Phillips Theological Seminary, Tulsa, Oklahoma, USA. A US citizen, she is a lay member of the United Methodist Church (USA). She teaches across traditional residential, online, concentrated and immersion formats of theological education, in addition to leading seminars in professional societies and local faith and interfaith communities. Her publications include *Misunderstanding Stories: Toward a Postcolonial Pastoral Theology* (Pickwick, 2013). She is a trained clinical ethicist and returned Peace Corps volunteer.

Jonathan Y. TAN (PhD, Catholic University of America) is Archbishop Paul J. Hallinan Professor of Catholic Studies at Case Western Reserve University, Cleveland, Ohio, USA. Previously, he taught at Australian Catholic University in Sydney, New South Wales, Australia, from 2011 to 2014 and Xavier University in Cincinnati, Ohio, USA, from 2002 to 2011. His publications include *Introducing Asian American Theologies* (Orbis Books, 2008), *Christian Mission among the Peoples of Asia* (Orbis Books, 2014), *World Christianity: Perspectives and Insights* (co-editor with Anh Q. Tran, Orbis Books, 2016), and *Theological Reflections on the Hong Kong Umbrella Movement* (co-editor with Justin K. H. Tse, Palgrave Macmillan, 2016).

Jenny TE PAA DANIEL (PhD, Graduate Theological Union) is Co-Director of a consultency specializing in Higer Education and in Public Theory. She is the former Principal of Te Rau Kahikatea at St. John's Theological College in Auckland, Aotearoa, New Zealand, and the first indigenous woman to hold the principalship of an Anglican seminary. She is a lay Anglican, who has served on many Anglican Communion committees such as the Inter-Anglican Theological Doctrinal Commission and the Archbishop of Canterbury's Commission on Theological Education. Her publications include *Anglican Woman on Church and Mission* (co-editor with Judith Berling and Kwok Pui-lan, Canterbury Press/Morehouse, 2012).

Mona WEST (PhD, Southern Seminary, Louisville, Kentucky) is Director of Formation and Leadership Development for the Metropolitan Community Churches, in which she is an Elder. Her publications include *Take Back the Word: A Queer Reading of the Bible* (coeditor with Robert E. Goss; Pilgrim Press, 2000), *The Queer Bible Commentary* (co-editor with Deryn Guest et al.; SCM Press, 2006); and *Queering Christianity: Finding a Place at the Table for LGBTQI Christians* (co-editor with Robert E. Shore-Goss et al.; Praeger, 2013).

CPSIA information can be obtained
at www.ICGtesting.com
Printed in the USA
BVHW071920260821
615320BV00001B/120